D0130759

Something's Rising

SOMETHING'S RISING

Appalachians Fighting Mountaintop Removal

Silas House
and
Jason Howard

Foreword by Lee Smith

The University Press of Kentucky

The oral narratives in this book reflect the experiences and opinions of the interviewees and do not necessarily reflect the views of the authors or the University Press of Kentucky.

Scholarly publisher for the Commonwealth,
serving Bellarmine University, Berea College, Centre College of Kentucky, Eastern Kentucky University, The Filson Historical Society, Georgetown College, Kentucky Historical Society, Kentucky State University, Morehead State University, Murray State University, Northern Kentucky University, Transylvania University, University of Kentucky, University of Louisville, and Western Kentucky University.

Editorial and Sales Offices: The University Press of Kentucky
663 South Limestone Street, Lexington, Kentucky 40508-4008
www.kentuckypress.com

13 12 11 10 09 5 4 3 2 1

Library of Congress Cataloging-in-Publication Data

House, Silas, 1971–
Something's rising : Appalachians fighting mountaintop removal / Silas House and Jason Howard ; foreword by Lee Smith.
p. cm.
Includes bibliographical references and index.
ISBN 978-0-8131-2546-6 (hardcover : alk. paper)
1. Mountaintop removal mining—Environmental aspects—Appalachian Region, Southern. 2. Landscape protection—Appalachian Region, Southern—Citizen participation. 3. Environmentalism—Appalachian Region, Southern. 4. Celebrities—Appalachian Region, Southern—Interviews. 5. Appalachian Region, Southern—Environmental conditions. I. Howard, Jason, 1981– II. Title.
TD195.C58H68 2009
338.2'7240974—dc22 2008049846

This book is printed on acid-free recycled paper meeting the requirements of the American National Standard for Permanence in Paper for Printed Library Materials.

Manufactured in the United States of America.

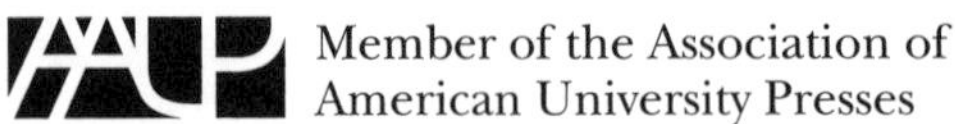

Member of the Association of
American University Presses

For Cheyenne and Olivia:
This is your heritage; protect it.
S.H.

For Garrison and her fighting spirit.
J.H.

We offer this book in honor
of the coal miners in our own families
and to all the children of Appalachia
who witness injustice in its many forms.

Something's rising
Up on Cranks Creek
People rising to turn the tide
Something's rising
Up on Cranks Creek
People say it won't be the water this time.

—Bev Futrell, "Cranks Creek"

Who's gonna stand up?
And who's gonna fight?

—Hazel Dickens

What's folks going to live on when these hills
wear down to a nub?

—James Still, *River of Earth*

Contents

Foreword

Silas House and Jason Howard are both sons of Appalachia, their family lives intertwined with coal mining. *Something's Rising* bears witness to the people they love and the lives they have lived—and still live, with great courage, right here in Appalachia.

House and Howard present a straightforward, knowledgeable, and cogent explanation of exactly how mountaintop removal came to be, and exactly what it is: "an entire mountain is blown up for a relatively thin seam of coal," followed by giant machines that push dirt, rocks, and trees into the valleys below, destroying streams, wildlife, and the lives of any people in the way. They trace the legislation that has allowed this to happen as well as the history of social protest in the region and the problem of insufficient media coverage both nationally and locally. They present the radical idea that censorship has to do not only with the too-familiar hillbilly stereotyping and the deep pockets and utter ruthlessness of big coal, but also with "class . . . and a spreading national prejudice against rural areas and the people who live there." It has to do with Appalachians' own ingrained apathy and powerlessness as well as our unwillingness to "rock the boat"—or to be perceived as "unpatriotic."

So it is *hard,* what these boys are doing here, publishing this book, which comes after years of tireless activism for both of them—writing and speaking out everywhere, running tours into mountaintop removal areas, joining and leading public demonstrations, forming and performing widely with their band Public Outcry.

Natural storytellers every one, the people profiled and interviewed in this book are all taking a personal risk when they stand up and speak out in these pages—as they are doing every day in their lives. Their stories put a human face on this urgent issue;

their stories add a human voice to the dire statistics. Their stories make it real.

Jean Ritchie tells about her own idyllic childhood, in a time before mountaintop removal mining: "Sometimes, I think of when I was a little girl there, in that place. The mountains circling around us like we were down in a little bowl. My happiest memories are of the times I was walking out in those mountains. . . . I had a special rock that jutted out, just big enough for a seat. I'd take me an apple and set there and I'd talk out loud, to the trees and flowers." Contrast this with Judy Bonds's story about taking her grandson to play in the creek, where he found "this white gooey stuff in the bottom . . . polyacrylamide. It's absorbed through the skin . . . it causes burns on the inside of your body, it causes cancer. They all use polyacrylamide at the preparation plants." Judy also tells us that "the kids here are sleeping fully clothed at night, plotting out escape routes, just waiting for the next Buffalo Creek."

Something's Rising is a moving document of human hope, love, and determination. Let's hope that "courage is contagious," as House and Howard believe. And let's do everything we can to help them get the word out.

Lee Smith

Acknowledgments

We offer our heartfelt thanks to all of the following, who helped in manners large and small, whether it be by offering tips on good subjects, singing songs that inspired us, passing along news, telling stories of their own, or serving as a guiding spirit: Lisa Abbott, Josiah Akinyele, Pat Beaver, Wendell Berry, Kate Black, Teri Blanton, Richard Bradley, Brooke Calton, Scotty Cox, Robin Daugherty, Pam Duncan, Dorothy Emery, Ashley Judd Franchitti, Amanda Fretz, Frank and Norma Garrison, Jan Goff, Ricky Handshoe, Harold and Ann Hayden, Marcy Hayden, Judith Victoria Hensley, Jane Hicks, the Hindman Settlement School family, Chester and Kathy Howard, Kate Larken, Burt Lauderdale, Lincoln Memorial University, Don London, Denton Loving, Sylvia Lynch, George Ella Lyon, Maurice Manning, Representative Harry Moberly, Myrtle and Debbie Moore, Mike Mullins, Ann Pancake, Representative Don Pasley, Kevin Pentz, George Pickow, Erik Reece, the Reel World String Band (Bev Futtrell, Karen Jones, Heather Roe Mahoney, Sue Massek, Elise Melrood, and Sharon Ruble), Eleshia Sloan, Lora Smith, Ben Sollee, McKinley Sumner, Patty Tarquino, Neela Vaswani, Marianne Worthington, Jack Wright, Colleen Unroe, and Aimee Zaring.

Among the heroes who inspired this book are Ollie "The Widow" Combs, Dan Gibson, Judy Hensley, Aunt Molly Jackson, Florence King, Florence Reece, Bill Strode, and Nellie Woolum. We were especially moved by the dedication of the more than 1,200 people who participated in I Love Mountains Day 2008; we extend all of them our gratitude. And we offer a tip of our hats to Angela Collins's fifth-grade class at Crestwood Elementary, who refuse to abandon their fervent belief that mountaintop removal is wrong and ought to be stopped, even in the face of bullying by those in power.

We are blessed to work with such people as our editors, Laura

Sutton and Donna Bouvier, and everyone at the University Press of Kentucky, who care about this book as much as we do. Most of all, we thank the subjects of this book—for welcoming us into their homes, for sharing their stories with us, and for standing up for what they believe in.

Introduction

"Despite all the riches under ground, the most important riches of the area are above ground: they are the people . . . It is your understanding coupled with your creative thinking that can find the creative solutions to the problems that exist. You can find the opportunity in the problem, open it up, articulate it, and bring new things into existence. And by doing so create a new, brighter future."[1]

These words were spoken by Senator Robert F. Kennedy at Alice Lloyd College in Pippa Passes, Kentucky, on February 13, 1968, during a fact-finding mission of sorts. Over the course of two gray February days, Kennedy traveled more than two hundred miles over winding mountain roads to hear from Appalachians about the economic and social challenges they faced and how their government could help them. It was not a campaign trip; Kennedy had not yet declared his candidacy for president. He came to the mountains because he cared, because he believed in mountain people, and because he knew that change was possible.

Some Appalachians still believe Kennedy's assertion—that the greatest wealth in the region is its people. Fortunately, many of them have strong voices, and those voices are rising up against the biggest threat to Appalachia today: mountaintop removal mining.

Mountaintop removal is a radical form of surface mining. The term is concise and straightforward: an entire mountain is blown up for a relatively thin seam of coal. This destructive method of mining requires large areas for disposal of the resulting overburden, or "waste"—topsoil, dirt, rocks, trees (almost never harvested so the coal can be extracted as quickly as possible)—which is then pushed into the valleys below, burying the streams, trees, and animals. This activity is neatly described as "valley fills."

Although the coal industry's loudest defense of this practice is that mountain people need the jobs mining supplies, the truth is that Appalachia's mining jobs are being buried with the overburden. Mountaintop removal is done by giant machines; draglines, bulldozers, and dynamite don't require as large a number of employees as deep mining. According to *USA Today,* this mechanization has resulted in a net loss of over 48,000 jobs in West Virginia alone during the period from 1978 to 2003.[2]

Ironically, mountaintop removal began as the result of a law intended to slow the rate of strip mining and its resulting environmental devastation. As strip mining increased throughout the 1960s and 1970s, many Appalachians began to speak out in protest. In response, Congress passed the Surface Mining Control and Reclamation Act of 1977, which required coal companies to restore the mined land to the "approximate original contour." Having been vetoed twice by President Gerald Ford, a more stringent version of the legislation was signed by President Jimmy Carter, fulfilling a promise he made to Appalachians while campaigning in the region during the 1976 presidential election.

Although enacted in good faith, the law contained a loophole that coal companies soon began pulling wide open. The legislation allows for an approximate original contour variance, in which the site can be approved for post–mine use in residential, commercial, and industrial development.[3]

Statistics from the Environmental Protection Agency (EPA) on mountaintop removal are sobering. The EPA estimates that more than 700 miles of Appalachian streams were buried by valley fills from 1985 to 2001. Many more mountain waterways have been lost since then. The study determined that if this practice continues at the current rate, over 1.4 million acres of land will be lost by the end of the decade.[4] And at the moment, there is no end in sight.

As a parting gift to the coal industry, which includes many of his largest donors, President George W. Bush, in the final year of his second term, proposed to relax the 100-foot mining buffer zone around streams. In essence, with this change, valley fills would be specifically written into law. Appalachians turned out at numerous hearings throughout the region to protest this action. In acts of unparalleled bravery for governors of coal-producing states, Kentucky governor Steve Beshear and Tennessee governor Phil Bredesen publicly condemned Bush's proposal in November 2008. Despite their pleas, the EPA approved the measure shortly thereafter.[5] Nationally, according to a recent poll, two out of three Americans are opposed to this change.[6] This widespread opposition, however, has yet to register with most Appalachian politicians. Coal is the "third rail" of Appalachian politics. To touch it means certain political death.

Coal holds no political loyalties. In the coalfields, there's plenty of moral cowardice among Republicans and Democrats alike. This became especially evident in 2005—when the anti–mountaintop removal movement started to gain political traction—to 2008, when the fight intensified, becoming too important and visible to ignore. This was a fever-pitch moment in the struggle, and for that reason this period bears closer examination.

The turning point in the legislative process against mountaintop removal came in 2008, when landmark bills were introduced in Kentucky, West Virginia, and Tennessee to severely regulate, or even ban, the practice.

Kentucky's House of Representatives saw a committee vote on the Stream Saver bill, legislation that would ban the dumping of overburden into any "intermittent, perennial, or ephemeral stream or other water of the Commonwealth."[7] The bill had been bottled up in committee for three years by the powerful chairman of the House Natural Resources Committee, Jim Gooch (D-Providence),[8] who consistently refused to give it a fair public hearing.[9] It was finally introduced in a different committee by Representative Harry Moberly (D-Richmond) in March 2008.[10] Ultimately, the resolution failed 13–12, with three lawmakers abstaining. One lawmaker exited the room just before the vote, returning shortly after the roll call.

A similar situation happened the following month in neighboring Tennessee, when an undecided member of the House

Environment Subcommittee left the room prior to the vote on legislation that would have banned mountaintop removal. That, coupled with a lawmaker who changed his mind and voted against the bill, led to its defeat in a 3–5 vote.

Such legislation didn't fare any better in West Virginia. On Ash Wednesday in early February 2008, State Senator Jon Blair Hunter (D-Monongalia) introduced Senate Bill 588—legislation that would end valley fills—and offered his fellow legislators an emotional confession: "To intentionally destroy God's creations, be they human or a mountain, is a Sin of Commission. To stand by and do nothing is a Sin of Omission. On this holy day . . . I wish to confess my sin of omission, and I promise to sin no more . . . God created our mountains . . . And, yes, God also put the coal in those mountains. But I firmly believe He did not intend for us to destroy the mountains, the streams, the forests and His people to mine it. Coal can be mined without mountaintop removal, Mr. President."[11] Later that month, the Senate Energy, Industry, and Mining Committee held a public hearing on the legislation before an overflow audience. Despite a majority of witnesses testifying in favor of the bill, it was not voted out of committee.[12]

Many of the region's politicians conveniently blame such legislative failures on public support for mountaintop removal. In a now-infamous article in the *Lexington Herald-Leader,* Gooch was quoted as saying, "If there were wholesale destruction of the mountains I think there would be more of an outcry. I've gotten a few letters from Louisville and Frankfort and Lexington, but not from where mountaintop removal is taking place."[13]

Despite Gooch's claim, the people of Appalachia were crying out. The *Lexington Herald-Leader* received sixty letters in response to his statement, pointing out that Appalachian citizens had been increasingly outspoken about mountaintop removal.[14] Less than a year later, in February 2008, approximately 1,200 people gathered on the front steps of the Kentucky state capitol to support the Stream Saver bill.[15] In response to this huge public outcry, nearly a month later about 1,500 miners and industry supporters marched on Frankfort in opposition to the bill. The governor met them on the front steps.[16]

Even in the face of these daunting political odds, grassroots environmentalist groups soldier on. The Alliance for Appalachia, the Alliance for the Cumberlands, Appalachian Voices, Christians for the Mountains, the Coal River Mountain Watch, the Keeper of the Mountains Foundation, Kentuckians for the Commonwealth, the Ohio Valley Environmental Coalition, Save Our Cumberland Mountains, the Southern Appalachian Mountain Stewards, and other organizations have mobilized to fight mountaintop removal in the Appalachian coalfields. In addition, countless individuals quietly toil away on their own on this issue. Most of them never appear in the newspaper, yet they are there, and they keep fighting.

Opposition to mountaintop removal has developed into a full-fledged movement, with several different factions fighting to change laws, debate the coal industry, and tell the stories of the people affected by this destructive form of mining. Over the past five years the term "mountaintop removal" has evolved from being an obscure industry description to a household phrase throughout Appalachia.

The region's artists have become increasingly important in this fight. Writers in West Virginia and Kentucky—the most affected states thus far—have put out books and CDs to increase the public's awareness of the issue. Large groups of writers tour mountaintop removal sites, attend community meetings, and report on what they have seen and heard, striving to keep the issue in the media.

Individual Appalachian artists involved in the struggle are bringing more attention to the issue as the fight intensifies, especially in the past two years. West Virginia author Ann Pancake's novel *Strange As This Weather Has Been* received wide acclaim after its release in late 2007, being named to several Top Ten lists and winning the Weatherford Prize for Literature; coal miner's daughter Shirley Stewart Burns released *Bringing Down the Mountains* in 2008, hailed as a major study on the topic and described as "clear and impassioned" by Denise Giardina, an author who has been at the forefront of the movement; Public Outcry, a band composed of Kentucky writers and musicians, released an entire album of protest songs about the issue in 2008. Mari-Lynn Evans, a West Virginia native and the creator of the widely viewed PBS miniseries *The Appalachians* is currently filming the documentary *Coal Power,* a portion of which will focus on mountaintop removal.

The movement is growing in southwest Virginia and East Tennessee as well, where mountaintop removal sites are increasingly appearing on the horizon. Citizens there are speaking out, trying to get ahead of the practice, which has already kicked into high gear in their areas but is not as advanced as the destruction that has befallen Kentucky and West Virginia.

Appalachians have written editorials, letters, and features that have been published in the *New York Times,* the *Washington Post,* the *Chicago Tribune,* and many other national newspapers. While the *Lexington Herald-Leader*[17] and the *Charleston Gazette* are the largest newspapers read in the region, only the *Gazette* has investigated the issue in depth, thanks to Ken Ward, who was writing about mountaintop removal when hardly anyone else was. Recently, the *Lexington Herald-Leader* published an editorial against the practice.[18] The addition of reporter Cassondra Kirby-Mullins, a native of Eastern Kentucky, has increased that paper's coverage of rallies and community hearings with fair and intelligent articles. The *Courier-Journal,* located in Louisville, is not widely read in the region, but it continues to give the issue prominence. And Tim Thornton of the *Roanoke Times* has written a series of investigative reports, including an exhaustive explanation of mountaintop removal and articles on the importance of women in the opposition movement and on the issue's increasing prominence in the curriculum at some of the region's colleges.

Although most regional newspapers have been slow to voice their own opinions about mountaintop removal (the exceptions being Whitesburg, Kentucky's *Mountain Eagle,* which is known for bucking the status quo, and the *Corbin Times-Tribune* [also in Kentucky], under the leadership of managing editor Samantha Swindler, who has been vocal in her opposition), national magazines have not; plenty of pages have been devoted to the subject in such major international magazines as *Vanity Fair, Harper's, Orion, O, Mother Jones, People,* and *National Geographic.* Many within the region, however, read only local newspapers.

By determining what is news with their story choices, the media act as gatekeepers of information. This in turn also makes them agenda setters, determining what issues are discussed by the public and consequently what appears on the political agenda.[19] The lack of information that has been made available about mountaintop removal has restricted the public's response to the issue.

This trend is historical in nature. According to John Gaventa in his classic social study *Power and Powerlessness,* such gatekeeping was a major issue during the coal mining strikes of the 1930s. The local media were eager collaborators with the coal companies in determining what would be reported as news and thus restricted the scope of the conflict. As Gaventa wrote, "By shaping certain information into the communication flows and shaping other information out, the gatekeeping capacity could combine with the repressive capacity to *isolate, contain* and *redirect* the conflict."[20] In the case Gaventa was referring to, the local newspaper, the *Middlesboro Daily News,* played down the extent and the significance of the miners' strike, effectively discouraging others from joining in the collective action. The regional and national media, however—led by the *Knoxville News Sentinel* and the *New York Times*—chronicled the conflict as widespread and important.[21] Gatekeeping was used, then, by the different levels of media to perform different functions: the local media used it to restrict the scope, intensity, and visibility of the conflict, while the regional and national media did just the opposite.[22]

The difference between local and national coverage continued in November 1965 when a frail, sixty-one-year-old woman named Ollie Combs—widely known as "the Widow Combs"—

was arrested after she lay down in front of bulldozers to stop mining on her Knott County, Kentucky, farm. The news made the front page of the *New York Times* and was picked up off the wire and printed in large papers across the country. *Courier-Journal* photographer Bill Strode (who was also arrested that day) won a Pulitzer Prize for news photography for his series on strip mining, which included pictures of Combs's arrest. The pictures shocked America. However, many newspapers throughout the region failed to report the incident or buried it well inside their pages.

In some ways, this situation has not changed much today: regional newspapers fail to report many of the protests, assemblies, and community hearings about mountaintop removal. The Internet, however, has greatly changed the way Americans get their news. As more people have turned to the Internet as their primary news source in recent years, newspaper circulation has declined dramatically. Due in part to the twenty-four-hour news cycle that cable news and the Internet have helped to create, there is such a wealth of information available to consumers nowadays that they are unable to process it all. In addition, newspapers, which are increasingly owned by large media conglomerates, no longer carry the political clout they once did.

Despite the widespread national coverage that mountaintop removal has received, the media still have not embraced this environmental issue enough to make it part of the national consciousness. The term "mountaintop removal" has yet to become a household phrase in America the way it has in Appalachia. Perhaps politics has something to do with it. Project Censored, a media watchdog organization, ranked the issue as the tenth most censored story of 2006.[23]

But we believe that this censorship—or lack of interest—has more to do with class, with an increasing national prejudice against rural areas and the people who live there. Appalachia is openly referred to as "flyover country" by many in the United States, and this is surely one of the reasons that this issue is being ignored by the citizens of an otherwise caring nation. Today's culture puts little stock in a rural place like Appalachia, a place people think of as consisting entirely of "rags" when what they are really interested in are the "riches." Perhaps it is this lack of national interest that causes many national publications to do large spreads on the issue and then move on, failing to sustain their coverage of the continued fight against mountaintop removal.

Not many people know about the Martin County, Kentucky, sludge spill, when 300 million gallons of sludge—an oozing mess of black coal waste—were dumped into waterways, roads, and homes.[24] The Exxon-Valdez spill, by contrast, involved 10.8 million gallons of oil into Prince William Sound off the shore of Alaska. Though it involved a tiny fraction of the number of gallons dumped in Martin County, the Exxon-Valdez oil spill became worldwide news.[25]

Why else do so few people know about the three-year-old child who was killed in southwest Virginia when a boulder dislodged from a mine site crashed into his family's trailer and crushed him in his own bed? Despite the fact that those seeking to increase awareness of any issue are aided by having a memorable image to present to the public, those fighting mountaintop removal have refused to use the child's name and likeness in protests or rallies so as not to exploit his memory. Still, the media have mostly ignored his tragic story. If this child had come from a more affluent community, we believe that the incident would have been more widely publicized, and would likely have sparked national outrage.

Even fewer people are aware of the ongoing protests against mountaintop removal throughout the region. Many arrests resulting from these protests are not widely reported. In 2003, four people were arrested in Kentucky for unfurling banners that opposed the practice. Two years later, nine people were arrested while protesting the destruction of Zeb Mountain in Tennessee. March 2007 saw thirteen arrested in Charleston, West Virginia, while protesting a sludge pond that services a mountaintop removal site just above Marsh Fork Elementary School, which keeps a single school bus parked in front of the building for a potential emergency evacuation.[26] In August that same year, five demonstrators were arrested in Asheville, North Carolina, for protesting outside the Bank of America, which has loaned nearly $1 billion to Massey Energy and Arch Coal, two of the largest mining companies in the nation.[27] June 2008 brought the arrest of twelve more in Virginia who were protesting the building of the Dominion power plant, which would increase pollution and the use of coal mined as the result of mountaintop removal. These are only a few examples; numerous other protests and arrests have occurred in the region.

Given these events, it is clear that people are sick and tired of putting up with whatever the coal industry and the government dishes out. They're also tired of not being heard, which means that their voices are bound to become louder and louder. These are not people who can be silenced.

Something's rising in the mountains of Appalachia: the voices of the people.

As we have educated ourselves on the topic of mountaintop removal, what has struck us the most are the individual stories of those affected by it. We have included in this book those whose stories have affected us the most. We believe that their stories perfectly illustrate the complexities of this subject. Mountaintop removal is not by any means just an environmental problem. It also has political, social, ethical, economic, and—most of all—cultural ramifications.

We have assembled twelve very different witnesses against mountaintop removal who have one great thing in common: they are speaking out for what they believe in with passion, intelligence, and wit. They are stepping out on a limb to voice their opinion. They are fighting to make Appalachia a better place for themselves, for their children, for their neighbors, and, especially, for generations to come.

These twelve have different backgrounds, classes, and occupations. They range in age from a man of twenty-three to a woman in her mid-eighties. They represent many professions and activities: nurse-practitioner, social worker, singer, college student, writer, miner, mine-inspector, and politician. Some of the people in this book are just starting to speak up. As they have learned more and become more concerned about mountaintop removal, despite being quiet by nature, they feel the need to make their worries known. Some of them feel a moral obligation to speak out. Others have been so affected by the ravages of mountaintop removal that their survival depends on standing up for themselves. Some are working alone, others are organizing their communities. Some have worked on the issue with the nation's most important environmental and political leaders.

All are Appalachians, a fact that is very important to us.

Poet and activist Don West once wrote: "If we native mountaineers can now determine to organize and save ourselves, save our mountains from the spoilers who tear them down, pollute our streams, and leave grotesque areas of ugliness, there is hope . . . It is time that we hill folk should understand and appreciate our heritage, stand up like those who were our ancestors, develop our own self-identity. It is time to realize that nobody from the outside is ever going to save us from bad conditions unless we make our own stand. We must learn to organize again, speak, plan, and act for ourselves."[28] Although West wrote these words over forty years ago, they could not ring truer today. The fight against mountaintop removal can only be won when the majority of Appalachians are willing to rise up and say, "No." Our interview subjects are speaking out, and with this book we intend to give them the opportunity to share their stories with a wider audience. By enabling them to tell their stories, we hope to encourage other Appalachians to speak out, too.

One of the main reasons we have featured only Appalachians in this book is that despite the widespread public outcry by so many of the region's residents, there are still many others who have failed to come out against mountaintop removal. Many Appalachians find it difficult to oppose this practice because of the coal industry's long history of convincing people that to protest any form of mining is to oppose an industry that has long been a major supplier of jobs within the region. This is not unlike the convoluted and confining definition of patriotism that more and more people seem to have adopted. In today's political climate, those who speak against war are often branded as unpatriotic or against those in the military. In a similar fashion, some Appalachians tend to believe that speaking out against any form of mining is biting the hand that feeds them.

Coal has long been a major employer in Appalachia, a region that is not economically diverse. Perhaps those in charge of the coal industry believe that making residents dependent on them will assure its continuation. Maybe politicians and those in power believe that keeping people under their control means convincing them that they have no other alternatives. Perhaps the environmental devastation caused in part by mining has kept other forms of economic growth, such as tourism and sustainable resources, from developing in the region, thus allowing it to remain the coal industry's private playground.

Over and over, the coal associations of Kentucky, Tennessee, West Virginia, and Virginia remind people that coal provides jobs for the region. However, the coal associations conveniently, purposefully, and wisely choose to *not* remind people of the many mining jobs lost to the mechanization crucial to mountaintop removal. In this context, it is worth noting that the counties that produce the most coal in Appalachia are often the poorest. Take, for example, Boone County, West Virginia's biggest coal producer, whose county seal boasts "Where coal was discovered in 1742" and which hosts the annual Coal Festival. According to the 2000 U.S. Census, the median income for a household in the county was $25,669, as compared to the national average of $50,200. The county produces an average of about thirty-three million tons of coal a year. In 2000, the average price of coal per short ton was $16.78.[29] That means that coal produced in Boone County was worth about $5.5 billion in the same year that the median income for a family in the county was half of the national average. In addition, the price of coal has risen sharply over the past decade, while median incomes have not. In 2008, a short ton of coal sold for up to $140 per ton, an 823 percent increase. Appalachians certainly have not seen a similar hike in their incomes.[30]

Yet the coal industry paints a different picture, which it feeds to Appalachians—and all Americans—in television commercials, on billboards and bumper stickers, at the workplace, and in the schools.

We believe that one reason we mountaineers so easily believe the coal industry has to do with manners. Appalachians have always been polite by nature. As John Gaventa observed, "the mountaineers were more interested in maintaining community harmony" when approached to sell or lease land to the coal companies in the early to mid-twentieth century.[31] This attitude persists even today, causing neighbors to become upset with those who speak out. Those who rock the boat are often criticized as being ungrateful—until the rocks from mountaintop removal sites rain down on the critics' own homes.

In short, the people you will meet in these pages have all taken a chance in speaking out. They're running the risk of being shunned or rejected by neighbors, friends, and family members. But they press on. They believe that courage is contagious.

Thus, our interview subjects are all Appalachians and they're all fighting back. These were our two main criteria for inclusion here. However, as this book took shape, we realized that these activists have two other things in common.

First, they all work quietly and efficiently, not seeking any kind of limelight or personal validation. In most cases their activism and dedication are either underrated or unnoticed.

Secondly, they all not only know how to speak up, but also have a natural instinct for storytelling, making this book a testament to the strong and beautiful oral tradition in Appalachia as well as a document of the fight against mountaintop removal.

The people you will meet here are storytellers. They all speak of stories as a force that sustains them, just as the tradition of storytelling sustains the entire Appalachian culture. All of them know that one way to fight back is to tell a story in your own voice, in your own words. Environmental devastation can take much from even a strong culture like that of Appalachia, but the last thing to be taken from these mountains will be the stories, because they are the lifeblood of their people.

We did not choose the twelve individuals for this book because we agreed with everything they had to say. On the contrary, we wanted to interview people who might have different views on the coal companies, their communities, and the government than we did. Mountaintop removal is such a complex issue that it is almost impossible for two people to agree on every aspect of the problem. However, we all agree on one thing: that this mining practice is deplorable and must be stopped.

In fact, however, Appalachians are used to deplorable activity. And despite their natural politeness and civility, they are used to fighting back. Appalachians were born of social protest.

After being ordered by the British Crown to abandon their settlement in the Appalachian Mountains in 1772, a group of pioneers met and decided instead to lease the land from the Cherokee Indians. The founding of the Watauga Association skirted the Royal Proclamation of 1763, which banned any settlement or purchase of land west of the Appalachians, and thus became the first American declaration of independence. Three years later, Mecklenburg County in North Carolina passed the first Resolution of Separation from Great Britain.[32]

This "renegade status" of its citizens has been reclaimed at various moments in Appalachia's history, often with coal at the center of the storm. The biggest squall happened in West Virginia during the turbulent 1920s. Simmering tensions between miners and company men over unionization resulted in the largest armed uprising in American history aside from the Civil War.[33]

The mine wars of the 1930s in Harlan County, Kentucky, continued Appalachians' legacy of fighting back. Again, the battle was over the right to organize. Following the miners' decision to strike in March 1931, coal operators hired gun thugs who terrorized striking miners and their families. The violence culminated in the notorious Battle of Evarts in May 1932, which left at least four dead and gave "Bloody Harlan" its nickname. Eventually, nine years of battles would result in eleven dead, twenty wounded, and the unionization of Eastern Kentucky miners.[34]

Music was a driving force in this social revolution.

"Solidarity Forever," a song written by Ralph Chapin during a West Virginia strike in 1915, is, Jeff Biggers has noted, "possibly the first labor anthem to be disseminated on a national level."[35]

The Harlan County strikes inspired Florence Reece, the wife of a striking miner, to compose one of the most powerful and enduring protest songs ever written, "Which Side Are You On?"[36] In the 1930s, Aunt Molly Jackson, a midwife and songwriter living in squalid conditions in a Bell County, Kentucky, coal camp emerged as "one of the more famous folksingers of the radical thirties."[37] Jackson traveled throughout the country spreading the word about conditions in the mining camps and was eventually banned from reentering Kentucky by politicians who were in the pocket of the coal industry.[38]

In 1932, partly as a response to the chaos occurring in Appalachia, Myles Horton and Don West founded the Highlander Folk School in New Market, Tennessee.[39] According to author John M. Glen, "its educational approach reflected Horton's conviction that a new social order could be created by bringing ordinary people together to share their experiences in addressing common problems."[40] Ever since its founding, Highlander has been active in Appalachian issues and organizing resistance to oppression across the South, including becoming a major force in the civil rights movement.

Despite advancements, tensions reemerged in Harlan County during the 1970s when more than 180 miners at Brookside went on strike to protest unsafe working conditions and the companies' insistence on including a no-strike clause in their contract. Immortalized in the Academy Award–winning documentary *Harlan County USA,* the miners eventually reached an agreement with the companies, but not before one miner, Lawrence Jones, was killed in the early morning hours on the picket line.[41] The success of the strike was due in large part to the women in the community. This reflected a broader trend across the region, according to Carol Giesen in *Coal Mining Wives:* "Women picketed, marched in demonstrations, lay down in front of trucks, wrote letters, and supported in other ways the workers' and mining union's efforts to change conditions in the mines."[42]

Nearly a decade before the Harlan County strike, the story of the Widow Combs caused such national outrage that it prompted then-Governor Ned Breathitt of Kentucky to introduce more stringent legislation regarding strip mining. Although Breathitt also called for a close examination by the courts of the mineral rights practice known as the broad-form deed, it took two decades for the practice to be declared unconstitutional.[43]

In the late 1800s and early 1900s, land agents from the northeast trekked across Appalachia seeking mineral rights to the land. With big talk and hefty payments—typically twenty-five to thirty cents an acre—they convinced many Appalachians to sell their mineral rights. With the advent of strip mining in the late 1950s, the sellers' descendants were often taken by surprise when a coal company showed up with a piece of paper that authorized them to mine coal by removing the entire surface of their land.[44]

These landowners had no immediate recourse in the legal system; Kentucky courts, for instance, repeatedly sided with the coal companies. Citizens groups began to form to protest the practice across Appalachia. In Eastern Kentucky, a group of disgruntled residents formed the Kentucky Fair Tax Coalition, later to become Kentuckians for the Commonwealth (KFTC). KFTC members began lobbying the state legislature in the early 1980s, and in 1987, in a split decision by the Kentucky Supreme Court, the law was struck down. One final avenue of recourse for the protesters at the state level remained: amending the Kentucky Constitution. Thousands signed petitions to protest the court ruling and to call for an amendment. At a rally in Frankfort, KFTC member Mary Jane Adams addressed the crowd: "The Constitution says that the government is the servant of the people. It doesn't say the government is the servant of the coal industry. It's time to speak out."[45]

Their voices were finally heard in November 1988. By a margin of four to one, Kentuckians voted in favor of the Homestead Amendment, which restricted strip mining by the mineral rights owner without the consent of the landowner. Five years later, the Kentucky Court of Appeals upheld its constitutionality.[46]

In neighboring West Virginia, citizens were fighting their own battle in the courts. One hundred twenty-five lives were lost and more than 4,000 people were injured and displaced when a poorly maintained dam at Buffalo Creek—used to filter massive amounts of coal slurry from a nearby plant—broke only four days after passing inspection. The disaster wiped out a valley of coal mining towns spanning seventeen miles, completely leveling the town of Saunders. Six hundred twenty-five survivors filed suit for $64 million against the Pittston Coal Company; two years later they settled for $13.5 million.[47] "We did some good," writes Gerald Stern, one of the attorneys for the survivors. "We made the company pay, and pay well. Maybe the cost of our settlement will make them a little more careful in the future."[48]

Other individuals in the mountains were hopeful that their actions would have the same effect. The late Hazel King is a prime example of these activists. After retiring from the military, King returned to her native Harlan County and began a tireless fight for the passage of the Surface Mining Control and Reclamation Act. Then, in 1977 she filed a complaint that resulted in the first act of enforcement under the legislation and earned her the moniker of the "law's chief citizen enforcer."

In her later years, King became an outspoken opponent of mountaintop removal. When her beloved Black Mountain—

Kentucky's highest peak—was endangered, she hired a helicopter numerous times at more than $1,000 a trip so people could view and photograph the mountain. Her work paid off; the coal companies relented.[49]

King had some young friends as allies in her fight to save Black Mountain. In 1997, students in Judith Hensley's seventh-grade class at Wallins Creek Elementary School in Harlan County heard about the proposed mining and chose to protest through a class project. Hensley's students began writing letters, prompting other classes at the school to join in. Other schools took up the cause as word spread across the region. Citizens groups joined the fight. After the students traveled to Middlesboro to protest outside of the Office of Surface Mining and appeared before the Legislative Research Commission in Frankfort, the state legislature intervened. A resolution was passed that compensated the coal and timber companies for their lost profits and protected nearly 12,000 acres of the mountain from being mined and logged.[50] National media outlets soon picked up the story, and the students appeared on ABC-TV's *Nightline.* On the show, one boy said, "It feels like we fought a war and won."[51]

But the war rages on.

The two of us come to this book as the children of that war and the children of Appalachia. One reason we decided to do this book together was that our family histories are so similar. We come from coal mining families that were able to rise up out of poverty in large part due to many of our family members working in the mines. To put our own stake in the issue of mountaintop removal in the proper perspective, we briefly offer our own stories.

Silas House: My grandfather, Johney Shepherd, worked for more than thirty years in the Leslie County, Kentucky, coal mines. After ten years in, he lost his leg during a roof collapse. After the accident, he was conscious the entire time until he was knocked out by doctors for the amputation. He spent a fidgeting six months recuperating and then went right back into the mines that had claimed part of him. That's how much he loved being a coal miner. Up until his dying day he spoke of his fellow miners as if they were his blood brothers.

My maternal uncle, Sam Hoskins, still wears the coal tattoo he was marked with when a rock fell from a mine ceiling, leaving a three-inch gash across his right cheekbone. I was always fascinated by this mark of survival. I grew up around men who couldn't wash the coal dust from their eyelashes so that they looked as if they were always wearing eyeliner, who came in from work with only the whites of their eyes and their teeth shining, who sat and told stories about the coal-mining life while they took supper.

There is plenty of coal-mining pride in my family. But there is another side to living within a place that has to sacrifice itself for the rest of the nation, and to survive.

I grew up with an active coal mine as a neighbor. My childhood was marked by the blasting, the dust, the constant groan of machinery, the monotonous shifting of gears as coal trucks raced up and down the road, carrying out their spoils. The hillside was flattened, and everything on it was gone forever. This was a place where I had watched lightning bugs rise up in summer twilights, where my father and I had gathered walnuts in the fall, where my best friend and I had ridden sleighs, had hunted crawdads in the mossy-banked creek. Suddenly it was blasted off the face of the earth, never to return. The mining company pulled out after a shoddy reclamation and the land has still not recovered; almost thirty years later, it is unable to support hardwood trees. Not much more than sawgrass grows there now.

Around the same time, my father's family homeplace at Happy Holler, Kentucky, was strip-mined, erasing our heritage and causing my aunt's grave to be pushed over into the creek and buried some fifty feet below piles of unwanted topsoil, clay, and low-grade coal—overburden, as the industry calls it. One of my earliest memories is of standing on a ridge overlooking the place that had once been the family burial ground while my father and a couple of his brothers stood nearby, silent except for the coins they rattled in their pockets. And they were never silent—never not telling tales—when they were together. My family bore witness to the way coal mining can lay waste to the land.

Jason Howard: I grew up next to the railroad tracks in Dorton Branch, a former coal camp, in Bell County, Kentucky. Some of my earliest memories are of trains rumbling by, rattling our windows, cars loaded down with coal. I spent hours walking those oily tracks with my father and grandmother, collecting pieces of coal dropped by the trains, hemmed in by the surrounding mountains. In the summertime, I placed pennies on the tracks with my friends, eagerly awaiting the distant sound of the train whistle.

I also listened to my family's stories about the rough side of the coal industry. My great-grandfather, McClellan "Clell" Howard, is the first name listed on the Kentucky Coal Miners' Memorial at Benham. He was murdered while in the mines because of a union dispute. His death is testimony to what fighting back could get a miner in the early union wars. My maternal great-grandfather, Garrett Garrison, went into the mines when he was only nine years old, driving a mule team, and worked there most of his life. As an adult, he worked in the Harlan County mines during the bloody strikes of the 1930s, and instilled in our family the belief that unionizing was the saving grace for a miner. He died an excruciating death by way of black lung. In their conversations, my family bore witness to the way coal mining can destroy a body. These stories marked my childhood as much as the coal miners I grew up around, as well as the boisterous stories they told of their workdays.

Being part of a coal economy is a complicated, conflicting thing. While proud of our coal-mining heritage, we both became keenly aware at an early age of the price that had to be paid for giving energy to the nation and the world.

We both know about the love-hate relationship many Appalachians feel about coal mining. We've not only seen it, we've lived it. When we first saw mountaintop removal, however, there was no love in the equation. After carefully examining the issue and learning as much as possible about this form of coal mining, we knew it was wrong. And even more than that, we knew we had to do something about it. This book is our way of fighting back.

While working on this book, we have been forever changed by the stories, images, people, places, and facts we have encountered.

We have seen communities devastated by the practice of mountaintop removal, abandoned by their representatives and their neighbors. We have met people whose faces bear the grief they have endured, grief not only for a lost mountain but also for a lost way of life. We've walked on years-old mountaintop removal sites, left behind after companies filed bankruptcy and were therefore not held accountable to properly reclaim the land before they moved on and filed permits under another company name. We have encountered evidence that caused us to question our own government and to shake our heads in wonder at how greed can distort and alter the landscape of a people and the integrity of an entire nation.

Yet we have been changed for the positive, too. Working on this book has made each of us find his own way to be a better part of the solution. We're both convinced that leading a simpler lifestyle is beneficial not only for the environment but also for the soul. The people we've met and the stories we've heard have caused us to agree more than ever that standing up for what you believe in makes you and your country stronger.

We have been changed by listening to the stories of our people, and we will be haunted by them. We will not let them go unheard.

The rate at which mountains are being leveled increases every day. Dissenters are not asking that the coal industry be shut down; they are simply asking for mining to be done with respect and responsibility, treating the place and its people with dignity. So far the coal companies have refused to listen to that request. Government officials refuse to require them to do so. As in so many other instances in history, our fate then lies within the hands of the people.

Thankfully, the people of Appalachia are rising up to make their voices heard.

In putting together this book we have spent many hours with each person we interviewed, observing them from afar before we ever approached them about being part of this project. After asking them if they would be willing to work with us, we then spent several hours interviewing them in their homes, on mountaintops, at local restaurants, on creek banks. More than one cooked us supper (proving the diversity of this region, we were offered everything from soup beans to homegrown strawberries to hummus). Some laughed to keep from crying. Others wept openly.

We want our readers to feel as though they have met these courageous people. We hope to accomplish that through the use of what we call the features that precede each oral history. In these introductory pieces, we present a feature-length story about the person, introducing him or her from our point of view before turning the book over to the subjects themselves, through their oral histories.

The people in this book are not only courageous fighters; they are also storytellers, poets, and stewards of the land. They are witnesses to a mining practice that is taking their place and tearing up their souls. Through talking about the environmental devastation that results from mountaintop removal, they have revealed the way their own culture, their heritage, their very memories are being scraped away, too. But their voices are rising, building in strength. They may now be only a murmur rolling over the mountains, but soon they will become a roar that will slide along the hollers and shady creeks, across ridgetops and cool cliff faces, until they are heard by everyone. These are their stories.

Jean Ritchie

The Preservationist

I come from the mountains, Kentucky's my home
Where the wild deer and black bear so lately did roam
By cool rushin' waterfalls the wildflowers dream
and through every green valley there runs a clear stream
Now there's scenes of destruction on every hand
and there's only black waters run down through my land
Sad scenes of destruction on every hand
black waters, black waters run down through the land.
—Jean Ritchie, "Black Waters"

Jean Ritchie's eyes haven't changed since she was a young girl. At eighty-six years old, they are as blue as blown glass, full of wisdom and cleverness and intensity and, above all, kindness. Kindness lights up Ritchie's entire face, so clear and real that it causes her to seem almost not of this world. Beatific. And she possesses the same kindness in her hands, in the slight, humble bend of her neck, in her beaming smile. And of course that kindness is what comes through the clearest, the cleanest, in her voice. It is there in her speaking voice, but also in her singing voice, the quality that has caused the *New York Times* to proclaim her "a national treasure" and the reason Ritchie has become widely known as "the mother of folk."

As soon as she enters the dining room of her home on the highest hill in Port Washington, New York, the natural illumination of her face is enhanced when she steps into the white light falling through the picture window over her dining table on this winter midday and she says, "Welcome, welcome," in her gentle way.

Jean Ritchie, Hindman, Kentucky. Photo by Silas House.

She pats her red hair, which she has just pulled up with a barrette on each side, her trademark part straight and exactly in the middle of her head. In that light, with a smile that covers first her mouth and then her entire face, for a split second she is a girl again. No matter all the knowledge those blue eyes hold: they must have been full of wisdom even then. For just a moment she is a child again, a girl frozen forever in time, the Singing Girl of the Cumberlands. Her eyes must have looked just this way at the age of twelve, as she described herself in her 1955 book, *Singing Family of the Cumberlands:*

> I watched the brightening sky and was proud that I could feel the frail beauty of it. I felt proud of my . . . lonesome feelings. I felt proud that I was who I was. I wondered if anyone would ever understand how much was in my mind and heart. I wondered if ever there'd come somebody who would know. You couldn't talk about such things. You had to talk about corn and dishes and brooms and meetings and lengths of cloth and lettuce beds. If you should start to talk about the other things—the things inside you—folks might think you were getting above your raising. Highfalutin. Maybe I was the only one. Maybe nobody else in this world felt the things I felt and thought the things I thought in my mind.

It wouldn't be long after having these thoughts that Ritchie would venture out into the world to find others like herself. But before that journey began, she learned nearly everything that would carry her through the rest of her life from her family and neighbors in the small community of Viper, in Perry County, Kentucky, where she was born in a cabin on the banks of Elk Branch in December 1922. Ritchie, the daughter of Abigail and Balis, was the youngest of fourteen, and a surprise to her mother, who was forty-four years old when Ritchie was born. "It's a mystery to me that the house don't fly all to pieces," her mother used to say, according to Ritchie. "I don't rightly know where they all get to of a night."

Ritchie, as the title of her book suggests, grew up in a singing family, a family who would gather on the porch every evening to "sing up the moon." They did everything together, singing all the while. "We'd sing while we worked and played, while we walked or did anything at all," Ritchie says. "We'd sing in the cornfields or over the dishes while we washed them." She can't remember anyone *not* singing. "We could all carry a tune," she says. The songs they sang were all handed down to them from family members and dated back to long before their ancestors crossed the ocean. Today the Ritchie Family is best known for preserving the song "Far Nottamun Town." In 1917 famed songcatcher Cecil Sharp found his way to the Ritchie Family and was sung to by Jean's older sisters Una and May.

When Ritchie was about four years old, she started eyeing her father's dulcimer, which he had bought for five dollars from a nearby dulcimer builder. No one in the family dared to touch it, knowing that it was Balis's prized possession, but often when he was in the fields, Ritchie says she would hide with it and play it. By the time she was seven, her father had caught on that she was sneaking around to play the dulcimer, but instead of punishing her, he sat down with her and began to show her a few things about playing the instrument. Over the next few years Ritchie taught herself to play. "I just watched him and did what he did," she says. Her singing was heavily influenced by the high, clear voices of her mother and sisters. She says that most of the time they didn't use musical accompaniment. "Instruments were just so hard to come by back then," she says.

An education was hard to come by, too, but Ritchie's parents—especially her father, a teacher—encouraged all of their children to graduate high school and to go on to college. "Dad wanted us to *all* go to school," Ritchie says. "He'd talk about this and people would say, 'Even the girls?' He believed in *all* of us."

Two of Ritchie's sisters went to Wellesley by way of the Hindman Settlement School,[1] but Ritchie didn't get the chance to board at Hindman since a new high school was built at Viper. She got a good education there, though, and went on to Cumberland College in Williamsburg, Kentucky, almost exactly 100 miles—and a world—away from home.[2] Ritchie then attended the University of Kentucky, where she received a degree in social work in 1946 (graduating with highest honors and a Phi Beta Kappa key). Immediately after receiving her degree, she moved to New York City, where she got a job at the Henry Street Settlement School on the Lower East Side, working with children.[3] "My plan was to go to New York and get some experience, then go back to the Hazard area to work," she says.

"We had to find a way to entertain" the children, recalls Ritchie, "so I'd teach them Kentucky games, and they'd teach me Jewish games and games from Italy and Puerto Rico." She also taught the children the songs she had grown up singing, accompanying herself on guitar and dulcimer. Students and coworkers alike became mesmerized when she sang. Before she knew it, and without even trying, Ritchie had acquired a following. She quickly became a popular guest at schools and parties throughout the city. At one of these gatherings she met George Pickow, an energetic magazine photographer who was making a name for himself with his pictures, which were a beautiful mix of reportage and art.[4]

"I had heard there was this great singer that was going to be there, but I didn't care too much about what she was singing. I don't think I even listened, because she was so gorgeous," Pickow recalls. Ritchie remembers that Pickow thought she was "putting on" her accent and that she wasn't "for real." He soon found not only that she was very much for real, but also that he loved her way of singing. He quickly became her biggest fan, and remains so today.

One thing led to another, and eventually Ritchie found herself singing for Alan Lomax, the preeminent folklorist and musicologist who had fostered the careers of artists such as Woody Guthrie and Leadbelly. "Jean's quiet, serene, objective voice, the truth of her pitch, the perfection and restraint of her decorations (the shakes and quavers that fall upon the melody to suit it to the poetry) all denote a superb mountain singer," Lomax wrote in the 1965 preface to Ritchie's book *Folk Songs of the Southern Appalachians.*

In 1948 Lomax set up a concert for Ritchie at Columbia University. By 1952 she had a contract with Elektra Records and had released her first solo album, *Jean Ritchie Sings Traditional Songs of Her Kentucky Mountain Home.*

In 1950 she had eloped with Pickow, and they began what Ritchie calls "our folklore-collecting travels; myself as a singer/dulcimer player/interviewer (gossip), and he as a photographer/filmmaker/sound recorder." Ritchie received a Fulbright Scholarship in 1952, and she and Pickow went to England, Scotland, and Ireland to "visit, swap music, tea-party and ceilidh with many wonderful folks," she says.[5] The result was the 1954 album *Field Trip,* which contains traditional songs as sung by rural people in the countries Ritchie and Pickow visited as well as Ritchie's interpretations of her own family's variants of the same songs. This album single-handedly preserved an entire culture that might have been lost otherwise. In the original liner notes, Ritchie wrote of meeting the singers of the British Isles: "I had the warm feeling that I was back home in Kentucky, that these were my kinfolks, and I knew I had found what I had come searching for—I had found my roots, and the sources of my songs."

On this trip she came into contact with a seventeen-year-old boy named Tommy Makem, who played tin-whistle but didn't know much traditional music. Makem went on to become one of Ireland's biggest recording artists (he is now known as "the Godfather of Irish Music") and has credited Ritchie with inspiring his interest in traditional music. Thus, once again she had her hand in preservation, no matter how inadvertently.

In 1955, Oxford University Press published Ritchie's childhood autobiography, *Singing Family of the Cumberlands,* with illustrations by Maurice Sendak. The book has as much to do with preserving traditional music as it does with preserving the storytelling tradition; in it, Ritchie examines forty-two of her family's most beloved songs. She had set out simply to save and explain her family's song variants, but she ended up writing a moving memoir of a time and place that was already forever gone. The book was published to wide acclaim, was excerpted in *Ladies Home Journal,* and is today considered a classic. It has never been out of print and regularly shows up on the syllabi of many Appalachian studies classes.

Ritchie went on to publish several songbooks that were interlaced with family and regional history. Three of them in particular—*Jean Ritchie's Swapping Song Book* (1952), *A Garland of Mountain Songs* (1953), and *Folk Songs of the Southern Appalachians* (1965) are indispensable texts for anyone interested in Appalachian music or culture. Together, they preserve more than 200 of the region's songs—some of which would have surely been lost otherwise. In all of them (but particularly in the *Swapping Song Book*) Pickow's accompanying photographs are themselves remarkable acts of preservation.

Ritchie became ever more active in the folk music scene and before long became one of the leading voices in the genre. Her involvement caused her to be incorrectly identified as a card-carrying Communist in a 1965 book called *Communism, Hypnotism, and the Beatles,* which named several singers as promoting Communism through their songs, and even earlier in small, now-defunct McCarthyite magazines.[6] Ritchie was shocked by the allegation, especially because of the way she found out about it. "I was performing at a college, sometime in the 1950s, I think," recalls Ritchie. "After the program, a young girl pushed this little magazine at me and said, 'Oh Jean—*why* did you ever become a Communist?' I assured her that I had never joined the Communist party. She showed me the magazine, and there I was, listed with other folksingers described as 'Pete Seeger and his ilk,' who sang leftist songs on the streets. It went on to describe the songs as 'left-wing' and 'pornographic,' songs like 'The Cherry-tree Carol.'[7] I swear that this is the song they had picked to illustrate the terrible filthy things that we 'Communists' were singing."

By the end of the 1960s Ritchie had recorded twenty albums, served on the board of and appeared at the first Newport Folk Festival (where her iconic performance of "Amazing Grace" is still talked about by anyone who was there), and was considered one of the leaders in the folk music revival. She had also single-handedly popularized the mountain dulcimer. Countless dulcimer players have given Ritchie credit for bringing their attention to the instrument.

In 1974 she recorded what many consider the first of her three true masterpieces (along with *None but One* and *Mountain Born*) out of her forty albums. *Clear Waters Remembered* contains three of the original compositions she is most often recognized for: "West Virginia Mine Disaster," "Blue Diamond Mines," and "Black Waters." It would also be the album that would solidify Ritchie's position as an environmentalist and activist.

"Black Waters" in particular became a rallying cry for the growing outrage against the environmental devastation being caused by strip-mining, which at the time was a fairly new method of mining coal. The practice was giving many Appalachians pause, especially because most of the coal companies were able to mine the coal with broad-form deeds, many of which had been sold decades before. Ritchie became a part of this movement with "Black Waters," which became an anthem for the movement against the practice. After struggling over its creation, Ritchie finally finished the song after being invited to participate in a memorial concert for Woody Guthrie. She performed it for the first time during that show and introduced it as something Guthrie "might have written had he lived in Eastern Kentucky." Besides being a powerful environmental song, it also resonated with Appalachians who might not have identified themselves as environmentalists but who had a love for the land in their blood.

Carla Gover, one of the region's most popular singer-songwriters and a current Appalachian Music Fellow at Berea College, remembers being at a crowded event in Eastern Kentucky when Ritchie performed the song in front of an audience full of working and retired coal miners. "Mountain men do not always cry easily," says Gover. "But when Jean sang 'Black Waters' there was not a dry eye in the house. Tell me, how many people can make a roomful of coal miners cry?"

Despite their obviously being social commentaries, Ritchie's songs speak to everyone as moving narratives. Instead of being accusatory and in your face, Ritchie's lyrics are simultaneously subtle and blunt, so that the listener realizes what is being said before he or she even knows it. "Her songs are powerful social statements, but in a way much different than, say, Bob Dylan's 'Masters of War,'" Gover says. "Jean is one of the most powerful, subtle, graceful, potent political songwriters ever to come out of this music-laden state, and she does it so effectively that there are many who probably don't even think of her as a political singer."

1977's *None but One* is Ritchie's most critically lauded album; it was even awarded the prestigious Critics Award from *Rolling Stone* magazine. The album contains two more of Ritchie's famous songs of social consciousness, "None but One," a treatise on racial harmony, and "The Cool of the Day," an ancient-sounding spiritual that demands environmental stewardship and which is now being widely used as one of the major anthems in the fight against mountaintop removal. It is a song that has already achieved classic status by being included in the hymnal of the Society of Friends. Ritchie allowed Kentuckians for the Commonwealth to use the song on their popular compilation *Songs for the Mountaintop,* which raises money for the fight against mountaintop removal. In 2007 Ritchie performed the song at the Concert for the Mountains, an event held in New York City with Robert Kennedy, Jr., in conjunction with a delegation of Appalachians who attended the United Nations Conference on Environmental Sustainability and spoke out about the devastation caused by this form of mining.

"I never feel that I'm doing very much to help our poor

mountains," Ritchie says, sitting at her dining room table with her hands folded before her. "Beyond making up songs and singing them, I don't know what else to do. I've never been good at waving flags and shouting through loudspeakers, so I'm wondering what there is of an activist about me. It seems an accolade I don't deserve." Ritchie grows quiet for a moment, her face turned to the white light of the window again. She grows visibly upset, but manages to contain herself. "Sometimes, when I think of how it's all gone . . . well, I better stop about there."

Ritchie is now able to look back on a life well lived, one full of music and service. Her accolades are many. In 2002 she was awarded a National Heritage Fellowship from the National Endowment for the Arts, the highest award given in the nation to traditional artists and musicians. She is one of only fifty-seven others to be given the honor, along with such people as Hazel Dickens, Bill Monroe, Wanda Jackson, and John Lee Hooker. She has received honorary degrees from the University of Kentucky and Berea College. An anonymous donor recently asked Lincoln Memorial University to organize the Jean Ritchie Fellowship in Appalachian Literature, a $1,500 annual allowance to an emerging Appalachian writer and the largest monetary prize given to a writer in the region. Her original compositions have been performed by such artists as Johnny Cash, June Carter Cash, Judy Collins, Emmylou Harris, The Judds, Kathy Mattea, Dolly Parton, Linda Ronstadt, and many others. Recently, a play entitled *Sing up the Moon,* a look at Ritchie's life and songs, opened in Pennsylvania and is preparing for a run in New York.

Ritchie says she's trying to slow down these days. "I'm trying very hard to retire," she laughs. But she can't help contributing to the fight against mountaintop removal in whatever way she can. More than anything else, Ritchie serves as a guiding hand for the movement, a figurehead whom everyone involved can look to for inspiration, and one whose eloquent wisdom is hard to deny.

Kate Larken is a writer, publisher, and singer-songwriter from Kentucky who has emerged as one of the leading musical voices against mountaintop removal. She says that Ritchie serves as "a light we can follow through all of this darkness." Larken, who often leads crowds in sing-alongs of "The Cool of the Day" at anti–mountaintop removal rallies and other events, depends on Ritchie's long-standing example as guidance.

"I'm inspired by Jean's generosity these last few years. Seems to me that she'll do whatever she can to help in the fight. Even in her eighties, she's not sitting back and letting others fight it for her; she's not fooling around—she's serious and she's active," Larken says. "I'll swear, I believe Jean Ritchie will walk 'til morning—if that's what it takes—to help lead us to where we need to be so we can all see this thing more clearly."

Although it has become harder and harder for her to get around—mostly due to a bad ankle—Ritchie tries to be as active in the struggle against environmental devastation as she can.

In May of 2008, Ritchie traveled back home to Eastern Kentucky to receive another honorary degree, this time from Union College in Barbourville. She elected to not speak at commencement, choosing to sing instead. Her set came about halfway through the two-hour-long program, but before that, people were already restless. Those in the upper bleachers fanned themselves with their programs. Babies cried. Everyone seemed to be milling about, going in and out to smoke, staying just to see their friend or family member graduate. But when Ritchie sat down with her dulcimer and began singing "Shady Grove," the commotion ceased. No one moved a muscle. The more than a thousand people filling the gymnasium were all unified in listening to her, watching her, feeling her good spirit wash over them. It was a magical moment, and it grew even more intense once Ritchie decided that she wanted to sing one more song. She stood on her own and looked out on the crowd, making eye contact with almost everyone.

"I wrote this next song about thirty years ago," she said, "about something that I felt was very important. And it turns out that it's still about something important." Then she closed her eyes and sang:

> My Lord, he said unto me
> "Do you like my garden so fair?
> You may live in this garden if you'll keep the grasses green
> And I'll return in the cool of the day."
>
> Now is the cool of the day
> Now is the cool of the day
> This earth is a garden, the garden of my Lord
> And he walks in his garden
> In the cool of the day
>
> Then my Lord, he said unto me
> "Do you like my pastures so green?
> You may live in this garden if you will feed my sheep
> And I'll return in the cool of the day."
>
> Then my Lord, he said unto me
> "Do you like my garden so free?
> You may live in this garden if you'll keep the people free
> And I'll return in the cool of the day."
>
> Now is the cool of the day
> Now is the cool of the day
> O this earth is a garden, the garden of my Lord
> And he walks in his garden
> In the cool of the day.

At that point, the only sound in the huge room is that of people crying. They may not know that they've just heard an environmentally minded hymn, but they all are aware that they've just witnessed something very powerful. Perhaps a few of them have even been changed forever. Then they stand up, with none of the hesitation that usually occurs with standing ovations. Everyone is on their feet, and the applause is thunderous.

After commencement, on their way out, people push and shove to speak to Ritchie, to thank her, to touch her. She is treated like a prophet here in her homeland. One woman, dressed in a bright Sunday-best dress and tottering on white heels she is not used to, stands nearby but will not approach Ritchie. Her Appalachian hands—big, hard-working, liver-spotted—hold tight to the shoulders of her young granddaughter, who wears an Easter hat for the occasion of seeing someone, perhaps an older sister, become the first college graduate in the family. The woman leans down to the little girl and whispers, "Look, Cassie. That's Jean Ritchie. This is something to remember, baby."

Just as when she was twelve years old, Jean Ritchie knows who she is and knows what she believes in. So many years ago that little Singing Girl of the Cumberlands thought to herself, "I felt proud that I was who I was." But that child also felt alone. As a twelve-year-old, she could have had no idea that one day she would bring so many people together, making all of them realize that they were not alone. She could not have known how proud all Appalachians—and all people who believe in standing up for what they believe in—would one day be of her, too.

When the interview is over, Ritchie frets that her visitors have not had anything to eat, having dined just before arriving at her house. Like a true Appalachian, she can't stand the thought of us leaving her home with an empty belly or an empty hand. She produces a box of chocolates and insists that we take them. "You didn't have any coffee or a bite to eat or anything," she says, with concern.

She also can't resist the Appalachian tradition of following visitors out the door when they depart. She comes out on the porch with us as we load everything back into our car and prepare to leave. She talks to us the whole while as we arrange camera cases and backpacks and tape recorders, wishing us well, telling us about her next planned trip to Kentucky, where she has always maintained a second home in Viper, unable to completely move away. Just as we are fixing to leave her driveway, Ritchie leans on the porch railing and holds up her face so it can be touched by the surprisingly warm March sun. She closes her eyes for a moment, and she can't help but sing: "What wondrous love is this / O my soul, o my soul."

Upon reopening her girlish eyes, she sees that we are about to pull away, so she gives a hearty wave. Her smile is like a prayer.

Jean Ritchie talking . . .

My childhood home there in Viper was a place of a happy childhood. When you have a happy childhood you can romanticize your memories. The whole family was there. It was a beautiful place. The mountains really were our backyard. We were right there by the branch, and the mountains were all around us. They were the front yard and the side yard and the backyard.

There was a certain old path we used to take up to the cornfield. We'd all go up together to hoe corn, all the sisters and brothers, with a mule to plow around the hillside before we hoed. There was this certain little path we took, and I took it not too long ago, showing George exactly where we crossed the creek here and where we climbed the hill there, you know. We'd avoid the road by taking these shortcuts. You'd climb down a clift in one place. We used to go to the cornfield like that. We'd sing and talk.

I remember us carrying our dinners up to the fields. This one time, my sisters Colleen and Edna and Pauline ganged up and made up a story. There was a tree—there were a lot of trees like this, but there was a great big beech tree that we'd always pass, and it had big old roots that made little circles where they went into the ground. They told me that little people lived down in there, little fairies, who lived back under the tree, and they said the roots was their front porch. We'd take little gifts there—little coffee can lids full of water and honey. They had me believing this was true.

And to this day when I pass that tree I still want to put something down there for them, some kind of offering.

When my people first came to Kentucky it was just subsistence farming.[8] But by the time I was around, most all of the men worked in the mines. All my cousins and uncles, and people all around us. All the men.

My brother Raymond worked underground, and the thing we noticed most about his hardships was when he got appendicitis. His appendix burst, and he was just lying there in the mines for about fourteen or fifteen hours before they got anybody in to help him. We thought we were going to lose him, thought he's going to die, but he made it through that. It was just neglect, nobody from the company came to get him. They figured since it wasn't a mining accident they didn't have to worry. Poor man.

My other brother worked in the commissary, and I remember one time he came home with a can of condensed milk. We everyone stood around and took a drink, having a little taste. I remember that it was the smoothest, most wonderful taste. We used to long for him to bring that home. And he'd bring little treats home that we didn't get all the time. His name was Truman.

I first took note of the coal companies and injustice when they started strip mining. There was a big uproar when that started. People started fussing just like they're doing now over the mountaintop removal, but they didn't get very far, as you can see, because they just stripped all over the place. They kept saying, "Aw, it'll all come back, it'll all grow back." Then they'd throw down a few little grass seeds and they told everybody that the grass would grow and the trees would grow and so on but it never was the same after that. You can see all those bare places still, where they first did it.

The memories are all about little things, like the head of the holler. There was a knob that stuck up, and we called it the Tater Knob. It looked just like the end of a potato. There was a hole up there and you could throw a little pebble down it and you could hear it going and going and going. It was probably down in some old coal mine. But maybe it was a natural cave or something. It was a place we used to play, and they leveled that, they took away the Tater Knob. That's the thing you think of. I don't think, "Oh, what they're doing to the land!" I think, "They took away the Tater Knob!" It's that connection that's being lost that's so important, especially to the ones who remember that land, who know that land, who played in those places.

They're destroying our memories, but they're destroying our whole country—you know what I mean by that, that usage of that word, with "whole country" meaning our region.

I was raised to speak up and say what I believed in. That was part of our education. My dad used to read every book he could get ahold of. He had the Bible and the *Pilgrim's Progress* and a few other big tomes. Just anything he could get. He'd just read, read, read. And he taught school, too. He taught there, round home, and started a subscription school when there wasn't any school; it goes back that far.[9] He was all in favor of education. Even before we went to school we were taught that everybody was the same in the sight of God, no matter what color they were or what country they came from. And we all believed that. And the older girls went to Berea, and Berea was a big advocate for not having racism or anything like that. Dad wanted us to go to school, and many kids didn't get to go to school, they were encouraged to just stay at the house and worked in the corn. School had seasons when they would let you off for fodder pulling or planting. Lots of people would say, "I didn't go to school, so you don't have to go to school." Our family was different, and we were very lucky to have my parents, who told us to get an education. Hindman[10] used to send its best students to Wellesley, so I had two sisters who went there.

The first protest songs I ever remember hearing were by the Singing Miner, George Davis, who was always on the Hazard radio station.[11] He was real popular, and everybody listened to him.

Then the first song I ever wrote that could be considered a protest song was just my own reaction to what was happening. I didn't think anyone else would ever listen to it. "Black Waters" was the first one. George and I were going over Pine Mountain, and we saw some water that was polluted from the slag heaps. The water was all discolored, red or yellow, a lot of it was black. And when it flooded around people's houses it was all black from the strip-mining and such. So we were on that trip and we saw the water and I just started singing, "Black waters, black waters, run down through the land," and I went home and over the next few weeks I wrote it.

And then there was "Blue Diamond Mines," which George was real important on. We were driving on a big trip, and we went through a big pine forest. I was singing "In the pines/in the pines/where the sun/never shines,"[12] and George said, "Why don't you do a song called 'In the mines/in the mines,'" and I thought, oh, that's silly.[13] Then later on I felt, well, that is good, that's a very natural thing to sing.

I was very much aware that they were protest songs when I wrote them, and so I didn't want anyone to bother my mother, who was an old lady, like I am now. I didn't want anyone coming up to her and saying, "Your daughter's up in New York singing protest songs. What is she doing? She must be a Communist." So I took a pseudonym: Than Hall. This was in tribute to my grandpa, but also to protect my family.[14]

And those kinds of songs sounded better coming from a man than a woman, could be better accepted. Pete Seeger[15] never got over the notion that I only sang ballads. He'd come out and say, "Now Jean Ritchie is going to sing us a song in her high, clear voice, and she's going to make us all really feel wonderful. She sings these beautiful old songs she learned from her mother, these lyrical, high things," but I wanted to sing "Black Waters," so I'd go ahead and sing that and then the next time, he'd introduce me the very same way. Your reputation that you make in the beginning is very hard to change. I would get up there and say, "This is what's happening to our mountains, and we want it to stop." That song made a big impression on everybody, and everybody always wanted to sing on the chorus.

I certainly do think mountaintop removal is morally wrong. Kentucky has one of the last great watersheds, these headwaters. It's being torn apart, it's being desolated. Every time we fill up a stream and kill a little river, you're causing terrible things for the future, as far as living in it. It's all going to be like Kenmont[16] someday, that whole part of the country. They've taken away all the houses out of Viper, on the right side of the road, by the river. When you drive up to Lower Viper, why, there's nothing there. The big trucks are coming out of Mace's Creek and turning down in there.

The children of today don't know the kind of experience growing up I did, I don't guess. They have television, whole walls of television, the schools go in more for sports than anything else, they have all these things to occupy them. So I don't believe they're as connected to the land as people once were, which might make it easier to happen.

Ever since I was a little girl and we would go with Mom and Dad to the Old Regular Baptist Church, no matter what happened, people would always say, "Ah, it's God's will. It's God's will and he's got a purpose for it, so we ought not question it." I think while it's a wonderful old religion, and the songs are good, and the beliefs are good, I still think that religion has influenced people to be apathetic. I think that maybe times are changing, though. People are starting to see what's going on and what happens when certain things are done to the land. But that old feeling of "It was meant to be," it's still there, I think.

Legally a landowner can do whatever he wants to with the land. But he ought to think about the result, about what his home is going to be like in a few years. He should think about what's going to happen to his neighbors, his river, his waters. He should think about others. He should think about the fact that there are no trees left to draw the water down. So legally it may be okay, but where it really matters, morally, I don't think so. The coal companies count on people thinking that their jobs are going to be cut out if they quit mining in a particular way. But my dad always went and dug that coal out himself to heat our house, and that didn't hurt anybody, it didn't hurt the land. But this large-scale stuff . . . well, we have to change our way of thinking. We just have to.

There have been times when I've felt like I was fighting my own people. I always wondered how people around where we lived would accept "Black Waters." When I was home, once in a while somebody would say something to me about it. Nobody ever threatened me or anything about it, but I think they thought I was a woman, so it didn't mean much. I don't know why I got by with it, but I did. And I never tried to say it was something else.

I still have land up in the holler. I guess we have about thirty-five acres. They've mined all the way up the holler. You can climb one mountain and see what it looks like on the ones hemming us in.

Do you remember being a young 'un and having a big sore on your leg, and it wouldn't get well, it kept draining? That's the way I feel when I see that land. I feel like it's a big, open sore on me somewhere. No matter what you put on it, no matter if you go to the doctor, it's still there. I don't know what it's going to take to heal it. I do what I can.

One time, I was up at home and I was complaining about the subsidence of our creek. The coal company had done something underground, and all the water went out of our creek, and they came up and looked at it. They waited until it rained and then they came up—they never would come when it was dry, that's how they do. From them I got the feedback that since I didn't live there year-round I shouldn't care what was going on.

I don't think I've ever really left Kentucky. So many thoughts are there, my family is there, my memories are there. The songs that I learned, people are still singing them there. I go quite often to visit, as many times as I can, and spend time there in my cabin. I feel that I'm still a resident of Kentucky. This is just the way I am, the way I talk, the way I act. I can't be anything else.

I talk the way we talk, and I wrote my book[17] that way, too, wrote it in our way of speaking. I had a helper, an editor at Oxford Press, he oversaw all my stuff and gave me advice and he said, "Jean, you know some of these words you're using, nobody's going to know what they are." And I said, "Well, you can tell by the sentence structure what they are. That's how we say it." He said, "You ought to change it and put this word in instead," and he'd suggest New England words. He was from there. And I said, "Well, I'm not from New England. This is the Kentucky word." So he just said, "I'm going on vacation and in three weeks I'll have a decision about this," and when he came back he had decided I was right. I don't know how I got the nerve to do that. That was my first book; I didn't know how nerve-rattling it could be. But I just wasn't going to do that, to change. And you know, when the book was reviewed, that was one of the main things they picked out to say that I did a good job of, capturing the language.

I guess I can claim Kentucky, because every once in a while they claim me. Just here recently they've named a road after me. Two miles of road.[18] I don't think they've done it yet, but the governor said he was going to.[19] They put the road fourteen foot higher on the hill. There was a big curve there where people were always having accidents. So they used that as an excuse to do the road over. They did improve it, but in doing it they denuded three or four mountainsides, all the way to the top. I don't know why they did that, but I think it's so they can mine it. I kept writing to Frankfort and asking them to not do it, telling them they were doing a terrible thing. Because they condemned everyone's houses, made them move, tore them down, desolated the land. I wrote letters and said they ought not do that, that they should fix the other road. I never got a real answer. When the governor came, he knew he had been getting letters from me, but he didn't know why; he hadn't read them. When they took the first shovelful of dirt he said he was going to name the road after me. When people told me this, I said, "Well, he sure wasn't reading my letters." He must have thought the letters were telling him the road was a wonderful thing. But they weren't.

Now I realize that in a way I'm an activist, but I sure never thought of myself as that way. Never thought of myself as someone who stood on lines and went to rallies and things like that. I'm a very shy person, but when I get on stage and am talking to my audience, that's different because I feel like it's one big person out there and we're just having a conversation. But I wouldn't get up and put on sequins and dance around with my microphone. I wouldn't go on like that. I just get up there and do what I do.

Shortly after I came to New York, it was about 1947, there came May Day, that used to be a big rally day in New York City. We were trying to organize the place I worked, the Henry Street Settlement, down on the Lower East Side. It was a place that was trying to help people, not a place that manufactured. But we didn't make a lot of money. Everybody said you shouldn't be doing this, but we said, "We want the workers at Henry Street to have better salaries and better places to live," which was true. It was a fairly large outfit. We were having a rally, and we were carrying this big banner and walking down the street, and Pete Seeger gave me this megaphone and said, "Here, sing a song." I said [*whispers*] "I can't do that, they won't listen to me, I can't do that." They had a truck with a stage, and he was wanting me to go up there and make a speech, sing a song. I said, "I'll march, and I'll carry a sign, but I can't do that, sing a song like that here." He pushed me out and made me—I was so nervous, so worried, that I just started singing, and the audience just talked. It was true, they didn't listen to me. It was just my personality, my belief in how good I was. In those days I really thought I was nothing, and still do, in some ways. I couldn't force myself to do it, it was something that my persona couldn't do.

But nowadays. Well, I'm again[20] not saying anything. I think we have to make people more aware of what's happening. The reason more people are not doing anything, I imagine, is because they think they can't win. They think, "Well, that's the way the world's changing." And that's the way the coal companies want them to think. They say, "Ah, we're bringing you stores and commerce and such; what do you want with this old country way?" And people believe that. And it's easier for them to not say anything. I think people just think it's a monumental thing, that they won't make any difference. They think they're small and this is large, and they think they're not going to get anywhere, that they'll just be beating their heads against a stone wall.

Sometimes, I think of when I was a little girl there, in that place. The mountains circling around us like we were down in a little bowl. My happiest memories are of the times I was walking out in those mountains, on those trails. I had a special rock that jutted out, just big enough for a seat. I'd take me an apple and set there, and I'd talk out loud to the trees and the flowers.

The memories, they just push right down on me sometimes. Everybody who was there isn't there anymore. Nowadays I think mainly about how it looks now, and how it used to look. The rest of it is all going to be destroyed now—unless we can stop it.

Port Washington, New York, March 14, 2008

Denise Giardina

Mother Jones's Great-Granddaughter

> The notion that a radical is one who hates his country is naïve and usually idiotic. He is, more likely, one who likes his country more than the rest of us, and is thus more disturbed than the rest of us when he sees it debauched. He is not a bad citizen turning to crime; he is a good citizen driven to despair.
>
> —H. L. Mencken

> I'm Mother Jones's daughter and she
> taught me to stand tall
> For the rights of working people
> and justice for us all.
>
> —Sue Massek, "Cosby"

Denise Giardina is a radical. Perched on the worn couch in her cozy home in Charleston, West Virginia, Giardina doesn't shy away from this term, a death knell in modern politics. She certainly doesn't fit the stereotype. Her wardrobe doesn't consist of military fatigues. There are no pictures of Che Guevara on her walls, no "Lyndon LaRouche for President" fliers lying on her coffee table. That's just not her style. Instead, Giardina looks to Henry Thoreau, Dietrich Bonhoeffer, and Mother Jones as her guideposts for revolutionary change.

Mother Jones is of particular importance to Giardina. Nearly one hundred years ago, Mary Jones was called before the United States Senate after organizing thousands of miners in a series of bloody strikes against the coal operators, most famously in Paint Creek, West Virginia. Senator Nathan Goff, a West Virginia Republican and a longtime supporter of the coal industry, scorned

Denise Giardina. Photo by Page Hamrick.

her in front of his colleagues as "the grandmother of all agitators." Mother Jones smiled. "I hope to live long enough to be the *great*-grandmother of all agitators," she replied with defiance.

Giardina is one of these spiritual grandchildren. Now in her fifties, she has been building on Jones's legacy of agitation against the coal industry since the 1970s. In the 1990s, she became one of the first public figures in Appalachia to publicly oppose mountaintop removal mining; this was an unpopular and risky stand for a writer with "favorite daughter" status who continues to live in the region. Since then, Giardina has been on the forefront of the issue throughout Appalachia, inspiring other artists to fight back. So groundbreaking were her early protests that she is often referred to as "the godmother of the anti–mountaintop removal movement."

The forcefulness of her advocacy sometimes catches her admirers by surprise. A self-admitted introvert, Giardina is a writer more in the tradition of Harper Lee than Truman Capote. Shy and reserved, she doesn't court publicity, doesn't enjoy being in front of large crowds, doesn't relish making small talk at receptions. Instead, her passions come alive in more intimate settings.

Her living room invites a level of ease. Hers is a writer's house, unapologetically lived in and worked in. Books and other objects of importance dominate; a copy of Ian McEwan's *Atonement* lies on her end table. Giardina is a West Virginian to the core; a DVD of the recently released movie *We Are Marshall* sits on a bookcase. Her beloved animals—one dog and three cats—creep around corners and hide under tables at will. Phyllis, her loyal mutt, rests her black-and-white speckled head on Giardina's lap. "Phyllis is just full of love," Giardina explains, scratching behind the dog's ear. "That's how she got adopted. I went to the pound and all the puppies were playing, but she came and just looked up at me, like, 'Play with me.'"

Such compassion is surely behind her objections against the coal industry; compassion for her people, compassion for her native land. Giardina's is a Christ-centered identity: "to bind up the broken hearts and set at liberty them that are bruised," in the words of Isaiah. But her theology of mercy has its limits. Out of this river of sympathy runs a steady stream of righteous indignation more akin to Christ's cleansing the temple. It's certainly something she'd like to see happen in West Virginia.

"I will be as blunt as I can be," she once wrote in the *Charleston Gazette.* "Mountaintop removal is evil, and those who support it are supporting evil . . . I puzzle over the modern-day difference between a terrorist and someone who supports mountaintop removal. One destroys with a bomb, the other with a fountain pen, dynamite, and a dragline. God help us."[1]

Such language illustrates that Giardina isn't your average protester. Her rallying cries come from a very deep place, a cavern of faith that she has found refuge in since childhood.

Reared in the Methodist Church with its Wesleyan creed of service, Giardina eventually gravitated toward the Episcopal denomination. During college, she began discovering the works of theologians such as Bonhoeffer, a Lutheran pastor who became involved in the German Resistance movement and a conspiracy to assassinate Adolf Hitler. The plot was eventually discovered, and Bonhoeffer was hanged for his participation. Giardina found Bonhoeffer's witness so inspiring that she based her fourth novel, *Saints and Villains,* on his life story.

"The church radicalized me," Giardina says. She was so taken with her faith that she eventually received a Master's in Divinity degree from Virginia Theological Seminary in Alexandria. More recently, she has become an ordained deacon or, as she prefers to call it, "a sort of servant minister."

"The phrase in the prayer book is 'Interpret the world to the church and the church to the world,'" she says. "It's a totally different way to advocate, with a spiritual point of view."

But Giardina's advocacy has always focused on the spiritual. A large portion of her faith and activism rests on the concept of environmental stewardship, or the responsibility of Christians to support the "protection of the environment and . . . the sanctity of creation."[2] It is also the inspiration behind her choice to agitate through her art, in the many articles, op-ed pieces, and novels she has written over the years.

One of those novels, *Storming Heaven,* published in 1987, chronicles the fight for unionization in West Virginia during the early 1900s, in particular the real-life Battle of Blair Mountain, an uprising of 10,000 West Virginia miners. The striking miners, after years of enduring low wages, poor working conditions, sickness, and even starvation, take up arms against the mine owners and the corrupt state government. The federal government eventually intervenes, sending in troops and airplanes with bombs, and finally quelling the rebellion.

"The U.S. government dont give a damn what goes on down here," one of Giardina's characters laments. "They dont even know we're here." Another, in agreeing to fight against federal forces, responds, "So what? Hit's a lousy bunch of Republicans is all it is. Hit's a rich man's government and hit's a coal operators' government. We dont have to take nothing offn it. Aint yall never heard of the Declaration of Independence? Hit's our god-given right."

The God-given right to unionize is something that appears repeatedly in Giardina's work. Like many in the mountains, the union is something she holds dear, which is why she laments the absence of its once-stabilizing influence in today's mining industry.

"The union has disappeared from Eastern Kentucky and West Virginia," says Giardina. "Cecil Roberts is a big part of that problem. Unions on the whole have lost power, but he's been really ineffective."[3]

On the subject of the union, Giardina continues: "They've really sold out to the companies on mountaintop removal. That was the worst thing they ever did, when they let surface miners be part of the union, because they didn't used to be. That was a disaster. And the unions have been in the pockets of the strip mines ever since."

The subject of unionization was also a major theme in Giardina's follow-up to *Storming Heaven. The Unquiet Earth* was released to widespread critical acclaim in 1992, winning Giardina an American Book Award for fiction. *The Unquiet Earth* picks up where *Storming Heaven* left off, documenting union-busting efforts and further abuses of power by the coal industry. One such transgression is a neglected slurry impoundment that is near a community. In a chilling climax, the dam bursts and washes away nearly 150 lives. Once again, Giardina uses fiction to remind readers of an actual event, in this case the Buffalo Creek Disaster, which killed 125 people and left thousands more homeless in Logan County, West Virginia, in February 1972. The final scene, describing a character's evacuation by helicopter, remains eerily relevant: "The mountains are falling away below us. They are ripped and torn like a rumpled gray quilt where the cotton batting shows through. The crown of Trace Mountain is gone, a flat rock moon pocked by green ponds of acid water."

Like the devastation of mountaintop removal, that disaster might have been avoided had more people raised their voices in dissent. Giardina believes that Appalachians have been disenfranchised for so long that they no longer feel empowered to fight back.

"We're fatalists in the mountains," she says. "It's all up to the good Lord. People pray and get saved and wait for the Lord to fix everything. I think that attitude grows out of powerlessness. If we were Vermont or New Hampshire, we'd have town meetings and local political control and own our own land. This wouldn't be happening. But we're not, we're a third world country."

Such civilizations require visionary and moral political leadership to lift them above their social woes. Like many other states throughout Appalachia, West Virginia has historically been lacking in political leadership. Traditionally a Democratic state, most of its politicians at both the state and federal levels pledge some sort of allegiance to the coal industry.

Giardina challenged this conventional wisdom when she made the leap from art to politics in her run for governor in 2000.

Knowing she'd never make it past the starting gate as a Democrat, Giardina ran as a third-party candidate in order to get into the general election and force a dialogue on mountaintop removal and other issues at the debates.

Her intentions had the Democratic Party in an uproar. Fearing she'd siphon valuable votes from their candidate, two Democratic officials asked her to lunch. In exchange for dropping her gubernatorial bid, the party would guarantee her a seat in the state legislature for her district. Giardina left the meal shocked and disillusioned and even more committed to her candidacy.

As the Mountain Party candidate, she ran on a platform of strict populism, the likes of which had rarely been seen in West Virginia since Hubert Humphrey and John F. Kennedy campaigned in the state in 1960. Championing such issues as better access to health care, smaller schools, and greater regulation and taxation of the coal and timber industries, Giardina barnstormed the state to gain support.

As the powers that be would have it, she managed to appear in only two of the debates. "Twice on statewide television I got to get up and talk for two minutes on mountaintop removal. A year and a half of work to get to speak for two minutes," she recalls wearily, running her small hand down her frowning face.

Her frustration in the gubernatorial race was all the more galling, Giardina says, because of what she decries as the lack of backbone among West Virginia politicians at the federal level. "[Senator Robert] Byrd is terrible on all coal issues," she says. "He's such a Constitutionalist, he took a good, principled stand on the war, but he's never been good on coal. And [Senator] Jay Rockefeller has always been spineless on coal."

She sighs in exasperation at the lack of presidential leadership on the issue. "I can't stand George W. Bush, but I'll have to say, he's not any worse than Clinton or Carter on mountaintop removal. Carter may have thought he was going to stop mountaintop removal, but clearly he didn't. Reagan, Bush, Clinton, none of them ain't worth a damn thing when it comes to coal."

In the end, Giardina received 2 percent of the popular vote for governor and a decade's worth of disillusionment with the political process. She also became pessimistic about the prospects of mountaintop removal being banned any time soon.

Her job, she believes, is to keep sounding the battle cry. And like her spiritual great-grandmother Mother Jones before her, Giardina hopes that she also can give birth to a new generation of agitators.

Denise Giardina talking . . .

I grew up in the Black Wolf coal camp in McDowell County, the southernmost county in the state.[4] The damage to the land was already starting to be evident, although mountaintop removal hadn't started yet. But even as a small child, for example, it made me mad that I wasn't allowed to play in the creek, because the creek was full of mine acid and all that. I remember one time my brother and I were mad at another kid, so we made Kool-Aid for him out of the creek water. I was aware for as long as I could remember. Living like that didn't seem right, and it didn't seem like things like that happened in other places, from my reading about them. There was already some strip mining, and I didn't like that either, but actually during that time period the most vivid sort of environmental damage was from gob piles.[5] I remember thinking as a kid how bad they stunk and how awful they looked, and I couldn't understand why they were allowed to put them there. I don't remember anybody talking much about the environment when I was little, except to say the creek was dirty or something like that.

My mother learned how to drive just so she could take us to church, since my dad had no interest in it. I always took church seriously, and I took the Bible seriously when it said that we should take care of the earth. My mom had a lot to do with teaching me about the environment and how that had a connection to our spiritual life. We weren't allowed to litter and things like that. She always made it clear that was wrong. I guess I extrapolated from that that if it was wrong to throw your pop bottle out then it was also wrong to dump coal just wherever you wanted. I just assumed that was wrong. I thought of it as a "do unto others" thing.

I grew up in the Methodist church. I always got a sense from my mother, and from my Sunday school teachers, that, again, you're supposed to take ethics seriously. You're supposed to take care of each other and the earth and care about what happens to others. Jesus stood up, and he expected you to do the same thing. That was always the model for me; even though it wasn't real political in that little Methodist church, I always felt like it should be. And just watching the evening news, just seeing people like Martin Luther King. During that time period, that kind of stuff soaked in. Nowadays it's Jerry Falwell and the Religious Right who get all the exposure but back then there was a Religious Left that got exposure, too. I think I soaked up that.

My mom had the most impact on me during that time. Her name was Leona. She was from Grapevine, in Pike County, Kentucky. My mom just was always outspoken about a lot of things. The first act of speaking out or being defiant that I remember most had nothing to do with coal mining, but it did have to do with her. She had the first integrated Brownie troop in the state of West Virginia. She wasn't trying to make a big statement, she was just starting a Brownie troop and she thought everyone should be able to be in it—black kids, too—so she just invited everybody. I actually talked about this at her funeral; she died two years ago. We had our picture taken and she sent it to the state headquarters, here in Charleston, and they apparently went through the roof when they saw that picture. I was only seven at the time, so I only remember it vaguely. They told her she couldn't have black children in the troop and she was like, "Well, why not?" and there was a big rigmarole about it. She didn't back down. So finally they told her she could keep the troop if she would destroy all the pictures because they said if the *Charleston Gazette* got ahold of them it would be all over the state and then everybody might want to integrate a troop. And they didn't want that, of course. She said okay, but she didn't destroy the picture, so I showed it at her funeral.

She was just real feisty. She didn't like being pushed around. She was that first generation of young women who had all kinds of experiences. She was a nurse, she joined the U.S. Army and went to the Philippines during the war. She had all these experiences rather than just being in Pike County all her life. She got out and saw the world, and she never shut up after that. She stayed independent.

When I was a child there wasn't much going on in my county to do with protesting coal or anything like that. But I think I internalized a lot of stuff when I was a kid. I remember not only the creek and the pollution, but lots of injustice. I went to junior high at Gary, which was a U.S. Steel town.[6] They had a big sign, a big archway, over the road that said "Man Hours Lost to Accidents" and it had some kind of slogan about being safe, but they also had like a scoreboard that kept track of the hours had been lost. It wasn't keeping track of how many people had died or anything like that. It was all about the hours. And I remember, as a little kid, that really angered me. It seemed so crass and cruel, and I was aware and angry. But I internalized it. I think I was already a writer then. I didn't write it down, but I told stories in my head. And I was always observing.

I don't come from a long line of coal miners who led strikes and things like that. My Italian grandfather was a coal miner, but he wasn't particularly militant, I don't think. On my mom's side, one of my uncles was a coal operator, and my grandfather worked for a little while as a mine guard, which I was always real embarrassed about. He also ran a company store for a while. He was sort of on that side of things.

On my dad's side, my grandfather was a union miner and my uncle was a union miner who died of black lung, and he was probably the most militant and pro-union miner I knew. He was always involved in the union. My mom had an aunt, my great-aunt Carrie, who had three sons, and one of them was president of the local union in Pike County.

My paternal grandfather was from Sicily and my dad was born

here, but they went back. I learned in my family that it's a myth that everybody was just dying to get over here and be Americans. They really came because they were desperate, but they were so homesick they went back, to Sicily. They lived there seven or eight years before coming back here again. So my dad went there as a babe in arms and grew up there, but they were so desperate that they came back to find work. He didn't speak English, so he was put into a first-grade class even though he was nine years old. His teacher used him as the classroom policeman because he was so much bigger. If they got rowdy, his teacher would say, "Dennis!" and he'd stand up and look mean at the other kids and threaten to beat them up or something. So he was more or less a first-generation American.

There were a whole lot of different ethnicities in the coal camp where I grew up. There were Eastern Europeans, Italians, Hungarians, Russians, about a third black, about a third native Appalachians.

I've tried to live other places, but it never works out for very long. Sometimes I wish I had because I'll look at things that happen here and I think, Lord, it might just be easier to not know about what all happens. But I keep getting drawn back. I went away to school, I went to seminary up in D.C., altogether about five years. I lived for a couple years in inner-city D.C. I lived at the Sojourners' Fellowship, which was a commune sort of thing back in those days, run by the people who do *Sojourners* magazine.[7]

It was a real experience, but I eventually got homesick. The straw that broke the camel's back was that I had some friends from Mississippi who acted like Appalachians. They were like us, they even talked like us. But then they moved back to Mississippi, and I started thinking about coming home then. There was a writing workshop starting up, with Mary Lee Settle and George Garrett, and I wanted to take part in that because I had started my first book. Even when I was in D.C., I was starting to get involved in the Appalachian social movements. I used to travel a lot from

D.C. to the Highlander Center. That was when the land ownership survey was starting up, and I took part in that.[8]

When I moved back, I was in Charleston a couple years. I was finishing up my novel *Storming Heaven,* and I wanted to live in a coal camp again. I wanted to have that feeling of being in a coal camp while writing those books, so I moved to David, Kentucky. Once there I made friends with lots of people from KFTC, like Joe Szakos[9] and Terry Keleher. I also wanted to reconnect with my own heritage, since my mother was from Eastern Kentucky, and those new friends were there, so I moved to David, in Floyd County, for several years.

As I started *The Unquiet Earth* I felt just the opposite: I wanted to get away. I wanted to feel homesick, for one thing. That book is about loss. Again, many of my friends had left. I decided to go to Durham, North Carolina. I still felt the pull of the mountains. I was so homesick again. I really liked being down there, I liked how many writers there were down there and the way the local media supported them. It would've been better for my career, probably, if I had stayed down there, but it just felt like I needed to be home. I felt like I could have more of an impact here, somehow. I think it's important to be here. And I missed the mountains. So I got a post as a writer-in-residence at Appalshop, and I went to Whitesburg, Kentucky. I thought, well, I can make up my mind if I miss West Virginia or Durham worse, and of course it turned out that I missed West Virginia the worst, so I came back here and have been here ever since.

My dad was very pro-company until he retired and then allowed himself to look at what was going on. He worked for the company who first did mountaintop removal in West Virginia: Cannelton Coal. I remember him in high school, coming home and talking about it. He was all enthused about it, saying how they were going to flatten the mountain and move the whole town of Montgomery up there. It's where the penitentiary is now. I thought that was the stupidest thing I'd ever heard. I asked why they'd do such a stupid thing. The town was already in a place, so why move it? But I don't remember hearing much more about mountaintop removal until the mid-seventies. That's when Ken Hechler[10] was fighting it in Congress and trying to get SMCRA[11] to be passed. From 1972 to '76 I grew more and more aware and more upset about it. I was aware of the broad-form deed, and I was involved with Highlander. That was also around the time the big flood hit Mingo County, in 1977, because everybody knew that strip mining had caused that flood. They were being surrounded by mountaintop removal at that point.

I went to seminary in 1976 and graduated in '79. Once I got out of college, I started being more aware, more active. I wasn't aware of much while in college. I was a very dull college student. Didn't party, didn't protest. I studied all the time, was too responsible. I was still a Republican at that time. My dad was a Republican, so I sort of followed in his footsteps for a while. Actually, I think the church radicalized me.

There was a place in Mingo County, up on Marrowbone Creek, where these nuns lived up on top of the mountain. You went to Kermit, then you went up a holler—Marrowbone Creek—and at the head of it you had to take a four-wheel drive, and you could see lots of mountaintop removal from there. I remember being just appalled by that. Once I moved to Kentucky I saw a lot more of it. It was during the broad-form deed fight that I became really exposed to more mountaintop removal sites. And I've been up to Larry Gibson's a lot.[12] It's right in your face, it's right there.

As a Christian, I believe God created all of this and made us stewards over it, which to me means we should take care of it. I think it's the environmental counterpoint to the Holocaust. It's the landscape, to the earth, what the Holocaust was to destroying people. These are some of the oldest mountains in the world, so whether you believe that the earth is 6,000 years old or several million, they are still among the first mountains He made, so mountaintop removal is a violation of everything I believe in, both religiously and in terms of how I think people should be treated, too.

The landscape is inside of me.

I remember the first time I left the mountains for a length of time, I went to England during a semester of college. I missed the mountains so bad. We flew into the airport here, in Charleston, and I could see them, the landscape, the contours. I started crying, realizing how much I'd missed them.

You grow up here and it's comforting. I go to someplace flat and I feel naked.

I remember the first time I went to Michigan, looking out at that flatness, and I thought, "How do people figure out where to put their houses?" I mean, really, how do you figure out where to put a town? I'm used to a place where the mountains make you put the town or the house where it wants them. I like a place that dictates that. I remember being little and seeing a tornado on the news and being scared, asking my parents if that was going to happen to us, and they'd say, "Naw, naw, the mountains'll keep you safe."

When I went off to college, I went to West Virginia Wesleyan, a church school. I had some faculty members there who had a big effect on me. My religion professor, for example. This is a totally different issue, but I was a freshman when Kent State happened.[13] There was this professor who made this really strong, religious-based statement against what happened, and the class stood and applauded. That kind of thing really affected me. When I came back here in 1974, I was thinking about leaving the Methodist church for a variety of reasons, and I was really drawn to the Church of England, so I got involved in the Episcopal church. I had always thought of it as a rich people's church—and it used to be—but it's pretty much not anymore. There was a new minister here, Jim Lewis, who, next to my mother, has had the biggest impact on my life. He's very outspoken, very politically engaged on a variety of issues. He and his wife are two of my best friends. He gave me books to read, introduced me to Dietrich Bonhoeffer.[14] He really got into my reading and my thinking. That's when I switched from a Republican to a Democrat. I went from thinking of myself as a fairly conservative person to thinking of myself as a radical. It was like a 360-degree turn in just a period of about two or three years.

We're a religious bunch, Appalachians. And so a lot of people in the mountains have adopted this attitude of: "Ain't no use worrying about the environment because Jesus is going to come anyway!"

It's very frustrating to me. I've seen letters from operators and miners about mountaintop removal saying, "This is our coal and God give us this coal and when Jesus comes back he'll fix it." Jesus is going to come back and kick your butt for the mess you're making, that's what I think. I go back to the old Upton Sinclair quote: "It is difficult to convince a man of something if his paycheck depends on his not understanding it."

We're fatalists in the mountains. "It's all up to the good Lord." "If it's your time to go, it's just your time." We're people who had families who went into those mines not knowing if the roof was going to fall or not, but leaving it in the Lord's hands. And some people think: the good Lord is going to come back soon and he's going to fix it so it don't matter if we break it. People pray and get saved and wait for the Lord to fix everything. I think that attitude grows out of powerlessness. That's a good word for what we all feel: powerless.

There's always been a strain of religion in the mountains that has been bought off by the company. But there has also always been a strain of real active religious groups, like during the early union days, when Holiness preachers would lead the strikes. But that seems to have disappeared for the most part. The Catholic Church used to be very active. There was a group of Jesuit priests and nuns in the Sixties who were very active in West Virginia. Also, down in Southwest Virginia, during the Pittston strikes, there were some nuns down there who were into everything.

I think apathy has infected the church as well as everywhere. There are some signs that that might be changing, though. Sojourners, for example, has always been a liberal evangelical group, and Jim Wallis has had some impact on fellow evangelical leaders to change.[15] I saw an article in the paper recently about a group of younger evangelicals who were getting involved in environmental issues.

Mountaintop removal needs everybody against it. Change is not going to come from this region, even. It's going to come from national and international pressure to stop mining coal this way. I worry because in this country there are a lot of people—including the Clintons—who are supporting and pushing clean coal technology and all this stuff. When that happens, then you can kiss the mountains good-bye. That's what I think. I hate to think that. That scares me to death. The mountains' only hope is if the world won't go along with it. If some of the projections are correct, in twenty or thirty years from now, people are going to be really aware of it and they're going to be mad when they find out what has been being destroyed here.

My brother is a conservative Republican, but he can't stand mountaintop removal. He says, "It's not a liberal-conservative issue; it's a smart-stupid issue." That's the way he put it. But even the *Charleston Gazette,* which has always been a liberal paper, is pro–mountaintop removal. It's also a nonissue for West Virginia politicians. They don't even talk about it.

That's one reason I ran for governor, so it'd get talked about in the debates. I ran for governor just to get a dialogue going, not at all expecting to win. I did the third party thing, I got talked into it. The Mountain Party, which hasn't been too active since then. If I had ran as a Democrat I knew I wouldn't get very far, so we did the Mountain Party thing so I could get in the general election. To force the dialogue, to force the others to talk about it. I'm not sure it was a real smart thing to do in some ways because it just about wore me out and burned me out. I have a writer's temperament. Most—not all—writers are introverted. I'm not bubbly and outgoing. I'm quiet, I really value my quiet time. It was just like pulling teeth to go out and shake hands and all that. People are always asking me if I'm going to write a book about it and I think, “Are you kidding?” I don’t even like to think about it.

Partly why I ran was because I was curious as to how it would turn out. We had almost no money, but we got a lot of free publicity. We were in the *Washington Post* and the London *Economist.* A friend of mine was in Spain, and the cabdriver asked her where she was from and when she said West Virginia he said, “Woman running for governor with dog!” Because he’d seen me and Phyllis on CNN.

Look at John Edwards.[16] He seems like a good guy with principles, but he’s not going to speak up against mountaintop removal. I thought, “What if someone runs for office and actually *says* what they think, without worrying about what the unions say, or what the business community says, or what anyone says and just says what they believe?” I wanted to run as someone who wouldn’t dilly-dally. Someone who would be honest. I’m for this and that, I’m against mountain removal, and see where the chips fall. And I got the answer. Because I had 2 percent of the money and I got 2 percent of the vote. It fell out almost exactly. It made me lose hope in the system.

One of the most interesting things about that campaign is something I haven’t talked about. But at that time Ralph Nader was running and people were worried about him taking away Democratic votes from Gore and all that. We had an incumbent Republican governor, so that was in his favor. So some of the people within the state started to worry that a third-party candidate would take votes from the Democrats. That’s the conventional wisdom, but I argued that that wasn’t the case because I had a lot of Republicans who told me they were going to vote for me, too. I thought I’d take from both sides. The state co-chairs from the Democratic Party called me, took me to lunch, and offered me the seat on the legislature in this district. I mean, offered it to me. Can you believe that? “If you would not run for governor, you will be the next Democratic legislator in this district.” I played along out of curiosity, asked how much it paid. $20,000. They were dead serious, the two of them. They were buying my lunch and offering me a seat in the legislature. That really blew my confidence in the system. What does that say about how our public officials get into office?

People were afraid of losing their votes, though, so they didn't vote for me. I think if you took a poll in this state, the majority of the people would say ban mountaintop removal, but that doesn't translate into action because people feel powerless. I bet you could get 60 percent of the people in this state to vote against mountaintop removal. But people just feel a lack of power. I feel that; I feel like I can't do anything. When I was out there campaigning for governor it was like banging my head against the wall to get anything done. I got shut out of all but two of the debates. Twice on statewide television I got to get up and talk for two minutes on MTR. A year and a half of work to get to speak for two minutes.

The first year we spent just getting on the ballot. It probably would've been better if I had run as a Democrat because I wouldn't have had to spend so much time doing all that preliminary stuff. I could've gotten into all the Democratic debates and wouldn't have been so burned out when it was over. And probably would've gotten 25 percent of the vote. I probably shouldn't have let myself get talked into it. I'm glad I ran, though. I'm glad somebody ran and brought the issue up. It got more press nationally than it did locally, which always seems to be the case. The *Washington Post* had a huge piece on it. People here in West Virginia don't know enough about it.

That sense of disenfranchisement goes all the way back to the beginnings of coal. You voted the way your boss told you to. You registered as whatever party the company told you to. My mom was a county school nurse and the county was Democrat so she had to register Democrat to keep her job. The poll workers would stand over your shoulder and watch how you voted.

We love the land, we're attached to the mountains, yet we let them be blown up. We convince ourselves that that's necessary. We swallow it whole, accept the lies. We need that flat land so we can build things on it! It's going to take several thousand years to fill up what we've already flattened. We just take it, we just put up with it. I don't know why. It used to be, when the union was feistier and stronger, they used to be able to get people feisty, too. But not anymore. And some of the kids I teach, I just want to shake them. They don't care about anything. They don't care about Iraq, about mountaintop removal. They don't read the newspaper, they don't watch the news.

I think it's like the civil rights movement. That wasn't just a Southern issue, it was everywhere, but it was worse in the South, the segregation. But that wasn't something that white people in the South could solve, it just was not going to be solved that way. It took a national effort to solve that. I think it's the same way with mountaintop removal. It's not going to be solved by people here. Because we're too politically isolated or we're too tied into the system or we're too apathetic. It's going to have to be banned on a national level.

If this was western North Carolina everybody'd be outraged. If it was upstate New York everybody'd be outraged. Because it's West Virginia and Kentucky nobody cares. Nobody even knows we're here, first of all. And if they do, they think we're just a bunch of dumb ignorant hillbillies anyway. I can't imagine anywhere in this country that would allow this kind of thing to be going on.

Americans are so self-centered, and we don't care what happens in another country. "Oh, kill them Iraqis," people'll say. And we're the same way, Appalachia, to them. *We're* just another country.

Look at Buffalo Creek. If that had happened somewhere else, everybody would still know about it, and remember it. Or the Martin County spill. I've talked about that before, told them it was the worst environmental disaster in the South, and nobody had heard of it. And it's because of where it happened. Someday they'll look at this region and they'll say, "Oh look at how they tore that place up; isn't that a shame." Then they'll go back to what they were doing.

They say I'm anti-coal. I'm not loyal to my culture. I'm a traitor to the state, to the economy. You get treated like an outsider even though you're not. My Italian daddy was just as hillbilly as they come, and he always told me not to get above my raising. And sometimes people treat me like I don't belong anymore, because of the stand I've taken. I've written letters and columns, refuting that, telling people, "Hey, I grew up in a coal camp, don't tell me I'm not from here."

Even in this state, one of the most active groups is the Ohio Valley Environmental Coalition, and they're in Huntington. Half their members are in southern West Virginia, but they named themselves after the valley. So people talk about them and say, "Why, they're from Ohio, they're from out of state!"

We're the Mountain State. Our state song says, "Oh, the West Virginia hills, how majestic and how grand/with their summits bathed in glory, like our Prince Emmanuel's Land." And the state motto, "Mountaineers are always free." The football team is the Mountaineers. We're destroying our whole identity! Psychologically, it's much like the way the German people convinced themselves they weren't responsible for what they did during World War II. It's self-delusion.

People bring up the economy. Well, our economy has already collapsed. We are killing any future economy we might have had. If we hadn't been practicing mountaintop removal we would have more tourism, a place that we could possibly entice other businesses to come and set up. Why would any business want to move to Eastern Kentucky or southern West Virginia, with mountaintop removal? When Toyota came to West Virginia, they didn't want a mountaintop removal site. We're not creating places that are going to bring in economy. No big business is going to want to locate somewhere that is not served by roads and good schools and recreational facilities. These places are being trashed, not improved. The coal industry has destroyed our economy. For the last 125 years it's kept out any competition. If it wasn't for coal, we could be like Vermont or New Hampshire, or western North Carolina. Instead, we've got this wrecked economy that was wrecked by the coal industry 125 years ago, and it's never recovered. They stole the land, and now they're destroying it.

I've heard people in the coal industry say it doesn't affect the waterways. Mountaintop removal doesn't affect waterways because it just destroys them, period. The way to stop water pollution is to stop the water! Of course! They've got it all figured out.

We could still have another Buffalo Creek, too. That humongous thing in Boone County, with the grade school right below it. Can you imagine any other place in America allowing that? Can you imagine the parents in the Hamptons having to scream about their kids going to school beneath a slag heap, with water behind it? It'll be on the national news when several hundred people get killed. For a little while, maybe.

To make it national, I think it'll take hundreds of people having to die. I hate to say that. But I believe that's what it will take. I've thought about, what if some of us went on a hunger strike? Or what if there was a suicide bomber? Would that bring attention to it? I wonder. Shortly after September 11, I was talking to my friend Jim Lewis and saying that I couldn't understand the logic of suicide bombers and he said, "Well, now, I don't know, you might have a little bit of that in you." And I thought about it and said, "Well, I might, actually." If it would stop mountaintop removal, would I strap a bomb on? Obviously I wouldn't, but I'd sure love to save a mountain. But I wonder if that would even stop it. I just don't know.

The authorities and the powers that be have figured out how to control us. It's not like the mass uprising you saw during the civil rights movement, when people just didn't want to take it anymore. Or during the Pittston strikes, that was such a community entity. Everybody was involved. I covered it for the newspaper. Gas stations wouldn't even fill up state troopers' cars so they could go out and patrol the strikes. Even the local county officials were standing up against the company. It was involvement from local government to the gas station attendants to the grade school kids. Everybody. I've never seen anything like that.

So many people have forgotten the land ownership study. The land is 80 to 85 percent corporate owned, and it is not for sale. They've taken what should be community-access land, and they own it, and they destroy it. If I decide, in this neighborhood, to take a ball and chain and start knocking this house down, I'm not allowed to do that. Because I have neighbors. I'm not allowed to move a dozer onto this property. I can't do just anything I want to. Just because it's your land doesn't mean you can destroy it. That's from a practical point of view. From a spiritual point of view I'd say, well, it's not your land, it's God's land. You're just caretaking it for a little while. From a Woody Guthrie point of view I'd say, "This land is your land, this land is my land."

I think the average West Virginia attitude is, "It's wrong, but there's nothing I can do about it." And that's real frustrating.

I don't see much hope. I hate to say that, but it's true. Part of it's that I'm getting older and crankier, and the governor thing took a lot of it out of me. But you just have to keep on fighting it. And I try to remain hopeful. I mean, in 1987, if you had told me that in five years that Eastern Europe was going to be free and the Berlin Wall was going to fall, why, I'd have thought that you were smoking dope. But five years later, it had all happened. So maybe some miracle will come. Maybe the good Lord's got some kind of a plan that he's just waiting to unleash on us, and it'll just snowball. And all of a sudden we'll look at this and say, "Well, we've lost some mountains, but we've got most of them, so now let's pick up and get on it with it."

Charleston, West Virginia, October 24, 2007

Bev May

Little Acts of Greatness

Did you really think that God got it wrong
when he put that mountain right there?
Do you believe Mother Nature had no clue
when she populated it so fair?
And what was the crime of Father Time
who set it all in slow, slow motion?
Still, you know best, don't you, little man?
Now where'd you get that notion?
—Kate Larken, "We All Live Downstream"

When we try to pick out anything by itself, we find it hitched to everything else in the world.
—John Muir

Bev May moves up the steep mountain much like she must have as a little girl growing up here on Wilson Creek, Kentucky. Her trusty dog, Rufus, a mixed breed with a noble profile, is barely able to stay ahead, although he seems intent on doing so. May's climbing is steady, her steps wide, and she never stops talking, eager to introduce us to the place she loves so much, the place she is terrified of losing.

Like that young girl, May is conscious of everything. She points out deer tracks, a single red leaf decorating the otherwise summer ground of the woods, a blue jay feather that has drifted down and come to rest on a rotting log. She runs her hand over the broad trunk of an oak, glances up at the sky, and comments on its deep, aching blue.

In an unfamiliar patch of the woods May gasps aloud and runs forefinger and thumb over a bluish-green teardrop-shaped

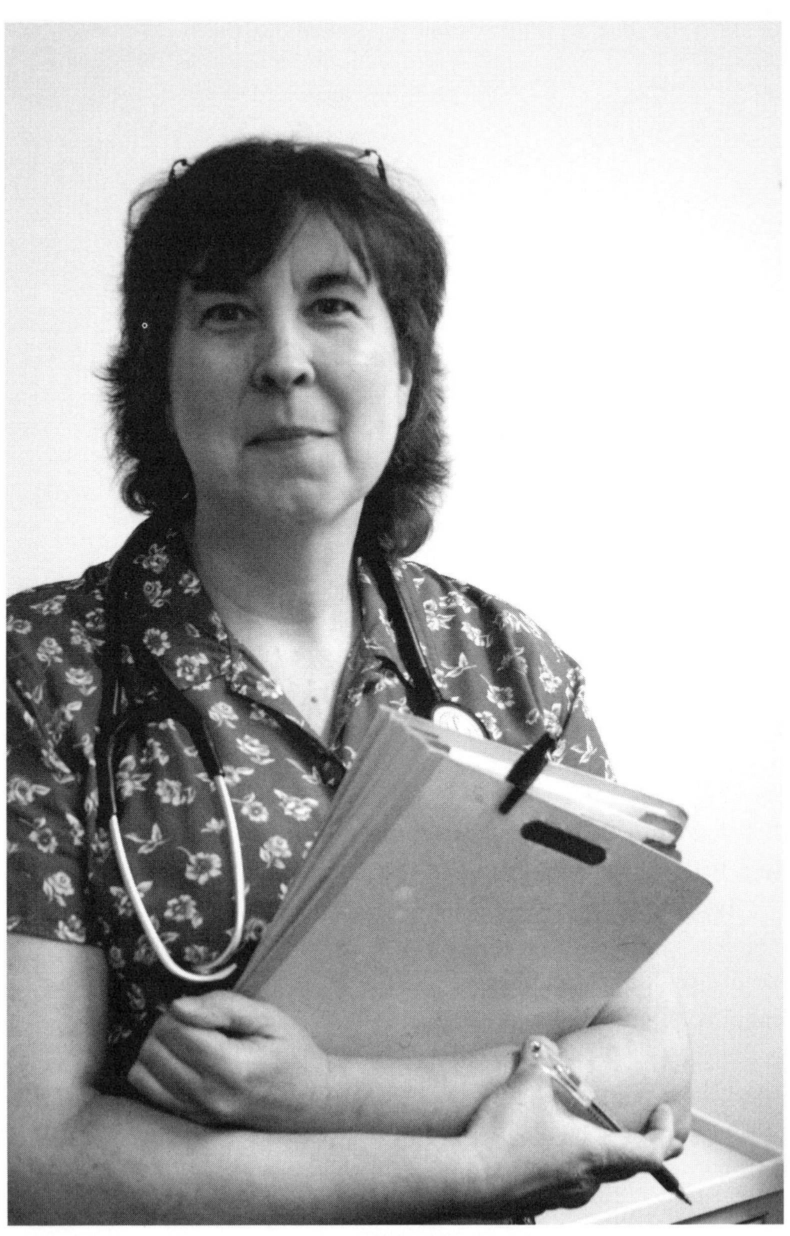

Bev May, Floyd County, Kentucky. Photo by Silas House.

leaf. "Why, it's a mulberry tree!" she says, laughing with joy. "I didn't know we had a mulberry tree up here. I *love* mulberries."

She is also very conscious of others, always holding the stinging limbs she passes through at the front of the pack so they won't fly back and hit whoever is hiking behind her, pointing to low clots of briars that might grab at our socks.

This woman is one with this mountain. They know and respect each other. This is apparent not only in the way May talks about the mountain, but in the way she moves up it with ease and grace, stepping lightly so as to disturb the least amount of earth as possible.

Even though she often says, "I can't get up here as fast as I used to," this is hard to believe. She reports that on Easter weekend she climbed this trail (which takes at least an hour) three times in two days. May is a woman who is used to being in motion; she is a medical professional, an old-time fiddler, and an activist. She moves with determination, her arms pushing at the air, her legs intent on their purpose, her feet on a mission. Today she is on her way to the High Rocks, her favorite place in the world, and although she wants to take her time and enjoy the walk up, she is also eager to reach the ridgetop, where she will once again encounter this natural castle of rocks, a secret world that only the inhabitants of this holler know, one they've been frequenting since the early 1800s.

When she does finally take a break, May sits on a scattering of small rocks on a steep bluff halfway to her destination, where she can see the tops of the opposite mountains, a blue haze through the trees. May is quickly joined by Rufus, who back-tracks to zoom in behind her and nudges his head into the crook of her arm. She took Rufus in after someone put him out in the nearby community of Maytown and her nephew found him. "He became sort of the living football of Maytown," she says, rubbing Rufus's head so that he turns to face her. She looks him in the eye. "And we can't have that, now, can we, buddy?"

May points to a mess of dead pine trees, most of them leaning or already fallen, victims of the recent beetle infestation that took most of Eastern Kentucky's shortleaf pine trees.

"You see them?" she asks. "My daddy planted them back in the sixties, after they broad-formed our land. They came in here and auger-mined this mountain, and those pines are standing there where they cut a road for the auger."

May is referring to a time when mining companies could come in on anyone's land as long as they could produce a broad-form deed, which was basically a document that gave the company possession of mineral rights. Often these deeds had been sold more than fifty years before by previous owners of the land, or shady family members, or people who had been told that their land would not be much disturbed.

"They left it a mess," continues May, "so Daddy planted the pines to keep the soil from eroding so bad. I hated it so bad when the beetles took the pines out, because he had planted them when I was little. I can remember it," she says, her eyes set on the land as if she can see a movie from her past playing there. "But then, once the pines fell I noticed that those little oak saplings just sprouted right up. So then I realized that the pines had done exactly what they had been meant to do: keep the topsoil from washing off, stabilize the mountainside, allow other trees to inhabit. And the pines dying just made way for the oaks to get more sunlight. So his work wasn't in vain at all."

Rufus has decided that it's time to forge on up the mountainside and has left us behind, so May stands and dusts off her hands. "Well, Rufus has determined we should go, so I guess we will," she laughs, and all at once she is a woman on a mission again.

In fact, May's mission is not only to take us to the High Rocks, but to *save* the High Rocks. They, like most of the land May has known all of her life, are in grave danger.

It all started one morning in November 2006 at the Graceway Methodist Church, when a neighbor bragged after the service that May Brothers Mining Company (very distant cousins to May) had approached him about buying his land to start mining in the head of Wilson Creek. This neighbor also claimed that three other families had already sold to the company.

Turned out the neighbor was misinformed; no one on Wilson Creek has sold anything yet. But the coal company is breathing down their necks, and as of this writing it seems certain that the company is intent on mining in and around Wilson Creek, including the long ridge that stands between that holler and Stephen's Branch, which runs parallel to it. And Bev May is not certain that her neighbors won't sell. "Money talks, especially when you need it," she says. "No doubt about it."

May, fearing that if only one neighbor sold out a domino effect might result, went straight into action. With help from KFTC, she secured space at a community center in Maytown and went door to door, inviting people to come to a meeting to organize and fight the coal company that seemed intent on invading their world.

Several months before this summertime jaunt up the mountain, May is presiding over the second meeting of residents from Wilson Creek and Stephen's Branch on a cold night in December. Concerned citizens are gathered in the Maytown Community Center, which was once the lunchroom for the Maytown Elementary School. Maytown is made up of about 200 souls, well-kept houses, an abandoned school, and four or five streets. An old camper serves as the community store, where cigarettes, pop, and candy are advertised in spray-painted handwriting on the exterior walls. The little town sits in a bowl near the railroad tracks, the mountains encircling it like gray, jagged arms. This night a thin snow falls like tiny feathers and the cold makes the night, void of a moon, seem even blacker.

The community center is freezing, but the furnace has been fired up and rumbles as everyone files in, brushing the snowflakes from their hair. The group is gathered close in a circle, not only to hear but to gain one another's heat. May sits on a couch that seems to want to swallow her up, silently watching for more people to arrive; the others are all caught up in various states of conversation. Their talking is punctuated by laughter and heads that shake with frustration.

"I guess we ought to get started," May says, so quietly that it is surprising when everyone stops talking at once and turns to face her. However, everything about May—her face, her carriage, the way she uses her hands to illustrate what she is saying—suggests kindness and intelligence. It's no wonder that people listen when she speaks: instead of demanding attention she simply respects everyone else's thoughts enough for them to pay extra attention to hers. Plus, she's a medical professional, and people in the mountains respect doctors. May is quick to point out that she is not the only college graduate in the group, however, and she's not even the only college graduate in her holler, despite stereotypes that would suggest otherwise. After the meeting, May also downplays her role as organizer of the group. "Oh, what happens is I tend to be the one that passes around the notices about meetings and calls people and tries to let them know what's going on. That's about it," she says modestly.

May launches into the meeting, intent on getting business done, but not aggressively. She wants to include everyone, to make sure all those gathered have a chance to say their piece. She goes around the room, allows everyone to introduce themselves, gives all those present the time to make their announcements. Many of the residents are here because they absolutely do not want the coal company to come into their holler. Others are here because they still haven't figured everything out and want all the information they can get. Some have already been lied to by the coal companies and are here to warn their neighbors. Others don't know what to believe. There are all kinds of rumors already.

Like many of the social movements in Appalachia, the rising chorus of Wilson Creek is largely made up of women. There are two elegant older ladies in crisp dress pants and sweaters, an earnest young woman who is new to the group and is taking into account everything around her, a vivacious woman in her sixties who is wrapped up in her husband's puffy coat and gives off a wonderful air of not giving a damn what anyone thinks of her. She is loudly relating how she told off one of the men who came to her house to try to talk her into selling. The circle around her collapses in laughter when she delivers her blunt reply to the man's encouragement. Several other women are there to represent their families, who promise to fight to the very end before they'll ever sell out to a coal company known for bullying people into signing away their rights. These are strong Appalachian women: tough as coal trucks, clever as foxes, as spirited as the music of these mountains.

A few men have turned out, too. One is from a neighboring county, and he has come to talk about the rich geologic formations—including the High Rocks—that stand on the ridges along Wilson Creek. He is a self-taught geologist, a man who reads books on rocks and minerals for fun, and he wants to offer any help he can. There are two teenagers who are concerned about their hunting grounds being destroyed, and a young man who is from the holler but is now enrolled at Morehead State University. He says he wants to study geology so he can someday serve as an expert witness in trials to prosecute coal mining companies. Ricky Handshoe, from nearby Hueysville, has come to tell everyone of his experiences fighting the coal company mining the land above his home. He is joined by Lowell Shepherd, who says he gave a coal company a lease on his land only to quickly discover that they weren't going to live up to any of their promises. He says that constant blasting[1]—much of it higher than the legal limit—has caused his house's floor to be so hilly that his grandchildren beg to roller-skate on it because it looks like it would be so much fun.

One of the young women is concerned about what will happen to her two asthmatic children if coal trucks start running up and down their road. "There'll be so much dust off that road," she says, looking around the room so that her eyes meet those of everyone else. She twists her wedding band around on her finger while she talks. Her hands are hard-working and chapped, hands that have known scalding dishwater and mopwater, hands that have scrubbed counters and carried plates, grabbed hold of hot skillet handles. This woman is worn out from just trying to get by, and now she has another aggravation, a threat to her children. Finally her hands become still in her lap. She looks down at them briefly, as if this manner of talk has worn her out, and then lifts her head to address everyone again. "If we let this company come in here, I just don't know what I'll do. 'Cause my children'll not be able to stand it."

"We'll just have to make sure they *don't* come in here, then," May says in her reassuring way, and many of the women nod, a gathering of strong forces, determined to fight back. May offers a reassuring smile, and some of the frustration falls out of the woman's stiff shoulders.

Over the next few months, the group works together to figure out ways they can fight the coal company before people start selling and before permits are filed. "It's pretty much been the case that if a permit gets filed, then you're already too late," May explains. "So we want to act before that permit ever gets on file." They stick together, and their strength in numbers has begun to work in their favor.

The group manages to persuade their newly elected state representative, Brandon Spencer (D-Floyd County), to attend one of their assemblies, and although he makes no commitments, he is impressed by their determination.

May brings in Kentuckians for the Commonwealth organizer Kevin Pentz, who works within the Canary Project, KFTC's arm that deals with coal issues. Pentz and May are all business at the meetings, but are actually old friends; May recently played fiddle at his wedding.

At Pentz's suggestion the group decides to pursue having the area declared as a land unsuitable for mining. To be approved as such, it has to be proven that an area is fragile or has historical and cultural significance, or that mining operations would affect the area's renewable resources, such as the water or food supply, or could endanger lives or property.[2]

The group decides to pursue the argument of the land's natural significance after many of the residents immediately mention that there is an abundance of wildflowers on the ridges along Wilson Creek and Stephen's Branch.

This is what prompted May's trek up the mountain three times in two days. One of those days she was accompanied by a group of students from Berea College, who chose to spend their Easter holiday searching for rare plants on this mountainside.

May is thinking of these students when she reaches the High Rocks on a fine summer evening several weeks later. In particular, she recalls one of the students, who came to understand, once she got up to the High Rocks, "what it's really all about. This is what you lose when you blow up a mountain. If you know where you're from, then it's not hard to protect it. But people who haven't ever been up to the ridgetops, well, they have no idea of how amazing this forest is." May touches one of the saplings that has sprouted up out of the rocky base of the cliffs. "It's not a hunk of rock. It's a living thing."

May is someone who takes living things very, very seriously. As a nurse practitioner, she has a job that is in high demand, giving her the opportunity to live pretty much anywhere she would wish to. But she chose to come back to Eastern Kentucky after graduating from the University of Kentucky in 1995 with a Master's in nursing.

"I feel a need to take care of my own people," she says.

She does just that in her job as the nurse practitioner and clinical director of the Little Flower Free Clinic in nearby Hazard, which offers free medical service to the uninsured and the homeless by way of a federal grant.

"In a lot of parts of the country no doctor will take Medicaid, so they have to have clinics for people with Medicaid, for poor people. Health Care for the Homeless projects are a small piece of that funding," May explains. "Within that funding, there's about a hundred Health Care for the Homeless projects, all of which are in urban areas, and they're working out of store fronts and church basements and take care of people that live on the street and under bridges and stuff."

The Little Flower Clinic is unique in that it is the first rural homeless clinic in the nation. The clinic operates on what May calls "a rural definition of homelessness," which might not mean that a person is sleeping under a bridge or on the street, like the stereotype of a homeless person.

"But if you're sleeping in what used to be the family's chicken coop, you're homeless," May says. "If you're sleeping in an abandoned school bus, you're homeless. If you're a family—say, a mom with three kids—and your husband's beat you and you go to your brother's so that there's five children and three adults in a two-bedroom house, you're homeless."

May says that some in the area question the validity of the clinic because they don't think of a rural place as having homeless people. "It's just that because we're hillbillies we think, oh, your family takes care of you," she says. "Well, they do. It's just that sometimes the family's not able to take care of you, and it puts the whole extended family into crisis."

The clinic is also supported by several churches in the area, and is named for St. Theresa the Little Flower, a revered Carmelite nun whose religious philosophy is best epitomized by her most famous quote: "I can do no great things, only small things with great love."

"We're down with that whole principle," May says. "That's what we are."

May has gotten so caught up in talking that she's refrained from going on to the top of the High Rocks, which she has been waiting to do all day. She takes in the magnificent collection of huge boulders and exposed cliff-face that look as if they have been stacked together for a giant's playhouse, accented by shoots of mountain laurel. The High Rocks are perched at the very top of the ridge, rising some sixty feet above the mountain's summit.

Their daunting size and stark beauty suggest a remarkable, open-air church, one assembled by God's own hands.

May moves up the rocks silently until she gets about halfway up. There she pauses, keeping her hand against the cool, gray skin of the rock. "I always think of my father, coming up here when he was little," she says, sighs, and then moves on.

Once May is settled on one of the cliffs' jagged edges, she looks out toward the land where her family has lived for generations. Her view is obstructed by thousands of trees, but this is a hindrance she is glad to live with. Somehow, though, May seems to look past the billions of leaves and all those swaying limbs. She is looking not only past the trees but also back over the years, back more than 100 years ago.

"In the late 1800s, my great-grandfather, Felix May, owned half of the holler that's nearest the mouth, here on Wilson Creek," May begins. "He worked rolling logs down the river to Cattletsburg, and one day he fell in. So in 1904, his wife, Suzie May, had nine children and one on the way, when he died of pneumonia," she says.

In those days, property rights reverted to the brothers instead of the wife. Suzie May became destitute while the brothers were suddenly very land-rich. Apparently they offered Suzie very little, if any, assistance. Despite the odds, she and her children survived, and she never remarried.

"She had a big bunch of boys who worked hard and helped her," May says, shaking her head at the determination of her ancestors. "She even had other family that came in and lived with her, and she had to help them, too. She raised lots of kids, not just her own, and eventually the land all got divided up and some sold out and now there's only about 100 acres left in the family."

Sometimes, May admits, she thinks about what it would be like to lose this mountain. "But then I can't think about it," she says, quickly, waving her hands as if to usher these thoughts away. "It makes me feel like I'm falling off the edge of the earth, to think of that. It's too painful. So the thing to do is to hope it doesn't happen," she says. "I realize that fighting the coal company is like David and Goliath, but I have to keep hope."

So that's what she holds onto. And every once in a while she reminds herself that in the face of impossible odds, David ended up winning his fight.

May doesn't understand people who can't see what's wrong with mountaintop removal. At the suggestion that there might be another side to the fight—say, a positive side to the mining practice—she grows fidgety, wringing her hands, a scornful grin on her face.

"It's morally wrong," she says. "Because every mountain in Eastern Kentucky is ours, really. Our heritage. In some cases, the only legacy we have. Whenever they blast another mountain, they're blasting away the future: the lumber, the watershed, the wildlife. Tourism, sustainable communities, everything. There hain't no putting it back," May says, laughing—maybe to keep from crying. "When we treat mountains like they're expendable, well, all I know is that it all boils down to short-time profits for the coal company and no justice at all for the people. The coal companies are all the time talking about overburden, you know," May says.[3] "Well, we're just overburden. Their job is to remove overburden and retrieve the coal. We're the first level of overburden, so we can't let them remove us, we can't give in."

May keeps looking at the trees, perhaps imagining them all pushed into a valley fill so that gigantic draglines can remove the overburden and make way for the extraction of coal. Then she turns, clenching her jaw, and her face is filled with defiance. She is fierce, determined, ready to fight.

"I just feel like we're being assaulted from all sides. That's what it's like, to live here," May says. "They're taking out gas and timber and coal all the time. There should be some balance. I believe they ought to be able to mine, but they want to level everything, and I'm not going to sit by and watch that happen. People ought to be able to live."

May looks up at the purpling sky, wonder playing out over her face. "Lord, it's getting late! I guess we ought to go back down," she says, with resignation. She hops off the edge of the rock, calls Rufus, and ambles her way back down the mountain.

Bev May talking . . .

When I was growing up we kept a garden, we raised cattle. What we had to eat and what was put into the freezer came out of the garden. And then we got our eggs, of course, from my Uncle Speed right next door there; he had a magnificent gas-heated chicken house. Did I tell you that he didn't have an inside toilet but he had gas heat in his chicken house? You know, because there's some things you ought not be doing in the house, right? So the man had priorities.

When I was little, living off the land was still very much critical to our well-being as a family. Having the land to garden and to hunt and to play in was just a huge part of my coming up. I can remember—we're talking in the seventies—I can remember my Uncle Speed plowing with mules, but I can remember a guy even plowing with an ox. There was still that sense of the preindustrial time. We still had the remnants of that, the good parts.

And it was also interesting because Maytown—the closest town to Wilson Creek—was there as a community long before there was a coal industry. So I feel really blessed I didn't grow up in a coal camp. I grew up in the woods with a real wonderful sense of where I belonged.

Uncle Speed died in the seventies and so my parents, me, and my brother and his children are the last of the family that are still on Wilson Creek. And of course all the others have moved off to other places or passed on.

I was real fortunate, I think, because me and my brother were the only cousins on both sides of the family to get to be raised as hillbillies. The rest of them on my mom's side, they went to Detroit and to Florida. And on my father's side they went to Lexington.

The ironic thing is that one of the reasons they moved off was in hopes of having a better education for their children, but I'm the only one on my mother's side of the family that ever graduated from college. There was no other option around here. You had to go to college. I mean you *had* to: either that or be poor. So that's one of the things I really appreciate about being a hillbilly is it gave me the little oomph, the little push to go to college. I think my cousins had other ways of getting work, and I knew full well that I didn't. I had to go to school. And the other thing that I learned from going to school around here is that nobody hands you your education on a silver platter. You've got to claim it for yourself. And so if you know that you can figure the rest of it out.

I think that when I was growing up that the people that had the biggest impact on me—now this may degenerate into some storytelling—were the ones who had been in the community their whole lives and had stayed put and had a real sense of commitment. I think that made the biggest impression on me.

As a nurse practitioner, I've got like twelve years of experience and I could work anyplace in the country that I wanted to, literally, but I want to be here because it's just so much more meaningful. I think I'm more effective because I'm a hillbilly. I'm taking care of my people.

And the same thing I think applies to being an environmentalist. If you know where you're from and what the stakes are, then it's not that hard to do whatever you have to do to protect it. And I do think that people that haven't been up to the ridgetops probably just have no idea of the richness and the beauty and the hundreds of little varieties of wildflowers and just the amazing thing that this forest is. And if you haven't seen it I don't know how I'd begin to explain it to anybody or how to make them value it. Because unless you've got out there and seen it, it's impossible, I think, to really understand what gets lost whenever you blow up a mountain. It's not a hunk of rock. It's a living thing that gets blown up.

Speaking of people that stay in one place, there was a librarian in our school named Shirley Stewart—she's still living—and she was a really dedicated educator. Maytown High School was a tiny little school. One of the things I remember is that there was one child in the whole school whose father was obviously black and the rest of the family was white. One little black child in the whole school, and she subscribed to *Ebony* magazine so that he would get some little connection there culturally. I think she helped him . . . he went to Antioch. Was it Antioch or Oberlin? Shoot, Oberlin, I think. She helped get him into college. And he's a lawyer now. That was the poorest family in the whole county. She was that kind of an educator. She was very independent minded, a strong woman.

One day at church—I was probably in about my freshman year of high school, I'd say—and it was the time that the Equal Rights Amendment was trying to be passed, and it came up for ratification in Kentucky. The opponents to this told all the preachers "This is going to mean unisex bathrooms, this is going to mean women fighting on the front lines of the army, this is going to be the end of Christian civilization as we know it." And our poor little pitiful country preacher stood up before the church and mouthed whatever it was that the state representative had told him. And Shirley Stewart stood up—I mean, he was doing this from the pulpit—she stood up and said, "Now preacher, I don't think we have enough information about this yet." She did it real respectful. It was the most amazing thing. I mean, you do *not* talk back to the preacher in Eastern Kentucky. You just don't. But she said, "Now this is what I've read about it. I don't think it means there'll be unisex bathrooms, I think it just means that women will be given equal status to men, and I just think we need to get some more facts about this before we make any resolutions on this."

It was succinct, it was respectful, it was erudite. I was probably about fourteen or fifteen. If there's a moment that just was defining for me, that was it. It was like, Wow, you can stand up and talk back to the preacher if you have your facts straight, and you can challenge authority.

And that's someone who has spent her whole life right here in Maytown just trying to do right by the people in her community. And I think it let me know, too, if you stay in one place in the mountains that doesn't mean you have to give up anything intellectually. If anything, it's a great jumping off point for learning about the rest of the world. You don't have to give up a single thing.

I've always been aware I was a hillbilly. And the way I knew I was a hillbilly was I knew there were people that were more hillbilly than me. And the way I knew that was that when I was a little kid, I remember there was some kind of commercial or something on TV about little children in Appalachia that "don't have no shoes." And I had shoes, so I was like, *Huh?* And all the kids that came to school had shoes. So, I thought, well, there must be someplace that's more hillbilly, that's more Appalachian than here. And whenever I would use "ain't" or some other "not proper English"—that being quote-unquote proper—my daddy would say, "You sound like you're from the head of Noggytuck." So I put it together in my mind that Noggytuck was where the hillbillies were, the ones without the shoes, the ones on the TV. So I knew I was a hillbilly, but there was people that was more hillbilly.

It wasn't part of the dialogue, being Appalachian. I think my family was of that generation where they were raised on farm life and not having a whole lot. My parents were very much of that post–World War II generation, I think, that were wanting really hard to be part of the American middle class. They had the jazz records and the family car and the frame-built house and were on the PTA and active in the church. Well, my mom was active in the church; my daddy's an agnostic. He's a heathen! He's a heathen, he really is. Heath*ern.* But anyway, they were of that 1950s generation that were trying really hard to make it into the middle class.

It wasn't hardscrabble for either of them. My mom actually had a little easier time of it because my grandfather was a supervisor for a gas company, and they had a pretty good-size house. They had a fairly comfortable life. My dad's family, they worked as farm people work. Milk the cows when you get up and go 'til daylight. A real strong work ethic.

But at the same time they valued pieces of the culture. My dad was a wood-carver, and the subject of his carvings were his memories from childhood—coal miners, women hoeing in the garden, preachers raising fire and brimstone—and so there was definitely a respect there. And because Daddy was a wood-carver he was in contact with people that did crafts.

He was an artisan, but he just said that he whittled. He sold them because my mommy made him. He just gave them away and finally she said, "No, these have value, you're selling them." Because of course as with all hobbies he was putting in more money than he was generating. There was definitely a respect for the tradition.

Now my mother, she likes old-time music now, but she called bluegrass music "catterwalling." Neither one of them liked bluegrass. They liked jazz and rock 'n' roll. I did some reading up on the history of Irish music, too, and their histories completely parallel. After World War II, every kind of ethnic music just about died out because of radio and television, this commercial music coming in. And a lot of World War II had to do with ethnic conflict, and people were just ready to put that away and assimilate and become a homogenous American identity. Appalachians wanted exactly the same things. Now there were some old folks that held out, the George Gibsons and the Lee Sextons and all them who knew that they had something worth hanging onto, but a lot of people were very much ready to walk away and forget because they'd been through hell.[4]

Which makes a lot of sense to me when I start thinking about my family history. It just makes a lot of sense how it fits in. When people pretty much threw down their culture, there was some logic to that.

I don't think I was ever ashamed of being from here, but I

felt really confined. I remember thinking: I can't wait to get to college and be anonymous. Nobody knows my grandparents, nobody knows me. I would just be myself, and I wouldn't have all this burden of history around me. And I just thought that would be so cool to be anonymous. It really wasn't cool. It didn't get me anywhere. I also wanted to meet boys. That was real important, too. That was a good motivator for going to college.

I remember feeling like the high school I went to was just not adequate. I knew I hadn't gotten too hot of an education. And I knew there was a bigger world out there. What that meant I wasn't sure. Once I found it I realized: geez, man, I left it all back home, the stuff that really matters. It's wonderful to go to a theater and get to see foreign films, that's cool, but it ain't nothing compared to getting to live on your great-grandmother's homeplace.

I was made to feel less when I went to college, up at Morehead. And that's an Appalachian school! I mean, they were good to me. I had some wonderful professors who were really encouraging. That first year I went it was like the red ink just bled all over my papers. It was awful, that first year. But then I started catching on and learning how to read and write and critically think and I had professors more than once say, "You know, it doesn't seem like you're from Eastern Kentucky." You know, when people say that they're trying to give you a compliment but what they're saying is, "Gee, I didn't expect you to do well in this class." That happened repeatedly. And when I went to UK.[5]

I majored in psychology at Morehead, that's what I graduated in, which qualified me to go out to Washington state and pick apples.

For a while there I traveled all over the Northwest and Canada. I worked in an apple orchard for three weeks. Busted my ass. And then I started working in a little restaurant, and from there somehow I found out about an opening in the women's shelter for the YWCA down in Seattle and I applied for that. For some strange reason I got that. I was an emergency housing counselor, which I actually was qualified to do. That was a really neat job, a real adventure. I had a lot of hillbilly moments there. That was my big adventure in the big city. So I came home to work for KFTC, and I think I was about twenty-three when I did that.

The homesickness, it was awful. It was sick. One time when I was out on the coastal Washington peninsula I stayed with this family for some time, and they had a little girl who was about eight years old. And I was standing washing the dishes and I remember I was singing "Blue Ridge Mountain Refugees," that Si Kahn song, just singing to myself. And this little girl comes over and hugs me around the waist and says, "It's okay, Bev, you'll get to go home again."

When I was in Seattle, what it did was affirm that I was from someplace. I knew where I was *from,* I knew what I was *about.* What I found on the West Coast is a lot of folks who aren't from anyplace in particular and don't know what they're about, so they're trying to create a new identity for themselves. When I was out there it seemed like there was a whole lot of women who were changing their names to Jane Whiteoak, and I was always like, "Honey, what's wrong with being who you are? There's nothing wrong with that." But I knew exactly who I was, and it took me living out in Seattle to understand what I had left at home.

I didn't want to be another unemployed hillbilly, so I was out there in Seattle. I read in *Progressive* magazine about the Appalachian Land Ownership Study,[6] which showed what we already knew: that almost all of the coal reserves are owned by multinational energy corporations and that the surface land is undervalued and undertaxed and a lot of that belongs to the coal companies, too, and that that's the source of poverty and inequity in Appalachia. I said, "Well, that's interesting, something's shaking back home."

So I started getting the KFTC newsletter, and somewhere or another the word came back to me they were looking for organizers.

I was an organizer, and my job was to try and get out the word. We were mainly working on two things as far as the legislature goes, which was the unmined minerals tax and the broad-form deed amendment. The broad-form deed amendment was nearest to my heart because, of course, I wanted someplace to come back home to. This whole holler was auger mined in 1962 and 1963. So my family was broad-formed then, and we were eminently threatened from then on out of being broad-formed again. I knew this could happen anytime, so it's the fear I've always had that I would lose my home.

So one of my little jobs was to do some local organizing around Somerset and that area,[7] but as far as the legislative session goes, my job was to try and get the word out about the minerals tax and the broad-form deed amendment to other counties in the west. So I did a lot of traveling. I went and did lobbying as all KFTC staff and members do, went and worked the legislative session. It was a great experience, a really good experience.

As an organizer with KFTC, you cannot take a leadership role, you can't be doing interviews with the press. You have to be in the background. I was liberated from that whenever I left KFTC and went to UK, when I went to college. So I would be called upon. Like when we did the big rally at the Rotunda, I was one of the speakers, which was mind-blowing because I have a terrible fear of speaking in public. But somebody had to do it, so I did.

So yeah, I was active during the fight for the broad-form deed amendment as a volunteer. That was a lot of fun because we won big. It's not every day that happens. It was incredible. We were optimistic going into the election. It was really cool on that night we had the election for the broad-form deed amendment. The primary was over—I think it was during the general election they had that—so Bush Senior was elected and that was a bummer. Every other election was just awful, but we were so happy because we'd won the broad-form deed! And we all got together at Hindman and had this wonderful party where it was just this huge sense of relief. And I couldn't believe that we didn't just win, we kicked butt. We won big. And it was the biggest vote for a constitutional amendment since the one to give eighteen-year-olds the vote.

This is relevant to the mountaintop removal struggle here. The key to winning it was really good on-the-ground organizing that covered the whole state, but there was a moral force behind us that was pushing it on. And wherever you were in the state, people knew strip mining companies were running people off of their land and treating people unfairly and destroying the land. And they knew it because the *Courier-Journal* had Nellie Woolum[8] being carried off of her homeplace and Bill Sturgill's mine,[9] where the house was going over the edge of the cliff. Folks had been seeing this for twenty years. They knew that strip mining was an abusive practice. So when they got down to the voting booth, 86 percent of them understood that they could vote against the coal industry. It was like a referendum against the coal industry, and all that we had to do was make them understand that that means a "yes" vote. Now, that's what we had to do because referendums are very confusing, all this really complicated text and you're in the voting booth for thirty seconds and you've got to figure this thing out. So we had to make people understand that a "yes" vote means you're voting to stop the broad-form deed. That was some really good, fast, on-the-ground organizing, but it had twenty years behind it. And that's where we're going now.

I think any reasonable person can intuitively understand that when you've blown the top off of a mountain you have forever destroyed it. People downstate, I think, can understand that more clearly. People here, they understand that, but they also understand that people have to make a living and that there's a limited number of jobs available, the economy isn't very diverse, so it's like a necessary evil that they're willing to accept because they have to have a job. The folks downstate don't have to deal with that end of it.

And the coal industry is always running its own campaign. They're always saying "We've created jobs, we've brought wealth to Eastern Kentucky, we put the land back just as good as it used to be." They have that same line. I've heard it all a thousand times. And it doesn't matter what the issue is when it's related to the coal industry, that's always what they say: "We've brought in wealth, we've brought in jobs, there wouldn't be anything in Eastern Kentucky if we weren't there." All of which are really offensive lies, but I think people can see through those lies and they do see through it.

Eastern Kentuckians like to say, "I can do what I want with my land." In the fight against the broad-form deed we had that feeling on our side. It is a major obstacle in the fight against mountaintop removal because what happens is the coal industry has a scam going on all the time. They've got the commercials showing the duck ponds and how nice they've put it back and they don't tell you the rest of it's wasteland and it's just dusty tabletops. They just show you the duck pond.

There's a mind-numbing amount of propaganda that's being put out by the coal industry all the time so that when they come around with this lease and say, "Okay, we're going to give you a dollar a ton for all the coal that we take out of here, that will be a half a million dollars. And we're going to put it back. You're going to have forty acres of flatland that you can do anything you want with. It's going to be beautiful. We're going to plant pasture grass, we're going to plant trees if you want us to, whatever you want. We'll put it back just the way you want it, and you'll get a half a million dollars."

So who doesn't want to believe this? When you're talking money, people hear what they want to hear, and this is a really seductive thing. Well, what they don't tell you is that they don't have to tell you a word of truth. They don't put it in writing. People here believe a person's word over a document.

And with the broad-form deed, the only people making money was the coal company. And now the landowner can, in theory, make some money out of it. What they don't tell you is that they don't have to tell you the truth about how much coal is on your property, they may not even want all the coal on your property. They may want your area for a load-out, which means you're going to get nothing. They may want your area for a haul road.

You're going to get plenty of destruction and you ain't going to get squat in the way of money.

They don't have to tell the truth. They may get your lease signed now and have no earthly intention of mining until the price goes up to who knows what, you may not live to see any of that money.

When people do business with the coal company, they're dealing with outlaws. It's like going to Vegas: you go and you think you can beat the house. You can't beat the house. They've got everything all tied up. They're going to make sure you can't beat the house. You can't beat the coal company. It's a big gamble, and they're not going to lose.

And if it's a local company, they have no more morals or sense of responsibility to the community. There's only one thing they're there for, and that is to harvest coal. It doesn't matter what's in their way. It doesn't matter if a cemetery's in their way, it doesn't matter if the homeplace is in their way, it doesn't matter if a hugely valuable forest is in their way. That's garbage, all of that is garbage. You can toss it over the hill. All that matters is getting the coal out and getting the coal out in as cheap a manner as it can possibly be obtained, and that's mountaintop removal. And that's why we've got this thing visited upon us.

One of the awkward things about organizing everyone on Wilson Creek is with the folks who have been approached to sign leases, and I don't really feel at liberty to talk with them a lot. It's like getting into somebody else's business. It's kind of awkward. I realize somewhere along the line that what I'd like to say to them is whatever you do we're still neighbors, we're going to be neighbors a long time after the May Brothers or after the Miller Brothers Coal Company comes through here. We're a community, no matter whatever happens. I would like to say that to some of my neighbors, and I haven't.

I don't believe any neighbors or family have gotten mad at me over speaking out, but they will. When this happens in a community, there's some larger landowners who stand to make some extra money and the smaller landowners that always get the damage, and what that can do is really tear a community apart. And the sad thing here on Wilson Creek is we're talking families who have lived here for four generations or more and we've all gotten along just fine. We all go to church together, respect each other, and everybody gets along good.

I think it's just tragic that it puts us in a position where all of a sudden people are almost pitted against each other. It's a real tragedy when a community gets torn apart that way. What happens is some people will sell out—I hope not here—or some people sign and let them mine. How can you not have hard feelings when the foundation gets blasted out from under your house and your neighbor has made who knows how much money? It's pretty tense.

When the May Brothers Coal Company representatives started trying to buy leases from people here back before Christmas, one of the ways to try and fight back we came up with was the idea of a "lands unsuitable for mining" petition. As part of that, we wanted to document the biodiversity that's right here on Wilson Creek and maybe find a rare species or two if we were really lucky. Some of these students in botany and agriculture came up from Berea in the early spring, and we went wildflower hunting, and this was the last place I brought them.

One of the students said that she had really wavered about coming because she had to finish a paper and it was due. Oh, this was Easter weekend. God love them, they gave up their Easter weekend to come and hunt for wildflowers, which I thought was incredibly sweet. So anyway, she decided she would come and she realized once she got up to this spot that it was exactly the right thing to do because now she knew; she understood what it's really all about. That made me feel really good. I hope I can do that for a lot of other students, because I think they really understood *this* is what you lose when you blow up a mountain. They went back all ready to join the fight, so I was really pleased with that.

Unfortunately people trust the May Brothers because they're local and they're respected as local people who have made a lot of money. Folks tend to respect people with a lot of money no matter what they did to get it. So that's kind of disturbing, because they can come around and talk to folks and get them to sign their leases even though, apparently, from what we can determine, they're not the ones that are going to do the mining. They want the Miller Brothers to do it, which of course means that what they tell people and what they're promising and what will actually be delivered by the Miller Brothers—it's a completely different company I'm sure—will be two very different things.

I think that we're going in the right direction. We're appealing to people across the state. A great strategy is the Mountain Witness Tours. We had one in August, and I think that's a really powerful thing. Like I was saying, you can't understand what you've lost or what's happening unless you actually see it with your own eyes. It's possible to say, "Okay, they're going to blow the top off of a mountain and they're going to shove all the dirt in the valley," but the human mind can't conceive of how huge an area that is unless you're just looking right at it and say, "Oh my God, it's everything I can see in a 180-degree direction." It's impossible to appreciate what a 3,000-acre mine looks like unless you've stood on a mountain and seen it, and when you do your life is never going to be the same.

I think that so many people have been touched or damaged by the coal industry, and yet at the same time they don't see a way necessarily to do anything about it. I've told the folks at work what I'm doing and they say, "That is so great. I'm so glad somebody is standing up to them."

Stand up with me! That's a harder step to take.

One of the nurses I work with, their foundation was cracked by a mine that was miles away and they've not been offered anything for it, they've not gotten anywhere with getting it fixed. They just sort of do what people do, which is just go on and hope it doesn't cause any serious structural problem. Which it will, of course. And she said, "I'm so glad you're doing this because it's not right."

People know it's not right that a coal company can cause damage to the foundation of every house for three miles, but what do you do? And people are, of course, beholden to the coal company for jobs, and when you're talking about somebody's payday, that's a great way to control their use of their civil rights.

One of the ways that coal companies around here will try to get leases from people is to promise a job to a relative or promise to fire a relative. It goes either way. So that's very frustrating because they've got them tied up economically.

This is my home.

I just put everything I've saved in my entire life into this house. I'm here because I want to be here. I could work anywhere. I really could. When you're a nurse you've got your ticket. But my family's here, my whole life is here.

It's not an accident that I play old-time music on the fiddle. Not even old-time music; *Kentucky* old-time music is my particular love. Or that I have chairs in my house that have had their bottoms caned by somebody down the road or a local guy that made my cabinets.

I live here, and I value and I love being in the mountains. This is home in the all-inclusive sense, and I will not be run off of it.

I know for an absolute fact they will never mine my place because they have to have my permission to do it and they're never going to get that. So that I know for a fact. But I know they can make it so uncomfortable and unlivable for you that they can force people out when they start blasting your house and poisoning your dog. It can get real ugly. I know that.

But I also know they can't make me sell. I know that for sure.

I just have no desire to live anyplace else. I want to be here because this is my life. There's just a lot of meaning to me in being here in this place. I've got work that is meaningful and peaceful, I've family nearby that look out for me and I look out for them,

I've got a community that I'm a part of. Where else in this whole country would I ever have that? I'd have to make it all over again, and it would never be equivalent. This is a blessing that I was given just by virtue of the fact where I was born. I'm not going to toss that away. I am certain in my heart that I am where I am supposed to be and doing exactly the work I am supposed to be doing. Why would I let a coal operator change that?

Wilson Creek, Kentucky, October 20, 2007

Carl Shoupe

Union Made

The fight is never about grapes or lettuce. It is always about people.
—Cesar Chavez

I'm sticking to the union
'Til the day I die.
—Woody Guthrie, "Union Maid"

Carl Shoupe is mad as hell. You can't hear it in his voice or even see it in his eyes. The clench of his firm, mountain jaw—his inheritance from his Cherokee grandmother—is the giveaway. As he stands to address the Bank of America shareholder meeting in Charlotte, North Carolina, he chooses his words skillfully, succinctly, ever the true Appalachian diplomat: "I came all the way from Kentucky because I am trying to save my homeland from total destruction caused by mountaintop removal coal mining, which Bank of America is a leading financier of. The southern Appalachian Mountains have some of the most biodiverse forests in the world. Mountaintop removal coal producers, funded by Bank of America, are exploding tops off these mountains and off our culture. This is not just about saving the climate, but also about the survival of our culture for our grandchildren and future generations."

Some of the shareholders and board members look at each other, brows crinkled in confusion. Many have never heard of mountaintop removal, let alone that their company, their own money, is subsidizing it. Others simply aren't used to such straight talk.

Carl Shoupe at Miners' Memorial Park in Benham, Kentucky. Photo by Silas House.

More anti–mountaintop removal activists who have come from across Appalachia stand up to speak. The face of Ken Lewis, Bank of America's CEO, is as red as a pickled beet. He has been ambushed.

And now *he's* mad as hell.

It is reminiscent of another corporate confrontation nearly forty years ago, when striking miners from Brookside, Kentucky, in Shoupe's native Harlan County, trekked to New York to say their piece at a Duke Power shareholder meeting. Chronicled in the Oscar-winning documentary *Harlan County USA,* it became a turning point in their fight for a living wage.[1]

Things are different today in Eastern Kentucky. The union has gone, having ceded its bloodied, hallowed ground to the companies and strip-mining operations. Deep mining is a lost art form; mechanization has long since taken over, replacing respectable underground miners with garish heavy equipment.

But in many ways, it's a place still at war over coal. The tactics of the coal companies remain the same: divide and conquer. On the other side, Shoupe and the grassroots organization he works with, Kentuckians for the Commonwealth (KFTC), find themselves fighting to bring people together in a broad coalition in the wake of the union's retreat.

"I talk about it daily," Shoupe says, seated—appropriately—at the Coal Miners' Memorial Park in Benham. "At the grocery, at the speedway, wherever. I had a conversation yesterday morning; a very respected man in the community. A professor. He said, 'You go, Carl, buddy, you get out there and you keep talking, you're doing a great job.' I said, 'Why don't you help me out a little bit?' and he said, 'Ah, buddy, I can't say much; they'd run me off.'"

He pauses long enough to breathe a shaky sigh of frustration. "So see, people know it's bad, that it's destroying our water, our culture, but like everything else, it's about money. People ain't speaking out about it. People are afraid of losing their jobs."

Shoupe, like so many others involved in this fight, believes that once again King Coal is using the big lie that is the biggest weapon it has in its pocket—in this case, that mountaintop removal provides jobs instead of replacing them with machines. And they're using it in full force.

Shoupe isn't about to back down from the fight. He responds with his own bombshell: "I'm a third-generation coal miner. If you can't deep mine it, it ain't worth getting out of the mountain in the first place!"

Coming from a family of deep miners, Shoupe has certainly earned the right to make such bold statements. This pledge of allegiance to his mining heritage is the foundation for Shoupe's current fight against mountaintop removal. His grandfather began working in the coke ovens around Lafollette, Tennessee, before moving to Wallins Creek in Harlan County and going into the mines. Shoupe's father, Buster, better known as Buck, followed him underground.

"My dad is a hero to me," Shoupe admits, gazing across the freshly mowed grass to the coal miner's statue.

Buck Shoupe was active in the legendary fight for unionization in Eastern Kentucky during the 1930s. While on the picket line at Crummies Creek, he was shot in the hand.

"Back in those days, they were these company baseball teams," he says. "Each coal company had their own team. Dad was a tremendous hind-catcher. He could've got a job anywhere, being a baseball player. But then he got shot. That ruined his baseball career."

The injury didn't wound Buck's determination. After he recovered and the strike ended, Buck Shoupe went back down in the mines. He also continued his fight for a better working environment through the United Mine Workers, even picketing with them in his old age during the Brookside strikes. He can be glimpsed, along with his son, in *Harlan County USA.*

"I don't know if I should say this or not, but, well, he's dead and gone anyway, so it don't matter: that shot of all them guns in the back of the car?" Shoupe recalls, describing a scene in the film. "That was my dad's car. He was old at that time, too, but he feared no man. He didn't fear anything but God. He was still fighting."

Buck Shoupe's son's blood also runs red with that mountain courage. Like many other men and women of a certain age from Appalachia, it's what carried him through the jungles of Vietnam just as the war began in full force in the mid-1960s. And like many other of his fellow veterans, his time in country is something that he doesn't like to talk about.

"That year-plus I spent in Vietnam, pretty much, it messed me up," Shoupe stumbles. He looks down at his brown sandals for a moment. "I didn't realize it at the time. I hain't going to lie about it; I still have problems with it today."

He dealt with his problems by coming home and drinking with buddies. Seven of them headed to Louisville to find work, all crowding into a two-bedroom apartment. Shoupe quickly returned. Homesick for his family and his land, he took up the family trade and went underground.

He looks back: "Joe Hollingsworth—he's dead and gone now—he liked my dad. He said, 'Yeah, that old Buck Shoupe's a good worker; you reckon you can work as good as him?' and I said, 'Yeah, buddy.'"

Shoupe remembers feeling confident going underground, believing he'd found his place. He relished that dawn of darkness, the rush of adrenaline that came with being a couple of miles underground.

"Coal mining as I know it, as it's been done around here for years, it's that risk," he says. "That's part of the culture. It's hard to explain what a deep miner is. You're a unique individual when you put that hat on and go underground and dig coal. It's a culture."

Shoupe wasn't able to enjoy this contentment for long. Ten months later, he was critically injured when three tons of rock fell on him, mangling his body.

"It was a horseback-type thing, a huge kettle bottom about

the size of a pool table," he explains. "I was lucky that they was enough fellers around to lift it up off of me and get me out from under it."

By all accounts, Shoupe should have been dead. But true to his tough, mountain stock, he survived. His legs, arms, and back are permanently damaged. His spirit has been affected, too. If you listen closely, if you strain to hear the backstory that lingers between his frank opinions and down-home mannerisms, you can almost hear a deep undertone of hard-earned compassion and sweetness.

He stayed in the hospital for a year and then spent another three years recovering at home in the care of his wife, Paquita, and his mother. During his convalescence, Shoupe began taking classes at Southeast Community College in nearby Cumberland. He became a full-time union man after graduating, working as a research assistant at the United Mine Workers headquarters in Fairfax, Virginia, just outside of Washington, D.C., during what he calls "the most miserable year in my life."

Shoupe moans, "I was so homesick when I was in D.C. I don't care to tell you, that just wasn't me. All that hustle-bustle. All them horns blowing and sirens. It took its toll on me."

He returned home to work as an organizer during the Brookside strikes, eventually retiring in 1986. After a number of blurry years—"I got burnt out," he says—he started noticing what was being lost around him: "If you go up the river there, you'll see that they've destroyed the very place I growed up. The places where I played in the creek and swung on the grapevines. That woke me up. I knowed that wasn't right, and for about three year now I've been fighting all I can fight."

What finally pushed Shoupe over the edge was an effort by Black Mountain Resources, an Arch of Kentucky subsidiary, to mine under Lynch's reservoir, which provides drinking water to more than 600 residents. He contacted KFTC after seeing its advertisement in a local paper.

"They helped us a sight," he recalls. "We started protesting it; we didn't know how to fight it. One night we had a permit hearing over at the college, and a big bunch come down from Frankfort and they had to change their permit."

That win was a moral victory for Lynch residents, some of whom followed Shoupe's lead and joined KFTC, forming the Harlan County chapter, which now boasts over sixty-five members.

The reservoir controversy also contributed to Shoupe's decision to run for a seat on the Benham city council in 2006, which he won handily.

It's easy to see why—he knows everybody in town. As he sits in the park, a lady wearing a trucker's cap to shade her face from the sun hustles by, walking her dog along the blacktop path carved out long ago by the phantom railroad tracks, another reminder of Benham's former glory in the heyday of deep mining.

"Hey, Louise!" Shoupe hollers.

"Howdy, Carl!" she calls back, pleased to see him.

"That's my neighbor," he explains under his breath.

Driving through town, he tips his chin or throws his hand up to many of the passersby. It's something that people like Colleen Unroe, Harlan County's KFTC organizer, have grown accustomed to seeing.

"Carl has a lot of connections with people in the community," says Unroe. "He is a powerful speaker who talks about mountaintop removal and valley fills in a way that people can understand. He consistently asks the hard questions of elected officials and community members alike and is always looking for an angle to get new people involved."

Unroe calls Shoupe's union background "invaluable": "Because of his work as a UMWA organizer, he intimately understands how the industry works. This context gives him a different kind of credibility and turns the industry's argument about jobs on its face."

Part of the reason Shoupe feels compelled to fight so hard is to compensate for the union's absence. He is still first and foremost his father's son: a union man.

"We set by and let the union slip away," he mourns, his face tightening in frustration. "The UMWA bears some responsibility for mountaintop removal happening. If I could talk to Cecil Roberts today, I'd say that the UMWA needs to get off their hind-end and stop supporting mountaintop removal. I'd say the union needs to get back to what it was built on: deep mining."

He scoffs when speaking of the new mines: "These guys up here on top of these mountains pushing dirt around, they're not coal miners. I won't give them the respect of calling them coal miners. They're earth movers."

Shoupe is indignant when he says this. His demeanor makes it clear that this is a personal insult to him, his father, his grandfather, and all the other deep miners who took such pride in both their job and their homeplace.

Such plain talk is remarkable for a politician, even on the local level. It's a trait that has served Shoupe well during his tenure on the city council, and he has combined that plain talk with bold, progressive ideas for his region's future.

"I'm trying to move toward another kind of economy," he says. "We have the technology to move on to alternative sources. We're trying to create a wind turbine program right here. It's really looking good. MACED is on board,[2] and KFTC, of course. It looks like MIT is going to get a summer intern to come down and work with us.[3] This could be ten or twelve good-paying jobs."

Shoupe's optimism is contagious. While many in the struggle become downcast at times, Shoupe responds by sticking out his Cherokee chin and digging in even more: "People can change things if they get together. If we have a cohesive effort, we can beat 'em. Our side is winning. Minds are changing here in Harlan."

Shoupe also believes that minds are changing on coal issues in the halls of Congress nearly five hundred miles away. In April 2008, he returned to Washington, his former home, to participate in the third annual Mountaintop Removal Lobby Week. Along with 125 other citizen lobbyists, Shoupe made his rounds through congressional offices on Capitol Hill to drum up more co-sponsors for H.R. 2169, the Clean Water Protection Act. Dividing into groups of four or five, the delegation visited over 110 House offices and talked to more than 30 senators or staffers about introducing a companion bill in the Senate.

As he walked the perimeter of the Capitol grounds, slowing to take in the sweet smell of the cherry blossoms in full bloom, Shoupe was encouraged by the turnout and enthusiasm of his fellow lobbyists.

"It's a good group this year," he smiled. "People from all over coming together. It shows that we can win this—eventually. We've just got to get some more of these knotheads up here to support us. Now, buddy, that's a hard job."

Back at the group's headquarters, located just behind the Supreme Court in the basement of the Lutheran Church of the Reformation, excited organizers rang a bell each time a group returned to report a new co-sponsor. You could hear their whoops and hollers all the way out onto East Capitol Street.

Shoupe joined in each time, shaking hands and hugging necks. But unlike some of the younger activists, there was a slight reticence to his celebration, and for good reason. He has seen enough in his life to know that to create change, one must be willing to pay a great price. It's one that his family and others like them have paid down through the years in the mountains, time and time again, their willingness forged in the coke ovens of East Tennessee, on the picket line at Crummies Creek, in the Number 32 Mine in Harlan County.

"I believe it'll come down to laying down in front of bulldozers," Shoupe says with sadness. "I really do. Unless the coal companies start to talk to people, start being part of the dialogue. I'm not against a good fight."

Back in Benham, as he looks beyond the statue of the coal miner, his eyes rest on the slab of black granite that bears the names of miners killed in the line of duty. And his jaw clenches.

Carl Shoupe talking . . .

I'm a third-generation coal miner, and I've lived in Harlan County all my life, with the exception of five years. This is my home. This is my culture. This is my life. I love these mountains, and so do a lot of other people in this area. I guess I'm just one of the ones who might be a little more outspoken about the situation. I'm proud that I can stand up for what I believe in.

My family has been in Harlan County, Kentucky, at least a hundred years. Originally my ancestors migrated in here from Germany. My grandmother was a Cherokee woman. My grandfather worked down around Lafollette, Tennessee, working on the coke ovens, and he come up here when they started mining in Harlan, over on Wallins Creek. My dad was involved in the union activities back in the thirties. Matter of fact, on April 2, 1940, he was shot on the picket line at Crummies Creek, Kentucky. He never did tell me, but I'm assuming he got a gun shot out of his hand. I'm just assuming that.

The union was very much a part of our life. My mother, uncles, dad, grandfather. We've been a union family all of my life. I grew up in a captive coal-mining town, Lynch, Kentucky. U.S. Steel owned the town of Lynch. Just to be frank about it, we were blessed because we had a lot of the necessities of life right there in Lynch. We had our own hospital, our own school, our own movie theatre. We even had outhouses that had septic systems, cisterns. U.S. Steel kept them good and clean.

Back when I grew up, ye made ye own fun. I had a wonderful childhood. We played in the mountains. We swung on grapevines, dammed up springs. We'd go skinny-dipping in the swimming holes. Just fun, buddy. Just anywhere you wanted you could get a drink from the springs or eat the berries from the mountains.

My dad was a hard-working man, a union man. My dad—now I ain't bragging—but he took nothing off no man. He was a mean man, he was. He had to be, back then. He was very well respected in this community. A lot of the old people, still living, they'll tell you that. Back then they paid in scrip. I remember Dad taking me with him to get his pay. He'd take me with him. He'd get into heated arguments right there in line, arguing about the union, him standing up to company people. A saying he always had, he told me this a lot: "You know, son, I don't want to drive a Cadillac. But I'd like to have me a little Chevrolet every three years or so." And what he meant by that, what I took from it, was that he did a honest day's work and he wanted honest pay for it. He worked hard, and he wanted what he deserved.

I graduated high school in 1964, that's about when things was starting to gear up about Vietnam. What it was back then, being a poor coal-miner's son from Eastern Kentucky, either you joined up and got what you wanted in the service, or you got drafted. No other way around it. So, old dumb me, I signed up for the Marine Corps. I served four years. Thirteen months and nine days of that I served in country, in Vietnam. I-Corp, around Da Nang, Marble Mountain, Hue Phu Bai, around in there. Then I returned back to the States. I went back for a year and spent that in Okinawa.

It's ironic, it's weird, because where I was stationed at, I was up in the mountains, and it reminded me of home. It's strange to think, but it looked a lot like home. We'd take sniper fire, all kinds of fire in that jungle up there. You couldn't see the enemy a lot of the time. The Ho Chi Minh Trail was up in there. So they came up with this Agent Orange and they'd spray it on the mountains and—it's a little exaggeration, but not much—the next day you'd wake up, and poof! The mountain would be bare. I'd get sad, seeing that. I imagined how strange that would be, to see home looking thataway. And lo and behold, I tell ye, now, this mountaintop removal they're doing now, it's not that different from what that Agent Orange did in Vietnam. God forbid, but that toxic stuff in that Agent Orange . . . well, since I've been involved in this fight, I've found out more about the chemicals and the toxins these companies are using on mountaintop removal sites and well, it's a no-brainer, now: they're killing us. They are killing us.

Seeing what I saw in Vietnam, I didn't realize it at the time because I was nineteen years old and I thought I was invincible, but looking back on it now, I see that it was just like it is today. Looking back I can see that there was that wealth. That capitalistic wealth. Five or six percent making all the money off the war. Back in Vietnam, it's the same like it is over there in Iraq today. We were out there getting sixty dollars a month, hazardous-duty pay, getting shot at, mortared, everything else, and then the civilians were back on base, in Da Nang, driving the bulldozers and building the airports and all that, they were making all the money and we were protecting them, more or less. That's when I learned that the poor man is going to fight the wars and the rich man is going to prosper. And the poor men are expendable.

It's just like in the coal mines. If an accident happens, the company, the industry, had much rather for a miner to get killed than to get maimed up. If they get killed they pay you a certain amount, your family is screwed. If you get maimed, they have more expenses.

I got out of the Marine Corps in August of 1968 and come back and I'll be very honest with ye, I laid drunk for about a month. Just laid drunk. A lot of my buddies was getting back from Vietnam around the same time. One of my buddies—he didn't have to go to Vietnam—came back from Germany and we all laid drunk about a month. Big bunch of us. Seven of us. We all decided we'd go to Louisville, Kentucky, and make our fortune. Back in that day, you could get a job anywhere in Louisville. GE. The railroad. Paramount Pickles. You could walk out of one job and get another'n.

But then, about that time in history, the coal started picking back up. The workforce here was getting old, and they needed more miners, so I come back here and started aggravating them until they gave me a job. It made it easier to get a job because they all knowed my dad. So they hired me on the third shift. This would have been May of '69 when I went to work for U.S. Steel. Then I met my wife, and we got married in August of '69.

Back in those days, buddy, working in the mines was hump

and grunt. It wasn't any of these buggies taking supplies in. Back then it was all done by belt. All ye timbers and tools and everything came in by belt. I was a roof-bolter. I thought I knew everything about coal mining. Eventually I went to work on the second shift.

On March 10, 1970, I was pinning top at the 32 Mine and the world fell in on me. The roof fell in on me. Just by the grace of God am I setting here talking to ye. I stayed in the hospital right at a year. It busted my back up, tore my chin off, mashed my arm up, mashed my leg. Oh man, I was just lucky that it didn't mash my head. It mashed 'bout everything else. I's the only one hurt. It was a freak accident. They estimated that it weighed about three tons.

At that time I got a lot better outlook on the companies. U.S. Steel was a good company to work for. They really were. They respected the union, the union respected them. You can go check the records, they was always good production, good union relations, when U.S. Steel run the mines up in here. I was under constant care. My mother and wife would come and help me eat, see to me. And U.S. Steel, the personnel man told my mother and wife to keep their receipts for their gas and eats and all, and they reimbursed them. That's unheard of, really. They was just a good company to work for, and that's why I have a lot of problems with these companies nowadays. You can't respect them anymore. They're renegades. They don't care nothing 'bout nobody, 'bout nothing but a dollar.

I never did go back in the mines. As I was rehabilitating myself, I went to college. Around this time the union got into some turmoil. Yablonski and all that.[4] And I guess because of my upbringing, I got involved in that. I started working on the election of Arnold Miller in the UMW.[5] I had my two-year degree, and there was some openings in the union, so they hired me. I worked out of the main office in D.C. I worked up there almost exactly one year before the Brookside strikes started. I begged President Miller to let me come home, and he let me. I worked quite a bit on the Brookside strike as a union organizer. I'm in the movie, but never named or anything. It's just a flash, but I'm there. My dad's in there, too.

I worked for the union a long time, and I got burnt out. I retired in 1986, and I became a drunk. I'll just be honest about it. I got fed up with life or whatever, and I laid drunk for about fifteen years. I didn't care what the companies did.

Looking back on it now, I know that my drinking was a result of having gone to Vietnam. There was no history of alcoholism in my family. It's hard to explain how that messes with ye mind. I was nineteen years old, thought I was invincible. You see things, you do things yourself, that you wouldn't do no way in the world . . . you block it out by drinking alcohol. By numbing yeself. Now that I'm sober, it comes back some.

Finally I got back to myself, found the Lord, and I got to looking around again and I thought, "Man, I've laid drunk all this time and look what's happened."

I am a Christian, first and foremost, and the way I read the Bible is that God don't want us to let his planet, his earth, to be destroyed. I'm not trying to make this a Christian issue, either. This is a human rights issue. If we choose to be mountain people, we have to protect our watershed, our mountains, our animals, our way of life. I know the companies own the land and the coal, but it's the simple fact that this is a deep-mining culture. They're taking that culture and destroying it, too.

This is Appalachia. I'm proud to be Appalachian. It's a way of life. We are a unique people. It's hard to explain. I've been around the world three times and shook hands with everybody twice and I can tell you that there's nobody that talks like us, or eats the food we eat, or acts like us. You can be your own person. It's just a different outlook on life.

This is a culture that this mountaintop removal is destroying. I've got eight grandchildren—four boys and four girls—and I'm not going to be able to take them out in the mountains and show them ginseng and yellowroot. This mining practice ain't just ruining the land but it's ruining who we are. It's changing everything. We stay scared to death when it rains, scared the mountains will wash down on us.

I get aggravated with people in my own community who will put up with this crap. Lots of people won't fight because they think, "Well, if it ain't in my backyard, it ain't hurting me." Right this minute, it's not affecting me directly. But I live here. I've got friends that live up there by a mountaintop removal site. He had a beautiful place, a big nice house, and then one day they turned a big pond loose on him and ruined everything. And he's been fighting them two years in court.

Some of my neighbors question my activism. I don't believe any of them have turned against me. Basically, right in this area, people know that it's wrong. It's hard to explain. They just don't want to come together and really fight it. The companies know exactly what buttons to push. The company has got these miners for sixteen hours a day. And they take their foremans to classes, how to combat a union drive, they've got the money to do all that. These coal miners are hearing this stuff, hearing this stuff, hearing this stuff from the company side. So what I'm trying to do in my own little way is to get my side out, but my side gets heard very sparsely.

I'm a progressive. I'm very proud of that fact. This is a democracy. This is majority rules. That's why I get so upset, because it's not that way anymore. Now, it's like one percent owns the rest, the ninety-nine percent. It's just like when we put that Stream Saver bill up, not one Eastern Kentucky legislator signed on, and that right there tells you that they're in the pocket of the coal industry.

Until I got involved with this a little bit I couldn't hardly spell the word "environmentalist." And now they call me an "environmental extremist." I personally take that as a compliment. If they want to call me that because of my love of the land that I grew up in, that's a compliment to me.

I've tried to talk to my deep mining friends. They need to

know what's going on. The bust will happen, I try to tell them. Once the bust comes, they'll all be starving to death again because there's no other industry. The companies will be gone, the mountaintops will be gone, and here will come the floods and we'll all be flooded again.

I've got a son and a son-in-law that works in the deep mines right now. They work 'em like dogs. They work 'em sixteen hours a day, seven days a week. The poor old miners don't have time to think about what's in the future. There's no extended health benefits for them—they say you have a health policy, but if you use them too much they'll fire you. They're sure not in as good hands as I was with U.S. Steel. They took care of me, and I've got checks coming in good now. Good health benefits, but my poor little grandchildren, they're not going to have that. These companies ain't providing for the miners the way they should. I think eventually they'll try to get around deep mining completely.

Cecil Roberts and his crew needs to set down with these coal companies and stop this criminal activity that the coal companies are doing.[6] Right here in Eastern Kentucky, there's more coal being mined right where we're setting today, there's more coal going out of this immediate area than ever before, and not one lump of it is UMWA coal. If this coal was being mined union, maybe retired miners' checks would increase a little bit. But no.

The company plays on this type of information. When the 1,200 miners marched on Frankfort, I know why they did that. My son and son-in-law work in the mines, so I know. Everybody knows it. They were told that they either go down to Frankfort or they'd be fired. At least one company told them if they didn't sign that petition they wouldn't get their paycheck. That's the non-union companies for you.

If you try to unionize now, the company will say, "You don't need them union bosses in here telling you what to do." Them leaving made it look they'd just leave the miners high and dry. What am I supposed to say?

The union is only as good as its local union, as the men in the mines. So if you're going to work unsafe even though you have the backing of the union, then what good's the union? But if you have the union, at least you have the right to work safe. But now, without a union, the way the administration is now, you just don't have any protection.

Even though I got hurt in the mines, I have to say that it was a safe mine. My accident was a freak accident. It all comes down to if a company wants to do the right thing or not. When I was just a young whippersnapper, first going in the mines, there was this old Italian miner who would say: "You clean him up, you timber him up, the coal, she comes." Now what he meant by that was that if you mine safely, then you're going to mine good coal. But if you go in there and halfway do it and try to be greedy, it's going to screw everything up. That all depends on the company.

Coal mining in this area used to be a very respected profession. You wouldn't even know that coal was being mined around here a lot of times. Because of one little simple fact: all the companies had their own bathhouses, places for the men to get cleaned up. You very rarely ever seen a miner with a dirty face. But now you see them in the grocery stores, in the stations, with their dirty clothes on. To me, I don't know how to say it, but that's being disrespectful in a way.

The sad part about it is that the people right here in Eastern Kentucky who are mining the coal, they don't have time to see what's going on on the broader scale. It's not only hurting our culture here in the mountains, it's hurting a lot of people elsewhere, even in third world countries.

The coal companies own it all: the timber rights, the coal rights, all of it. All this logging that's being done, it's part of the coal mining industry. They go in and clear-cut and then they mine it.

We are unique in this little area because we've been able to fight a lot of this. If you'll notice, since we've been sitting here, you don't see any big coal trucks coming through by us, because we've kept them out. But if you go down the road about three miles here, there will be trucks running every forty-five seconds; those big twenty-two-wheel trucks will be going through.

If all these mountains around me right now had been leveled, I'd be devastated. I'd probably—I hate to say I'd give up—but I'd probably just pack up and move. It just wouldn't be worth living here anymore, to me. It's sad enough to see it happening all around me. It just tears ye heart out, to see this type stuff going on.

Right here in this area, you've got your school board, your health care facilities, the newspapers, but there's no big industry but coal. Everything revolves around coal.

I honestly believe in my heart that if the environmentalists and the coal industry could set down together and get a dialogue going . . . we could change things. Coal ain't going to stop tomorrow. But there is a way we could communicate and clean things up and maybe even get coal to be a part of the equation. But the coal companies don't want to budge, they don't want to give anybody else a voice. They just don't want to lose a dollar.

Through the years, we have been beat down. Our politicians have not represented us. There was a big redistricting so that there are four representatives who represent Harlan County. It's divide and conquer. That's what's happening.

The companies' big showcases are Hazard and Pikeville. Yeah, they're doing well. But the surrounding rural areas are starving to death. Right here in this whole area of the tri-cities, there's not a red light. There's some stop signs, but no red light. If I wanted to go to Applebee's, I'd go to Hazard.

I just want my oak trees and walnut trees. I want to be able to take my grandchildren out in the woods and not have to worry about falling off a three-hundred-foot highwall. They're coming in on us. They're coming in from Letcher County, right over that ridge there. It's all on the other side of the mountain right now, but they're slowly encroaching. That's why I'm fighting so hard.

Benham, Kentucky, May 2, 2008

Kathy Mattea

A Light in the Dark

The green rolling hills of West Virginia
Are the nearest thing to heaven that I know
Though the times are sad and drear
And I cannot linger here
They'll keep me and never let me go
—Utah Phillips, "The Green Rolling Hills of West Virginia"

"There's a certain point in Eastern Kentucky, on I-64, when I'm driving home, where the mountains start to rise. Every time I hit it, still I feel it, it's way down deep, and something just lets go," Kathy Mattea says. "As I get closer and closer to home the horizon gets closer and closer until I can only see right around the bend, and that feels real safe to me, being nestled in like that. Home, in the mountains."

Mattea is a beloved, Grammy-winning singer who spent the last decade of the twentieth century as one of country music's most dependable and most respected hit-makers. Her songs are the kind that people know all the words to and sing along with when they come on the radio: "Eighteen Wheels (and a Dozen Roses)," "Where've You Been," "Walk the Way the Wind Blows." Mattea's personality has helped sell her records. People don't like just to hear her sing, they want to be her friend, too. In the new century, Mattea is emerging as one of the genre's most influential voices. She's also quickly becoming one of the more visible Appalachians involved in the fight against mountaintop removal.

Mattea has had the chance to talk about the issue a lot lately, because she's appeared in the papers frequently these days with

Kathy Mattea, Huntington, West Virginia. Photo by James Minchin.

the release of her latest album, *Coal,* one of the best-reviewed records of the year, in country or any other genre.

Coal showcases Mattea at the height of her powers as a singer. In covering classic coal-mining songs like Jean Ritchie's "The Blue Diamond Mines" and "The L&N Don't Stop Here Anymore," Hazel Dickens's "Black Lung," Billy Edd Wheeler's "Red-Winged Blackbird" and "The Coming of the Roads," and many others, Mattea has achieved something new in her already remarkable career. She has not only produced what might just be her best album to date, she's also returned in music to the home she speaks of with such eloquence, the Appalachia that she left physically when she was nineteen years old, but that she never left spiritually.

"This record reached out and took me. It called to me to be made. That's a different experience. It's like 'If not now, when?' and 'If not you, then who?' Nobody said that to me and I didn't think that, but you go through your life and you try to be open, you try to think how can I be of service, how can my gifts best be used in the world?" Mattea says, seated at the dining table of her Nashville home, which is simple and modest by the standards of entertainers of her stature. "If you ask that question every day, you find yourself at the center of something."

Mattea has found herself not only at the center of music at its highest power ("These songs provide a voice for a whole group of people, a place, a way of life. And that's a sacred use of music," she says), but also at the center of a growing environmental movement.

After becoming involved with Al Gore's Climate Project, Mattea found herself learning—and talking—more about mountaintop removal. It wasn't something that most country artists were talking about at the time. In fact, Mattea, Naomi Judd,[1] and Kenny Alphin (better known as Big Kenny of the duo Big and Rich) are the only country singers, Appalachian or not, to speak publicly on the topic despite constant lobbying from anti–mountaintop removal groups, who realize how powerful a famous country singer's words would be to people across the nation.[2]

Mattea is no stranger to stepping up to the plate when she's needed. She was the first country singer—and one of the first mainstream artists, period—to speak out against the government for not offering better funding to AIDS research and health care. She shocked audiences in 1992 when she spoke on the subject on live television during the Country Music Association awards (CMAs), a show known more for its flashy dresses and cowboy hats than its political statements. At the show, to the chagrin of the producers, Mattea wore three red ribbons to commemorate three friends of hers who had recently succumbed to AIDS. At the podium, she explained what the ribbons meant.

"I had lost friends and that's why I wanted to say something," she says. Although nobody else in the industry at the time was keen on talking about the disease publicly, she opened the door for others to do so. And she found that people were both receptive and supportive of what she had to say in her simple, nongrandstanding way. "For the next two weeks," she says, "people kept pulling me aside and thanking me for speaking up." She found support from many different corners, from the famously conservative DJ who privately told her she was his hero to the staffer on the popular *Ralph Emery Show* who told her his son was dying from the disease.

"I realized at that point was AIDS was touching everybody, but there was no safe way to talk about it. Before I spoke up, I felt alone; I felt afraid. I thought I might get blacklisted from the CMAs, but once I spoke up I could see right away that I had done the right thing."

She still gets scared when she thinks about this new issue—mountaintop removal—that she feels compelled to speak out about, but she knows it's the right thing to do. "I'm very scared about this; I'm not very comfortable," Mattea says. "I was not born an activist, but I try to live a life with some kind of integrity in it. So if you try to do that, if you feel called to do something, you can't say no. I can't live with myself if I say no. I don't want to be eighty years old in my rocking chair and thinking, 'Gosh, I really wish I would've done more.'"

Some people call themselves activists but actually *act* very little. Mattea is an activist in the truest sense of the word. She not only speaks her mind, but she also goes to action. After verbalizing her concerns about the government's reaction to AIDS patients in the early 1990s, she went to work on the issue. She immediately spearheaded efforts to create the album *Red Hot + Country,* a hit compilation record that gave its proceeds to benefit AIDS research and received two Grammy nominations. The success of the record led to a benefit concert held at the Grand Ole Opry. In two short years the issue had gone from being unmentioned to being discussed on the most hallowed stage in Nashville. Many people give Mattea credit for making this happen.[3] In 1992 *The Advocate,* the world's leading gay magazine, named Mattea as "Nashville's conscience on AIDS."

These days Mattea is active in several charities, including the American Foundation for AIDS Research, the Music City Cares AIDS Walk, the National AIDS Candlelight March, the S.A.V.E. AIDS Vaccine program, the T.J. Martell Foundation, and the West Virginia Task Force on Children, Youth, and Families. Besides her long list of awards for music (two Grammys, four Country Music Association awards, and many more) she has been honored for her work for others. She is the recipient of the 2001 Minnie Pearl Humanitarian Award as well as the 1994 Harvard AIDS Institute Leadership Award.

Mattea says that although she is speaking out against mountaintop removal, she believes everyone in this struggle deserves to be honored. In addition, she believes that no one will be served in the long run if one side is forced to sacrifice its needs for the sake of the other. "There has to be a shared strategy for the long term, honoring everyone involved . . . a creative vision where both sides brainstorm about solutions that are workable for as many folks as possible." And that's part of the reason she's doing this: to call attention to how jobs are being lost to the mining practice and how miners and their families are suffering at the toe of valley fills—not only to live with herself, but because she is loyal to the land she knows so well, despite having left in her early twenties.

"Even after you've gone away, it never leaves you, being Appalachian. It's like having a dual citizenship," Mattea says. "I used to not understand living as an expatriate, but being an Appalachian and not living there is sort of like being an expatriate in our own country."

She's also toured mountaintop removal sites. Always fair-minded, Mattea has agreed to tour such sites not only with environmentalist groups, but also with groups such as Friends of Coal, an offshoot of the West Virginia Coal Association. She says she has been greatly changed by seeing the devastation firsthand. But even more haunting than the unforgettable images of destroyed land are the stories of the people Mattea has met along the way. She refuses to be one of those celebrity activists who swoop in just to do a photo op. Instead, she has made a conscious effort to listen to the people who live with mountaintop removal every day.

"I have a lot of experience from my job meeting people after shows and hearing their stories, and I think that the biggest gift you can give somebody is just being totally present and listening with your whole self," she says, her lip trembling. "That's what I really try to do, and it's amazing what happens, the connections that you feel with people and the things people tell you. When I went to listen to them and they all started to talk, I felt myself fill up. And I just felt myself . . . it was, like, so much."

Mattea breaks down. Her home is silent, and the sounds of her grief are amplified by the quiet of the house and the ticking of the clock in the living room. Mattea's graceful hands wipe the corners of her eyes. In recalling the stories of the people, she is remembering their pain, too, and she feels it intensely, even now, a year after her trip. "It was just so much, what they were going through. How do you quantify story after story after story after story and you see people not giving up? It was amazing. I thought about how hard it had been for some of them to get there, to come tell me their stories. And it was really powerful and, yeah, it's emotional. Those tiny, individual stories, when you put them together, are the stories of a people and a place that need to be told. Houses being washed off foundations, and the kids being afraid of the floods, and being told you can't drink the water but you've still got to bathe your kids in it. Coming home and finding your front yard torn up because of somebody's backhoe. I don't know what I would do in that situation. I don't know if I could be that strong."

Mattea has also made the issue of mountaintop removal a central part of her oft-visited Web site (where she has even put up videos of anti–mountaintop removal testimony), and in March 2008 she lobbied Tennessee legislators in support of the Tennessee Scenic Vistas Protection Act, a bill that proposed banning mountaintop removal.[4] She has also recorded a radio commercial in support of the bill, has written about the issue for *Blue Ridge Country* magazine, and, perhaps most important, continues to talk about the issue everywhere she goes, with every reporter who interviews her.

Speaking out is not without its negative side, though. "Some people say, 'Oh, she just wants to sell records' or 'Oh, she hasn't been in the limelight in a while and she's just using this' or 'She moved away thirty years ago, well, who is she to talk about this?' I guess all those things are somebody's point of view, but it doesn't have anything to do with what's in my heart," Mattea says. "I grew up in West Virginia running trot lines and spelunking with carbide lamps and walking in the woods. I climbed the mountains and I went to Girl Scout camp and did all the hikes. I've been all over the state, and I grew up really digging into what it was all about. And it's like, you can't bring me up that way and teach me all of that and then expect me to keep my mouth shut. I love that place. It's part of me."

Mattea's family history with Appalachia—and with coal mining—is thick. Her mother, a second-generation American, was the daughter of a Welsh coal miner. Mattea's paternal grandfather was an immigrant from Italy who came to America as a stonemason and found work building coke ovens all over West Virginia. "They sent him down to Smithers, and the mines were booming there, and so he saw that he could make more money by going into the mines," she says.[5] "They had come from Italy because of the poverty; they worked so hard, it was amazing." Both of her parents grew up in coal camps.

Mattea's father was saved from the mines by an uncle, who helped him to go to college. "He found out the night before college was about to start. Uncle Wig told him he could work it off in the store," she says. "His life changed in an instant."

Mattea grew up in Cross Lanes, West Virginia, between Nitro and Charleston. She recalls a happy childhood steeped in family lore about the place and the mines. "One story I remember in particular is them always telling me how, in the wintertime, the miners never would see the light of day. They'd go in before daylight and come out after dusk. Around quitting time they'd watch for the miners to come home," Mattea says. "They'd see this string of lights in the darkness, coming down the mountainside, and they'd know my grandfather was on his way home. I love that image."

Her love for the place and its culture is palpable when listening to Mattea's *Coal,* which at this writing is the #2 album in the nation on the Billboard bluegrass charts and is being embraced as one of the best records of 2008 by reviewers from the *Boston Globe* to the *Los Angeles Times.* Her work on this album, which was produced by fellow traditionalist Marty Stuart, has helped Mattea to better understand her relationship to Appalachia, its mountains, and the way the place shaped her as a person. No matter that she had eighteen top-ten country hits under her belt, Mattea says that she really learned how to sing by doing the songs on *Coal.* Although she says she had to dig really deep to get to the dark and light places that held the power for her to let these songs come forth, she also found them to be "almost too effortless to sing." When Stuart heard this, he said this didn't surprise him a bit. "That's because it's in your blood, pal," he said.

Mattea likes this explanation. "I think there's a mystery there: that somewhere in me, in my DNA, there's my great-grandmother singing, and my grandmother, and my people, singing through me, with me," she says.

And that's yet another reason why she'll keep fighting for Appalachia and her mountains by raising her voice in song, and in protest.

Kathy Mattea talking . . .

I had heard about mountaintop removal, but it didn't really register.

Then I trained with Al Gore to be part of a group called the Climate Project that he started, which was a grassroots movement as a service project that he initiated to train a thousand people in this country to go give the slide show that *An Inconvenient Truth* is based on.[6] And so when we trained it was very intense. It was a weekend, and they encouraged us to personalize the slide show and make it our own and find our own kind of point of view so that we all weren't just trying to be Al Gore. It had to be more personal than that. I found this Web site, ilovemountains.org. And I was blown away. I made a slide for the show, of the Hobet Mine.[7] I took a picture of the footprint of the Hobet Mine superimposed over the island of Manhattan. And it took up half the island of Manhattan. I was dumbstruck. And when I began to put this in the slide show, you could hear audible gasps in the room. People couldn't believe it. Well, it sort of opened up a can of worms for me, and I began to meet people and learn more about this.

I went up and did this flyover with Mari-Lynn [Evans] and the Sierra Club, and then it turned into a press conference and all this stuff.[8] And if I had known, I might have done it differently, only because I felt a little bit like I didn't have time to process my reaction. It was sort of like not kind of getting to catch your breath. I literally had twenty minutes before I had to stand up and say something, and I was still pretty emotional. So when I went up with them, immediately Bill Raney, who's the head of Friends of Coal, kept saying publicly, "Well, we'll take her up. We'd like to show her the other side."[9] But I didn't hear from him. So I called him up one day. I said, "Take me. I'll go with you." So they took me up and I got to see a working site. I got to have lunch at a mountaintop removal mine with all the miners, I got to ride in some of the equipment and see how it's done. They showed me some of their environmental stuff. Some of the guys who do studies on the water and all that, they were there, telling me some of their stories. And so that sort of brought me to today.

The next thing that happened was *Blue Ridge Country* asked me to do an article on mountaintop removal. And I went back and read the articles, and basically what I keep finding is there is this set of people who are very active and then there's this other set of people who are like, "Hey, this is going on and isn't it sad and I hope they do something." And I feel like I don't want to just add my voice to the war. I don't want to keep screaming, "They're wrong, they're wrong, they're wrong, they're wrong, they're wrong." And I don't want to just say, "Wow, I sure hope they do something; I hope somebody does something."

And so I've really done a lot of soul-searching about where I feel like I can be of service in this whole thing, and I think somehow—just for me and the way I want to do this—when I decided to go and take a look at what the coal guys had to show me, I decided I didn't want to walk in with the idea that they're my enemy. I really wanted to try and be open. They showed me some reclamation that looked really good. I mean, you couldn't tell. And they showed me some reclamation and I was like, "That is *not* beautiful to me." But I tried to not villainize anyone.

Then I started learning about how coal contributes to global warming. All of a sudden, every rock I turned over had coal under it; that was kind of the way I described it. It is all put together. One of the thoughts that I had—and I don't know, I'm a chick singer, what do I know?—but when you fly over these mountaintop removal sites and even the reclamation sites, as you know, they're all flat on top and you can only build so many malls and airports and parking lots and shopping centers and golf courses. Especially when the grass won't grow. But, you know, you think, okay, it's decimated already and it's all flat. What if you just filled it with solar panels? What if you just filled it with wind turbines? It's like, okay, what could we do with this? We could create a whole other industry that could be something that would not have been possible before, but could be something that could move us forward to a point where . . . what if you built those things in West Virginia? What if you maintained them? What if you trained people to maintain them? You'd have a whole other industry that was sustainable, yet made something positive out of what's left from this negative impact. And I had this thought . . . I was talking to one of the people who was there, one of the activists, and he said, "I thought the exact same thing." And you think, who am I to throw this forward? But you just never know where a solution will come in.

Some friends of mine have come in contact with this guy who does conflict negotiations all over the world and has for thirty years. Palestinians and Israelis. People in refugee camps whose families have been murdered by their neighbors and they're trying to figure out how to live in this situation. Inner-city gangs and the police. Inner-city teachers and their students. Just people fighting for justice and the systems they're fighting against. His technique is called nonviolent communication, and it's in the tradition of Martin Luther King.

I've been learning a lot about this ability to communicate even when you don't agree. That's the space that I want to try and hold in this. If I can try to understand and let them understand where I'm coming from, *that's* where a new understanding comes in. And this guy, this negotiator, says when people can truly hear each other and hear the human need, the universal human need, behind why they are doing what they're doing on either side, it's amazing. Solutions tend to present themselves. And so I seem to be one human being who knows all these people, and I somehow feel like that that's a way I can help. I don't know if I can get coal operators and miners and the governor and legislators and activists and residents all together in a room with this guy or someone who does that kind of negotiating, but that's the best thing that I would be able to do. I don't have the skills to do it myself, but I sort of see myself as one person who knows all of these people.

It's very scary, because you can sort of feel the pressure to take a side, and I have very strong opinions. But I don't know that me just stating my opinions is going to be helpful, and I want to try and do something that's real and helpful. I think that if we can learn to say, "This is wrong. These are the facts and this is wrong," and have the discipline to keep from going to a place of hate, then that's the way the world changes. That's the way we don't have to have wars, either in our families, in our marriages, in our friendships, in our fighting against social injustice, or from country to country around the world. I've come to believe that that's the key. That's my fifteen cents.

It's a very scary thing for me to be able to sit here and say this. I don't feel equipped to do this. I don't feel that I know enough to do it, but it feels very much like what I'm being *called* to do. That's my prayer, that's my hope, is that that can be the template. Those kinds of struggles, that picture of that kid lying down in front of that tank in Tiananmen Square, or the picture of the marches with Martin Luther King that were peaceful. The pictures of Gandhi and how they did it over there. It is not accepting the unacceptable, but refusing to be a part of the violence, and there is a sacred space in that paradox that is where divine intervention happens.

I have experienced it in my life too much and it's miraculous. I do believe it can be done. I do. But I think that there has to be people in leadership positions that can understand that and can keep articulating that in the face of very high emotions—really, really high emotions.

I don't pretend to have some picture of some universal right or wrong. I don't think any of us do. The best way I can put it—I was thinking about that this morning when I was thinking about you coming—is I can remember when I was a kid and I was growing up in the Vietnam War. It was every night. And I can remember being like eleven and twelve and thinking, "This is going to go on for my whole life. Every night it's a report on the war and this is going to go on for my whole life. And the people who are grown-ups think this is okay. This is crazy." Then I got older and I thought, "Well, this is just the way of the world, and there's nothing you can do about it." And I think it's kind of the same with mountaintop removal. It takes a lot of discipline to hold the longer view. When we destroy our treasures in the name of the short-term goal, it's a stupid way to live. It's a stupid way to live.

I was reading somewhere where someone in the industry said, "Well, this is a very small number of people that we're affecting," but you know there is this thing about the people who choose to live in these places, and I know it because my family is really rooted there. It's an attachment to a sense of place like many, many people don't have anymore. And someone has to steward this land for us or we'll be out of everything. It'll be gone before we realize what we've done.

I have a friend who says, "Corporations have all the rights of an individual but not the responsibilities of an individual." So when it comes to a corporate environment, the success or failure is determined by the bottom line, financially. But how do you measure human costs? How do you measure environmental costs? How do you measure that other stuff if it's not even in the equation? And I think that's where we've really gone wrong not just in this industry, but as a culture, as a society, so that the people who are screaming about this can be looked at as Pollyanna or tree-hugger types or painted in certain terms when really every spiritual leader on the planet advocates going back to nature in order to stay centered and grounded. No matter what you believe, if you go for a two-hour walk in the woods, it changes something fundamentally in your point of view if you do that regularly. I don't know. That's the best way I can put it without villainizing anyone.

When I first got into this, I called one of my cousins, and I was talking to her and she said, "Kathy, the point of view around here is that they're disposable people." Nobody has to be disposable if we take the long view and we start looking at renewable energies and other alternatives. Okay, maybe we can't fix it tomorrow, but if we start to say today, "What can we do?" at least it makes us feel like we're not trapped. We have some sense of responsibility for where we're going.

We've gotten so far away, most of us, from a sense of connection with the outside world, nature. We live in our cars, we live in our houses, we go to office buildings, we ride elevators, most of us. Lots of people spend hours commuting to and from their houses, and much of the time don't have windows that can open in their house. So it cuts you off from something fundamental about being human and when that happens, you start to not see it anymore. You start to just not even notice it.

Nature will renew itself, but we have the ability now to do damage beyond nature's ability to repair itself. And that's the thing that's so scary. There are so many of us and we have such awesome technology that that's the reason that it's more important now than ever. And I learned that from the *Inconvenient Truth* slide show.

How can we find the balance? I think it's always about that. It's always about balance. But if we don't even have stewardship of the environment in the equation, and we're completely blinded by this kind of insatiable appetite we've built up for "success" and for energy, and to just feed this parasitic beast of our doing-ness as a culture, we're in danger. We're in danger in all kinds of ways.

And the danger of mountaintop removal, well, I think it's just because people don't know, but I do think that it's getting out there more and more. Even though I feel like there are days I'm so afraid I'm going to do more damage than good, I really want to add my voice in a way that makes a difference. But what I've found is when I'm being called to something I never feel like I'm ready. And when it's really what I'm supposed to be doing, it's like you put your foot up and the ground comes up to meet you. You have what you need when you need it, and you didn't know you had it sometimes.

Here's the thing: this is the crux of it to me. If I try to say, "Well, if I was a coal operator, how would I feel?" I'd be like, "Holy crap, they can't take us off coal. What am I going to do if coal goes away?" Well, I can relate to that because I'm passionate about the environment and global warming and what do I do? I transport my band around in a diesel bus. I can't afford a biodiesel bus; I don't own my own bus. So the lease company that I lease from doesn't have biodiesel buses, and when they get them they send them out on the big rock 'n' roll tours. So I'm getting eight miles to the gallon when I go out on the road and I've got a bus spewing diesel fumes and I'm thinking, okay, how can I be on the road and be responsible at the same time? There are things I'm doing, but this is a place where I haven't figured it out yet. Well, someone can come along and point a finger at me and say, "Well, see? Who are you to be able . . . you're not doing it perfectly."

But when we all sit and point the finger at each other at what we're doing wrong, we don't get to move forward with baby steps. We're not going to spring forth fully formed. And for that reason, that's what I think is dangerous about these sort of anonymous running commentaries online and the connection that has with gossip in general. It's like a place where people are free, they are given this forum to spew, nobody has to have discipline to try to understand. And so for me, it's like, okay, how can I not perpetuate that myself? How can I try to understand how I would feel if I was a coal operator? Well, if I was a coal operator I would think, "This is what I'm supposed to do. And if I try to talk about doing something differently, everybody's going to get scared, and suddenly I'm going to be without a job and the rug's going to be pulled out from under me." How do we create some kind of discussion where we can shut the world out and all of its running commentary, and say, "All right, let's all get in a room and get real. Tell me what you're afraid of."

And I'll bet you money that if you sat down in a room where people all felt safe to be frank, you'd find a lot of coal operators going, "Man, I don't like it either. We don't like doing this, but coal is up right now. We got to get it while we can because we don't know when the price of coal is going to go back down. We might not even have enough money to pay what we need to pay to keep going." So I think that there is a fundamental shift that is not about what we talk about, it's *how* we talk about it. I think that's where we'll begin to find answers.

I think any injection of sanity in the discussion is helpful. At the end of the day, I really believe that what we're all here to do is to use the gifts we've been given to try to contribute something to the world.

There are days when I lie in bed and think, "Who are you to say anything? Who are you? Just because you've got some tiny public forum of your own?" All of those questions go through my head, too. At the end of the day, for me, everything good that has ever come to me in my life has happened because I have tried to listen to my gut and lived my life from the inside out. It was the thing that told me I needed to quit school and come to Nashville.

There have been these moments of grace in my life when I've suddenly, clearly known what I was supposed to do. And so I have to trust that. And this is what I'm being led to do. It terrifies me. But I trust that voice inside, I've learned to trust it. And I've learned that no matter what happens, the ultimate result of that will take me to a place I need to be, even if I have to go through some rough times in between. And I think part of the reason that's hard for me is that, musically, I've not been one of those social activists through music. But I think that I'm an articulate person and I'm a thinking person. And in recent years, I've been asked to speak more and to teach and to write, and so I feel like I have this other voice which is aside from my musical voice, and I feel like that's sort of what I'm being called to use here. It's not something that I feel a sense of knowing about my ability to articulate ideas, but stepping into that in kind of a public way is new for me, so it does feel uncomfortable sometimes.

The only thing I can say is I can't imagine how I would feel if instead of a mountain in my backyard there was a valley fill. I've seen the good ones. They're not exactly beautiful, even the ones that are done well. And if my family had lived on that piece of ground for two hundred years, I'd be damn emotional. I'm emotional about it now.

I think this is the test for all of us. Maybe the coal companies need to be a little more emotional and we need to be a little less emotional, and we need to meet somewhere in the middle. I think emotions are fine. I think it's the facts that are going to tell as well. The facts don't lie.

For me, when I get angry about it, or I get really sad about it, I have to take that and not try to make myself feel better by blaming somebody. I don't think I'm going to do any good that way. I have to find a way to get my story out, and I have to find a way to channel that energy in a way that's positive. So I don't think emotions are bad. To me, it's the difference between . . . I don't know if I'll be able to articulate it. To me, anger means that there is action to be taken. Like when I saw Gore's slide show, I didn't sleep for a couple of nights. There were a couple of points that kept coming back to me that I didn't think were sensational, mostly about the population explosion combined with the technological explosion. I went to despair for a while. I was just paralyzed. It was like a screen saver in the background that had been turned on and I couldn't turn it off.

But once I started to take action, I began to sleep at night again. I can't change it all, but I can do *something.* I can do what I can do. That's where peace comes from, and I think that's the place to use that energy. And then we have to learn to, as my husband is fond of saying,[10] sit in the ugly spot, we have to sit in an uncomfortable place for a while and hold still and keep from clobbering each other to make ourselves feel better. Otherwise, we're just two sides of the same coin.

I am not optimistic and I'm not pessimistic. I don't know. I have no idea. All I know is I believe it's possible, but I think enough people have to come together with some kind of nonviolent approach in order to find a solution. I really do believe that. I think that if we just keep going, "You're wrong," "No, you're wrong," or "You're too emotional" or "You're not treating the people like people" or "You're trying to kill a whole industry," we're not going to get anything done. I think that people need to go to court; people need to go say, "Here is the law, here is what's being done, here are the facts," and let the system work. I also think that there is a larger discussion to be had, which is how do we all take responsibility for mapping the long-term road together ourselves. And we've got to come together in order to do that. Leaders from all parts of this have to be able to sit in a room together to do that. So I think that can be done. I don't know who can call that meeting. But I figure I'm going to take my tiny little ant-sized voice and throw it out there and see if it begins to take hold.

Nashville, Tennessee, February 11, 2008

Judy Bonds

The Endangered Hillbilly

> My people, darker than God sometimes, I see you
> in the shade of mountains, and if I burned a piece
> of coal to see you better, I would burn
> the darkness from it, but the darkness would
> return behind the nearest object; it starts
> on the other side of where the light runs out,
> but let's agree that is the harder side,
> where darkness makes another kind of light.
>
> —Maurice Manning, "Why Coal Companies Favor Mountaintop Removal"

There's a heaviness that hangs over the town of Whitesville, West Virginia. Like the fog from the nearby Big Coal River, it seeps through the streets, past the empty storefronts, on up the mountainside to the rows of houses that overlook the town.

It has become the invisible resident, a testament to the flight that has taken place over the years even as the profits of the mining industry have soared. Many of the buildings on the main street are vacant, pocked by broken windows boarded up with plywood. Only a few businesses barely hold on: an auto shop, a law office, a motel.

The sign for a local diner boasts hot fried baloney sandwiches, an Appalachian staple. Inside, a handful of people gather at the counter for their midday dinner. Even in the midst of the laughter that trickles out onto the street, one can hear the exhaustion.

People in Whitesville are tired. Although the town is located within Boone County, the leading coal-producing county in the state (and the county with the most mountaintop removal mines),

Judy Bonds, Whitesville, West Virginia. Photo by Silas House.

nearly 30 percent of residents live below the poverty line.[1] Ever the faithless lover, coal has left much of Whitesville high and dry.

"This town is dying," Judy Bonds mourns in the storefront office of Coal River Mountain Watch (CRMW). "Growing up here in the sixties, this was a pretty booming town. My mother tells me that in the forties it was even more booming. The more coal we mine, the poorer we get."

Such candor has made the fifty-seven-year-old grandmother a controversial figure around Whitesville and beyond. Coming from just up the road in Birch Holler, Bonds is used to taking her share of knocks. Her fierce hazel eyes and commanding voice are clues that she is descended from tough stock. It's something that has sustained her as the outreach coordinator for CRMW, a grassroots organization devoted to stopping mountaintop removal.

"I have the reputation of being a pretty angry person who speaks her mind," Bonds says. "Sometimes the words don't come out right. If it's a spade, I call it a spade. That's who I am. I can't apologize for that. I lost my diplomacy a long time ago."

Bonds was raised to speak her mind. The daughter of Oliver "Cob" Thompson and Sarah Easton Hannah—"pronounced 'Hanner,'" Bonds is quick to point out—she is proud of her country upbringing in the Coal River Valley, where her family has lived for ten generations. "My first memories was of my father and grandfather plowing the field above my home," she recalls. "I remember the smell of the rich, beautiful black earth. That's how it is in Appalachia—you are the mountain and the mountain is you."

Bonds also remembers playing with her father's mining gear and finding one of his paychecks, made out for only fifteen dollars. That discovery, perhaps more than any other, put a nagging doubt in her mind about ethics in the coal industry. Her father's pay was barely enough to provide for her family, she says, let alone to compensate for the risks to his life and health.

"I remember walking up and down the railroad tracks at night with a pillowcase picking up lumps of coal so that we could stay warm," she shakes her head. "My memories of coal are not good memories."

Bonds doesn't recall ever hearing her father grumble. "It was my mommy who complained, who railed and ranted against the company and the industry and how they treated the miners and the people. My mother was the one who talked about Matewan and Mother Jones and John L. Lewis."[2]

Her mother was also responsible for making sure her father finally received his black lung benefits. "My daddy got old and he was used up by the coal industry and he had black lung and needed to retire, but he still had children and grandchildren that he had to raise," says Bonds.

The coal company didn't take such things into account. They denied him compensation, giving him an ultimatum: go back to work or quit.

He went back in the mines.

Meanwhile, Bonds recalls, her mother hatched a brilliant scheme. "My mother thought, 'Well, I'll get life insurance on Cob.' So the agent come to the house and came back after a physical, and he looked at my mother and said, 'Ms. Thompson, we can't insure your husband. He very sick, he's ill.' And she said, 'Well, what's wrong with him?' And he said, 'Why, he's got black lung. He might live six months.'

"My mother said, 'Can you prove that?' He said, 'Yessir, Ms. Thompson, right here's the paper that proves he's got black lung.'"

Despite her requests, the agent refused to turn over the piece of paper. Not batting an eye, says Bonds, her mother pulled out a pistol that she had tucked away in the big pockets of her housecoat.

"She pointed it at the insurance man and she said, 'Sir, you're not leaving here with that piece of paper.' And so that's how my father finally proved that he had black lung."

Bonds decries that "a proud, rebellious people have kind of lost their spines," something she blames on the coal industry. "I'm awful proud to be a hillbilly!" she shouts and lets out a big grin. "I choose to call myself an Appalachian-American because people need to realize that Appalachians are a distinct ethnic group."

Her identity is something that Bonds always mentions in her speeches. At an anti–mountaintop removal rally at a church in Harlem in May 2007, she is filled with righteous indignation: "I never knew that America thought that I was an ignorant hillbilly until I went to Ohio when I was six years old and I found out that I was an ignorant hillbilly! It amazed me."

Bonds's feeling of inferiority has been buried deep inside her all these years. It bubbles to the surface whenever she thinks about mountaintop removal and the fact that it's destroying her culture. In fact, she is so adamant about preserving mountain culture that CRMW recently created a t-shirt emblazoned with the rallying cry "Save the Endangered Hillbilly." They can't keep enough in stock.

"Some people say if you're from a coal mining family and you speak out against coal you're betraying your heritage. Well, I pretty much say that these modern-day miners are the ones betraying their ancestors by destroying this land and who we are," Bonds says with her trademark bluntness. "God made mountains and mountaineers. Greed made coal mining. I'm sorry, but that's the truth."

Here she pauses and looks out the picture window at her hometown. A car sputters by every now and then. Somebody passes by on the sidewalk; she throws up her hand in acknowledgment. Leaning back on the worn couch, her posture softens.

"I've lost a lot of friends over speaking out," Bonds says. "Nobody in my family, nobody real close. I consider them people who were never my friend to begin with. My daughter bought me a stun gun for Christmas because I've been threatened a couple of times. You can't look down when somebody looks at you. You've got to look them right in the eye and keep going."

It's an old company strategy: divide and conquer. And Whitesville has been torn in two.

This, Bonds says, is a fact often acknowledged in conversations around the supper table and in line at the local Dairy Queen. There, a weathered man walks in wearing a t-shirt with what appears to be a man's face morphing into that of pig. A devilish mustache curls its way out from underneath the snout. What gives away the identity of the swine is the bold, black text above the picture, an ode to the state's largest coal producer: Massey Energy Sucks. The pig is Massey CEO Don Blankenship.

A patron looks up from his chicken strip basket. "Nice shirt."

"Thanks, brother," the man says, ambling over to extend his calloused hand. "He sure is a bad 'n."

Another customer rolls her eyes and giggles, nudging her friend across the table. She turns and shakes her head in disgust.

Bonds herself cackles at mention of the man in the t-shirt. "I'm so glad he was out today. Ain't he great?"

"Massey has been able to steal the spine out of people," she says. "It's a lot like battered wives, that Stockholm syndrome, where you identify with your abuser. That man beats you up, knocks you down, then he says, 'Oh honey, I didn't mean to do that, I love ye so much, let me help you up.' And then he kisses you. It's the same thing. 'Here's ye some coal sludge, here's ye some coal dust. Oh, I love you, here's ye a paycheck. Let's build a sludge pond above the school down the road here and send your children there.'"

Located about ten miles downstream from Whitesville, Marsh Fork Elementary School stands in the shadow of one of West Virginia's largest impoundments, which is operated by Massey Energy. Standing 385 feet tall, the Shumate sludge impoundment holds 2.8 billion gallons of coal slurry. Another impoundment, built just a few miles upstream from Whitesville in Marfork Holler, contains 8 billion gallons of slurry.

The ponds have surrounded Whitesville, making some residents concerned for their safety. Despite repeated assurances from Massey Energy, many, including Bonds, still have their doubts.

The disasters at Buffalo Creek, West Virginia, in 1972 and Martin County, Kentucky, in 2003 are still too fresh in their memories.

"We had better remember," she says, going on to blame the union's absence for the domination of the coal companies over area residents.

She recently witnessed the partnership between union and company when she traveled to Washington, D.C., to attend a congressional hearing on the oversight of the Surface Mining and Reclamation Act. What she saw stopped her dead in her tracks. "I was standing there with my 'Stop Mountaintop Removal' shirt and I looked over and there sat Cecil Roberts rubbing shoulders with Bill Raney and Bill Caylor.[3] Coming from a union family, I about puked. It makes me sick to know how corrupt the leadership in the union has become."

Bonds also refuses to cut the local churches any slack. A practicing Christian, she credits her faith with informing her views on the environment and fighting mountaintop removal. "Mountaintop removal is a destruction of God's earth," she says. "More churches don't fight back because they have coal miners in their congregations. And there's a history there. Most of the pastors in the old churches were owned by the companies. Churches don't want to divide their congregations."

Many mountain churches also are subsidized by the coal companies, she notes. "It's very complicated; it's not black and white. They just teach God, gays, and guns and don't talk about the environment. It's changing, but a lot haven't joined the fight."

Maybe more would enlist if they had been on the walk that Bonds took one day some years ago with her seven-year-old grandson. Like any other child, he wandered over into the creek to play. His hands full of stiffened shad, he hollered up at his grandmother, "What's wrong with these fish?"

They were dead.

Bonds panicked and began screaming for him to get out of the creek. The look of confusion on his little face cut her to the quick.

"Anybody who sees their grandbaby—or any child—in a stream full of dead fish under a corporate outlaw, there's no way it can't affect you," she says.

Bonds says that the coal company did more than just ignore her concerns. They laughed at her. "I called a lawyer right up the road here," she remembers. "He said, 'Well, Ms. Bonds, what do you want?' I said I wanted the trains covered, I wanted them to quit running them at night, I wanted the black water stopped, I wanted the blasting to quit.

"He said, 'This is coal country.' He went on and on. Forgive my language, but I said, 'I don't think you're the lawyer I'm looking for. I think you're a pussy.' So I didn't work with him."

Instead, Bonds joined up with CRMW in 1999 after seeing a flier for a rally. Formed the previous year by activists Randy Sprouse, Janice Neese, and Freda Williams, the organization has become a leading voice in the fight against mountaintop removal.

The cause keeps Bonds so busy that she barely sleeps. "It's overtaken my life," she confesses. "I write letters to the editor in my sleep. I spend a lot of time on the road. It's hard for an Appalachian to travel that much. I've had people tell me that I'm doing it for my children and grandchildren, but it's hard to give up that fishing, that family time."

It's also been hard to get the ear of the national media, which Bonds blames on prevailing stereotypes about the region. She has pitched an idea for a national media campaign involving celebrities, but so far to no avail: "People have tried to contact Jennifer Garner and Brad Paisley to speak out, but it's hard to get your foot in the door with them. It bothers me that people like that don't help their own state, their own region. I'd like to hear an explanation from them on that." Knowing Bonds, she'll confront them about it if she gets the chance.

As a folk celebrity in her own right, she has certainly earned that chance. Her honest speeches, coupled with her compelling biography, have garnered mountaintop removal national attention in the pages of *People, Vanity Fair, O,* and *National Geographic.* In

2003, she was awarded the prestigious Goldman Environmental Prize.

Bonds is using the attention to educate people about coal. In Harlem, she tells a delegation to the United Nations that she is outraged: "Most Americans think their electricity comes from an electricity fairy. That's what they think. You ask them where it comes from: 'Well, from the light switch.' Excuse me, but I know where it comes from because my blood, sweat, and tears pays for it. Every time you flip on that light switch you're blowing up my mountains and you're poisoning my babies. When you come to Appalachia, you're no longer in the United States of America—no, sir. You're in the United States of Appalachia, and King Coal rules with an iron fist!"

Bonds is determined to loosen the coal industry's grip in the mountains. To her, it's just as much about the culture that mountaintop removal is destroying as it is the mountains.

"They filmed parts of *Matewan* right up the road here," she points out the storefront window. "James Earl Jones was interviewed, and I think he put it best. He said, 'Mountain people are a different type of people, and their landscape makes them different types of people. They're not used to going anywhere the straight way. They have to be determined.'"

To that Bonds adds, "We have to keep working, keep fighting."

That has become Bonds's mantra: keep fighting. It's something she whispers to herself in quiet moments, a guidepost she uses to shout down her doubts. Looking out at Whitesville, surveying its despair, she has no intention of turning back now: "I'll be there every step of the way."

Judy Bonds talking . . .

My daddy was a coal miner; my granddaddy was, too. My daddy worked the evening shift and he'd come home all black, all around his eyes. I remember at that time, the house in Birch Holler—that's where I's born—we had one of them old oval wash tubs. We'd pump the water out and we'd heat up the water. We had a fireplace grate, and Mommy would put the washtub right there and hang a bedspread up between the living room and the kitchen. We'd take a bath and then my daddy would bath in that water last because he turned the water black. I didn't get to see much of Daddy except for on the weekends because he worked so much. He was the hardest-working man I ever knowed in my life. Him and my granddaddy would plow the field up above the house there with a mule. My very first memory—my very first—is of that rich black earth where they'd plow in that field. I'll never forget that in my life. Those was the happiest days of my life, living up there in Birch Holler, away from everybody else. But lo and behold, one of them carpetbagging land companies owned that land, so when I was seven years old they made us move. We moved on down the same holler. I remember all the coal dust. That was the first time I ever seen running water.

I always loved horses when I was little. I found a pair of knee pads that they'd give the coal miners to wear down in them dog holes[4] and so I found them in Daddy's stuff and I thought, "Hmm, what great toys," so I strapped them on and clomped around like I was a horse. It was a long time afterward that I realized what they were really for; they were for my daddy to wear so he could get on his knees and mine coal to provide electricity for everybody in America.

My mommy saved all the receipts in this big chest, and I used to get in it and look around. One time I found a paycheck stub for Daddy, from the Bethlehem Coal Company. That paycheck was for fifteen dollars. I just couldn't understand. Fifteen dollars for a man risking his life and his health. Fifteen dollars is what he gets for that?

If I had known then what I know now, I would've begged my daddy not to have been a coal miner. If he hadn't been a miner, he'd still be alive walking these hills with his health, if he'd just farmed or done anything else besides mining. Because he died of black lung. He never complained about the company. He worked hard, and he always brought us kids some kind of special treat home with him, in them lunch buckets they had, the kind that kept water in the bottom to keep their lunch cool. My father taught me about hard work. But my mother taught me a lot about speaking out, about talking back, because she voiced her opinion. I remember how angry she was when the Buffalo Creek Disaster happened. She was so very angry. Not only at the coal industry, but also at the politicians. I think that was my first awakening to how our government, instead of protecting the people, protects the corporations.

It was hard at first to speak out, being the daughter of a miner. But we have a mono-economy in West Virginia, Eastern Kentucky, and Southwest Virginia. It makes me angry just to think about it. When I connect the dots, the complexities of it, I know that I have cousins and neighbors who still depend on the coal industry because they have created a mono-economy here. That's part of the government's conspiracy with the industry: you create a mono-economy, take away people's choices so that they have to blast and poison their own neighbors, and indeed their own children, in order to stay where they want to stay. It keeps them divided. Jay Gould said, "I can hire one half of the working class to kill the other half."[5] They're all using the same handbook of oppression. It's so hard, so complex, in a way. But when you connect all the dots, it's so simple. And so evil. It's about profit and power. It's about ruling over us peons. Because the coal industry and even the government think we're just peons. The coal industry thinks Appalachia is their own little playground where they can do what they want. And they have.

They kept us divided, they kept our fathers working very hard to make a living so they couldn't fight. The mothers were taking care of all the kids and the gardens and washing the clothes. So the mothers couldn't fight. So it kept us divided. Then came the baseball teams that the coal companies sponsored, just another way to keep the natives from getting restless. When I figured all this out in my mind, it made me so angry. Right now I don't get a lot of sleep because it's in my head and it wants to come out, it's in my heart and it wants to come out. I'm pretty ticked off at how I've been duped all my life. My father kept his mouth shut because he knew he had children to raise. So he worked and he raised his garden. He was a true mountaineer. He loved this mountain life. He loved it. My family was mountaineers before they's coal miners.

We need to change things; we need to diversify our economy. We need to train these coal miners and give them choices to where they don't have to destroy their own homes in order to live here. What does it take to make a man destroy his own home, where he desires to live? What does that take? We need to give these workers another life, we need to give them hope. They have no hope, and they know that, but they won't admit it. Because if they admit it, they'd be admitting they're wrong.

It was through desperation that men became coal miners. If you go back and study history, these mountain men didn't want to be coal miners. They got duped and conned into losing their land to the industry and then they had no other choice. But to begin with they wanted to be subsistence farmers and hunters and mountaineers; they didn't want to be miners. That's the reason the coal industry had to bring in immigrants, because these mountain men didn't want to be miners. They wanted to be mountaineers.

Right up the road from where we're sitting, three miles from here, is Marfork Holler. Holler people walk. That's what you do, you know. You walk up the holler in the evenings, you get in the creek and flip over the rocks and look for crawdads. That's just what you do. The kids play in the creeks. You walk and talk. One evening me and my grandson, who was seven, were walking up the holler and he got over in the creek to play. And there were dead fish everywhere. I didn't notice them at first, but he did. He was standing there with fish in his hands, and I was screaming, "Get out of there! Throw them fish down! Get out of there!"

What do you do? It takes something like that for you to fully understand that that coal company above you is putting stuff out that kills you and your family, that's going to poison you. I started to see more blackwater spills. So I started to put together that they're not just poisoning us there in the holler. Not just in Marfork. They're poisoning everybody. People in Whitesville, people along the Ohio River and the Kanawha River. They're putting out mercury that's causing mental retardation. It was then that I began to understand that they don't care about anybody, no matter if it's a child or an old person or anybody at all. I was already angry at that coal company, but that was the straw that broke the camel's back. There was no turning back from there.

The coal company had to restock the stream with fish, and they actually admitted that it was a leak from a chemical they used at the preparation plant. But they said, "It's not harmful to human beings!"

About three years later, my grandson and I were walking along. He had stayed out of the streams for a while, but it was hard to keep him out of the creek. It's hard to keep a mountain child out of the creek. But he got in there and I saw this white, gooey stuff in the bottom of the creek. So I got him out of there. And I found out later that it's polyacrylamide.[6] It's absorbed through the skin, a chemical they use at the preparation plant, it causes burns on the inside of your body, it causes cancer. They all use polyacrylamide at the preparation plants.

If we could get the mass media to really look at this, to report on what an injustice this is, then mountaintop removal would have been over five years ago. It's going to take blood before anyone will notice, before the mainstream media will pay attention. But we can't get the national media to care about an Appalachian-American issue.

We're the only ethnic group you can still get away with making fun of. It's all over the place. *Squidbillies,* "Appalachian ER," "Hillbilly Moment."[7] It's all over the place. I call myself that because I'm proud to be an Appalachian and proud to be an American. I'm proud to be a hillbilly. I love that word. That word doesn't bother me at all. It's the words they put in front of "hillbilly" that demeans us. I want Americans to understand that we're a distinct culture that they should be proud of, too. Our place defines us. We're a distinct mountain culture, and our culture means something. This is a culture that has been handed down to us all the way from the Native Americans. This mountain culture is a very special culture that America needs to embrace and understand.

The mainstream media doesn't pay attention to us because of the stereotyping. In 1860, this army officer addressed the general assembly in Virginia and said, "To the west of here"—that being West Virginia—"lies a land with vaster amounts of coal than all of England, nay, in all of Europe. And the people there don't know the value of their land. So let's go steal their land and put them to work as cheap laborers."[8] And our fate was sealed. Then the railroad companies and the land companies and all that knew of the timber and gas and oil and coal in Appalachia. They knew that if they dehumanized the people, that'd make it easier for them to steal their land, to steal their culture, and to put them to work as indentured slaves, which is basically what they did when they started paying our granddaddies in script.[9] They painted us as inbred, ignorant, violent people—"Stay away! Stay away!"—and that made it easier for them to do what they wanted to in Appalachia, because they had sold us as being mongrels—that was a word that was used to describe us. The mainstream media believed that.

Appalachia is a bad taste in mainstream Americans' mouths. Because it's vast, it's stark, it's real. We're not this plastic society that Americans thrive on now, this materialistic place. We don't put on a show, don't put on airs. We're unhomogenized. We're not Photoshopped. We're unretouched. We're *real* people. And I don't think mainstream America likes real and stark and raw. That's my opinion of it.

I believe it will take someone like JFK or RFK to shine a spotlight on us. I'm hoping—and I have faith—that there are true Americans out there that will realize that these hillbillies, these mountaineers, that we are intelligent people, we're caring, we're friendly people. And they'll realize that maybe they ought to go beyond our dialect, beyond the way we eat and dress, and listen to us. When it comes to wars, who's the first people they want to fight their wars for them? It's us, it's us. It's always been that way, if you look at the history of Appalachia. We's born fighting.

I've lived here all my life—fifty-seven years—except for about six months when one of my husbands was in the service and he took me out to Kansas, of all places—Fort Riley, Kansas. And in that time, I've seen this town die. Bill Raney's association keeps talking about the prosperity of coal. Hell, I can't find it nowhere. I've looked everywhere for that prosperity. I can't find it. I can't find it nowhere. The more coal we mine, the poorer we get. Why? Can they explain that to me? I want my government and the coal industry to explain that to me. I just can't seem to get it. Maybe the coal dust is affecting my brain. I'm seeing, in this little town, buildings falling apart, boarded up. I've seen it all my life. The more coal we mine, the more mechanized they get, and the poorer we get. It's just about the same in every Appalachian town.

You take McDowell County, it was once one of the richest counties in the United States.[10] It's now one of the poorest. I just can't find that prosperity. The coal industry says, "Aw, it's your government, they're stealing that coal severance from ye." I say, well, let's go to the legislature and tell them we want the taxes to go back to the coal communities it come from. But they say, "Oh, no, you'll never get that, all the counties deserve that coal severance tax." But are all of them breathing the coal dust, drinking the sludge water we're drinking? They're all in on it together. In Appalachia, I think 98 percent of the politicians are corrupt. They owe their soul to coal.

We've been oppressed for 150 years. Our people have had to deal with that. Remember I said that mountaineers didn't want to become miners? Well, what happened was, they become dependent upon the things they could buy. I think that was a conspiracy. Our state motto is "Mountaineers are always free." Well,

I think that West Virginians in the coal areas have forgotten what that means. Mountaineers are always free because God gave us what all we needed to survive in these mountains. We didn't need no help from nobody. God made sure of that. But then them companies came in and said, "Here's ye some shoes from Sears. Here's ye some eggs from Connecticut." And slowly they became addicted to that, they became dependent on that. Being addicted to that kind of lifestyle, it becomes hard to remember what it means to be free. The coal industry and the government decided to make these so-called free mountaineers into slaves dependent on the corporations. You can't discount that people just wanted to feed their kids. But there are also all these people driving this economy who wants a new tanning bed and a new truck, a new four-wheeler and a new boat. America has adopted this materialistic culture, and the mountaineer has adopted that too. Combine that with our mono-economy.

So what happens is that not enough of us speak out. It's complex. But there are those of us who are standing up and speaking out. There are those of us who are saying, "What can you do to me besides kill me? You're poisoning me anyway." Those of us who are daring to speak out, we'll be able to stand before God on Judgment Day and I'll be able to say, "I tried." And there are many who won't be able to say that.

There's a history of fighting back in Appalachia. We've stood up, we've been knocked down, we've stood back up. But not as much of that happens because of the modernization, the materialistic nature of Americans. I was part of that. Before all that happened at Marfork, I was just as asleep as anyone else. But that woke me up to how this is all connected, how this materialistic society drives this.

I saw this bumper sticker the other day that said "Live Simply So Others Can Simply Live." I think that, as a culture, as a human culture, we all have to realize that. But Appalachia can be the poster child for how we have to change. That's why people are starting to pay attention to us at last.

We were pushed plumb out of Marfork. My family was the last ones to leave. The coal dust, the trains, the black-water spills, the constant traffic. There was an orange, grimy substance on everything that I later found out was a syn-fuel[11] plant that they had up there. Marfork is known as the Super Tipple. Their plans was for a nine-billion-gallon sludge pond that they built up above me there. When the DEP[12] started testing our wells for sludge, I said, "Uh-oh." I mean, that was our water. So finally, being the last ones up in there, I decided it would be best to get my child and my grandchild out of the way of danger. I knew that dam would give way eventually. The water was destroyed. And the dust was killing us. My grandson couldn't hardly breathe. We left there in 1999.

When I leave work here in Whitesville and drive home, I have to drive right through Marfork. And it's still hard. Sometimes I go up there to see the graves. I have to go through a guard shack to go to my family's graves. I go there—I drive real slow, sometimes with a guard right on top of me, following two inches from my bumper—and I remember things as a daughter, a child, a mother, a grandmother. I remember everything. But after I get to a certain point, it's like a strange land to me, although I lived there so long. Because it's gone. It's an alien land now. There's a big preparation plant up there, and I have to drive through that to get to where my grandparents and my brother are buried. It's hard. It's real hard, because that's where my heart is.

The graveyard is like a little island. It's the only green spot up there. I only go when the weather's cold so I won't notice that as much. There's periwinkle all over the place up there. That's a telltale sign of an old Appalachian graveyard because it keeps the grass down. It's real noisy up there now, with the trucks going in and out and the conveyer belt going through. There's coal dust all over everything on that little graveyard. I don't know how my ancestors carried caskets up that mountain. It's a little island, a little piece of green there amongst all that.

I noticed last time I was up there, AEP[13] had put up some new power poles. They're putting in new substations everywhere here. There are no new people moving in, we're losing population. But they're putting in more substations for the company. They're using more electricity to make electricity. That's what my grandma would call chasing your tail.

People will say the landowner has a right to do whatever he wants to with his land. What about my rights? Sure, the coal company has that right until it encroaches on what I can do with my land, and my water. The coal company never wants to talk about that. We just had this big deal here in West Virginia about landowners' rights, but it works both ways. What about when my land is destroyed by them doing what they want? If I set a charge off on my property and it blowed over on my neighbor's land? I'd be in jail. But that don't happen with the companies. You can crap on your own land all you want to, but not on mine. No.

Women have always been at the forefront of Appalachian fights. Traditionally, women have held down violence. I think women like to talk. Women can speak out. Women are protective for their children. Go ahead and fight for a mommy-bear's cub, or go for that hen's chicks. Yeah, go for it, buddy. Women are protective.

Lots of these churches need to start fighting back. They should read Genesis 2:15.[14] God said he put Man in the garden to dress it and keep it. Not to destroy. He told us to use what was on this earth, but he also told us to protect it, to be stewards. We can use it, but we can't abuse it.

Look at nature. Creation shows God's creativity. He gave me something in my charge to take care of. I have to answer to him for it. Which one of these mountains would God blow up? Which one would Jesus store his waste in? We will be held accountable for what we've done to this land.

My faith was always there, always on the back burner, but I've depended more on it for the past four years or so. Because of all the stress I've been under, all the frustration, the only peace I could get is when I'm sitting in the backyard, or fishing with my grandson, or playing with my dogs, or out in the woods. That's when God talks to me, through these hills, these trees. Over the last couple of years, talking to God has calmed me down somewhat. He restores my soul. I pray to God for the answers. I've looked for the answers in the Bible, and they're there. It's all there.

Everything God created points toward him. I look at that mountain that points me to God and I'm going to blow it up? Excuse me, that don't make sense. I heard this preacher one time—he called himself a preacher, anyway—talking at a stream buffer-zone hearing. He works on a mountaintop removal site. He said he'd been to the Grand Canyon and while he was there he thought, "Why, look at that. That's one of the Seven Wonders of the World." And he said he thought about how, back home, he was creating that, too. I thought, Lord, how blasphemous. Oh my, may God forgive that man. I thought, "You think you can create. That you can do a better job than God?" I thought: "Buddy, you better think about what you're saying."

Mountaintop removal is morally wrong.

Let's start with the fact that first they clear-cut the mountain and destroy all the trees that God's animals live in, all these animals that we need, that we treasure. Then the animals come down, and we have to fight with them. Bears and rattlesnakes. I've had to fight them.

Then they start the blasting and drilling, they're blowing up God's mountains. The dust comes down on the people, covers the air, the leaves, it gets in your lungs. The blasting literally makes you feel like you're in a war zone. My dogs will be walking across the yard and will stop, look around real confused, then, bam, you hear and feel the blast yourself. It shakes your house, damages your home. It's an insult to people, especially to people who don't have much of a home to begin with. But, by golly, it's my home. You feel like you're being attacked. It does something to your psyche. Because you *are* being attacked. Four million pounds of explosives a day. That's a lot of explosive.

Then you breathe that air, and the coal dust gets in your eyes and nose and lungs. The kids breathe it and get sick. The elderly breathe it. You breathe it, you get sick. Then you have to look at the destruction they've done, knowing exactly what it's done to the mountains and the animals and the human beings. That mountain was something special. It's been there eons. Forever.

They can go through some mountains in a couple of months. Here in West Virginia they've tried to hide it for the longest time—they don't even try to hide it in Kentucky—but we can see it now.

The part that's really hard on people is the flooding. The kids here are sleeping fully clothed at night, plotting out escape routes, just waiting for the next Buffalo Creek. It's an attack on your physical self and your emotional self, too. It's morally wrong to do that to people.

I don't mind being poor. I don't mind living in a holler. I love living in a holler. But I do mind being polluted and blasted. I don't mind being isolated. I love being isolated. But I do mind being poisoned. That's wrong.

There are lots of people who won't hardly grunt to me, who won't associate with me. I walk into a little store and I can feel the tension. They've tried to intimidate me. If they smell fear, they come after you. I just ignore it.

I believe in the purpose-driven life. I believe there is a glimmer of hope. Even if we can save just one mountain, if we can save something for our kids. I believe there's hope. Even if there's not any hope, I'm not going to do like the rest of these yaller dogs and hump up in the corner and bury my head in the sand and say, "I can't do anything." I'm not made that way. My mommy always told me, "Don't you hump up in the corner. You get a lick in so they know they been in a fight." So that's what I'm going to do. I'm going to get a lick in so they know they've been in a fight. Now ain't that what a true Appalachian does?

Whitesville, West Virginia, March 27, 2008

Pat Hudson

Called to Action

> But ask now the beasts, and they shall teach thee, and the fowls of the air, and they shall tell thee. Or speak to the earth, and it shall teach thee, and the fishes of the sea shall declare unto thee. Who knoweth not in all these that the hand of the Lord hath wrought this? In whose hand is the soul of every living thing, and the breath of all mankind?
>
> —Job 12:7–10

It's a cold Sunday morning in East Tennessee and the Church of the Savior is filled to capacity. The congregation stands; voices from across the crowded church harmonize and send the words of a nineteenth-century hymn soaring up to the rafters.

> For the beauty of the earth
> For the glory of the skies
> For the love which from our birth
> Over and around us lies
> Lord of all, to Thee we raise
> This our hymn of grateful praise.

As the organ swells with its last note, Pat Hudson and Dawn Coppock move to the lectern and invite the congregation to join them in the responsive reading.

> It is by grace that we live among God's mountains.
> You shall not defile the land in which you live, and in which I also dwell. (Numbers 35:34)

Pat Hudson, Knoxville, Tennessee. Photo by Silas House.

As the audience gives the response in a synchronized monotone, Hudson catches Coppock's eye. The look conveys what both women are feeling: This day has been a long time coming. It's the inaugural Mountain Sunday service, dedicated to "the spiritual value of our mountains" and to confronting the threat of mountaintop removal mining. They exchange a quick smile, a shared prayer of thanksgiving.

Looking over the congregation, the two women are pleased: a body of believers—men and women, black and white, gay and straight, young and old, Democrat and Republican—have come together to honor God and His Creation.

Where else could this happen? Hudson asks herself.

After all, this is not a church of judgment. It's a house of freedom, open to all who enter, operating on the belief that "where the Spirit of the Lord is, there is liberty."[1] This flock—a United Church of Christ congregation—believes in promoting not only Creation, but also creativity: Appalachian poet Marianne Worthington stands to read a moving essay about mountaintop removal. Jean Ritchie's anthem "Black Waters" is sung. The pastor, the Reverend John Gill, a calming presence with hair a little longer than most East Tennessee preachers, leans on the podium and eyes his congregants. He is a man known for challenging the people of the church instead of offering them platitudes. Although the look on his face is serene, he is also a man who has seen the harsh realities of the world and remembers all of them. Perhaps the memories have taken up residence in his eyes, which are sad and concerned. Grief is in his hands, too, which occasionally drift up to emphasize a point. He chooses his words with care and passion, challenging everyone in the audience to be environmental stewards:

"It's time now, with our understanding of how we're related to the whole earth community, that we really need to extend our sense of our neighbor to the earth itself," he says. "What we do to the earth directly affects our neighbor. If we allow this kind of destruction to happen, our human neighbors are affected. We ought to love the earth like a neighbor."

His words wash out over the pews and settle on the people's shoulders, where they are considered with intelligence and patience. Once Gill finishes, it's clear that his sermon has been their mountaintop experience. Like others in the faith before them—Abraham, Moses, Elijah, even Christ himself—they leave the spiritual ridgeline changed. As they walk to their cars, many are moved to tears, some to righteous anger at themselves for their role in a culture of consumerism. Others are lost in silent reflection, thinking of both the issue and the woman who initially brought it before the church: Kathy Lindquist, a woman who greatly influenced everyone who knew her.

"We wanted to do something to memorialize Kathy," Hudson recalls, barely rising above a whisper. She is someone who rarely raises her voice; she believes in the power of quietude. "We knew we wanted to combine her love for the environment with her deep faith."

Lindquist was a civil engineer for the Tennessee Valley Authority as well as a passionate Christian and environmentalist, who had lived with cancer for twenty years. As a member of the Church of the Savior, she led the senior youth group and wrote a column called "Earth Corner" for the church newsletter. Concerned about the alarming increase in mountaintop removal sites in Kentucky and West Virginia, and fearing that the practice would soon be multiplying in Tennessee, she addressed the issue in her final column before her death in September 2005. At her funeral, Hudson and Coppock decided to place a petition against the practice next to the guestbook. It was the beginning of their teamwork on the issue. After some initial prodding by a fellow church member, they founded the Lindquist Environmental Appalachian Fellowship (LEAF)—an organization they describe as "a Christian fellowship of Tennesseeans whose faith leads them to take action" for the state's environment. Once Hudson and Coppock announced the formation of a group that would stand up for stewardship in memory of Lindquist, they were overwhelmed by the outpouring of both moral and financial support from their church family.

On the surface, the two women's partnership might have seemed like a mismatch. Hudson is a soft-spoken freelance writer whose work has appeared in publications such as *Southern Living* and *Americana.* A poet, Coppock is a well-known adoption attorney in East Tennessee and never has to be asked twice for her opinion.

Such yin and yang often makes for successful working relationships. They quickly developed a packet of materials on environmental stewardship—the concept that "the earth belongs to God and we're only caretakers," as Gill puts it—and mountaintop removal, which they have sent to churches throughout East Tennessee.

"The idea was to identify somebody in a congregation who was willing to lead the charge or the educational efforts in that congregation and just turn them loose," says Hudson, referring to the way the packets were distributed. The packets contain written materials on environmental stewardship, as well as DVDs of the films *Kilowatt Ours* and *Mountain Mourning* and the book *Serve God, Save the Planet.*[2] They include a note to forward the materials to another church upon finishing, a sort of "practice-what-you-preach" philosophy that promotes reuse of the provided information. According to Coppock, the packets have reached more than seventy churches within the region. Five congregations are now holding weekly creation care meetings as an adult study in response to receiving a LEAF packet.

Both Hudson and Coppock say that they have made a conscious effort to target churches of all theological stripes. "LEAF's been the beginning of building bridges," Hudson says. "We didn't want to be simply preaching to the choir or talking to the converted. We wanted to plough some new ground and have it be people who hadn't heard this message before—people who wouldn't show up at a water quality hearing or hadn't heard about the environment as a spiritual issue."

A critical step in that outreach was bringing in Dr. Matthew Sleeth, an evangelical medical doctor and author of *Serve God,*

Save the Planet. His effectiveness at recruiting other churches prompted Church of the Savior to join Compassion Coalition, a group of primarily evangelical churches in the Knoxville area. It also garnered them support from the local chapter of A Rocha: Christians in Conservation, an international organization dedicated to stewardship for which Sleeth was executive director of the North American chapter.[3]

Another important step was joining with other religious leaders to view firsthand the damage caused by mountaintop removal. In 2006, Hudson and Gill participated in the Mountaintop Removal Tour for Interfaith Leaders, hosted by Kentuckians for the Commonwealth (KFTC). During their visit to Montgomery Creek in Perry County, Kentucky, the diverse delegation made a twenty-minute hike up a steep mountainside to view an active site. Hudson and Gill were silent as they made the treacherous climb over rocks and along the rugged path, which was lined by wild orange azaleas that no one below had noticed before. Pausing by the flowers, Hudson put her hand out toward them as if they were breathing cool air. Behind her came a crooked line of people of various ages, religions, and ethnicities. Their faces were lined with sweat and determination; McKinley Sumner, the mountain's owner, offered an elderly nun a hand up onto a particularly steep natural rock step. Although the nun was out of breath and obviously tired, she refused to turn back. No one else did either.

Finally reaching the ridgeline, the group straggled out on a green wooded peninsula. What greeted them was a panorama of destruction.

Some ventured to the very edge of the cliff, staring a hundred feet straight down into the valley of dirt and rock. Others were frozen by grief in the middle of the overlook. Their shock seemed comparable to how Moses might have felt if, after climbing Mount Nebo, he had realized that there was no Promised Land. After a few minutes, they all came back together without a word and formed a circle.

Collecting themselves, they joined in singing "Amazing

Grace." Down below, warning horns blared and sirens wailed. Everyone kept singing, sure that the site foreman was just trying to scare them off. Some closed their eyes against the devastation, many moved their mouths in silent prayer. Others raised their hands in the air as if in praise of this once beautiful place. The horns sounded again, a long, funereal drone. And then, once again, the sirens, shrill and high, as if the land itself was crying out. The song continued, louder, defiant. Suddenly everyone realized that these were real warning horns and sirens, because on the last verse of the song, a mountain just across the expanse of empty air from them collapsed in on itself, another victim of the charges set to bring it down.

"It felt like somebody had hit me in the gut," Gill says, remembering the moment the mountain blew up before his eyes. But for Gill, something even more haunting than that was yet to come. "Hearing the stories of the people who lived there," he says, "it started to connect the dots for me. My soul has been largely formed in the mountains of Appalachia. If you love your neighbor in Kentucky or West Virginia or North Carolina or Tennessee, you should care about how the earth gets treated in that place. If you love your neighbor downstream from you, you should care about what happens to the river in your region."

He stood up in the pulpit the following Sunday and told his congregation in no uncertain terms: "This is sin."

Hudson returned to Knoxville committed to doing more in the fight. She and Coppock began digging deeper, stretching their commitment: *What else can we do? Can we kick this up a notch? Can we be proactive?*

One idea they came up with was following KFTC's lead and sponsoring Mountain Witness tours in which interested churches or individuals are taken to a mountaintop removal site in Tennessee. Both women believe that an up-close look at the devastation plays an important role in a church's decision of whether to take action. After Hudson and Coppock organized these tours, even more congregations began taking up the issue.

"When you figure this started just three years ago and that much has happened already," Coppock pauses and shakes her head. "We didn't do it all, but I think we hit the first domino."

Their efforts were not confined to churches. They soon extended all the way to the state legislature. After discovering that there was no legislative effort to ban or regulate mountaintop removal in Tennessee, Coppock decided to take matters into her own hands. An adoption attorney experienced in legislative matters, she's used to being blunt about what she wants. "I was in Nashville in a meeting with Bob Tuke, personal lawyer for the governor.[4] He said, 'Legislatively, what can I do for you?' And I said, 'Well, I'd like a ban on mountaintop removal.' Bob, who is very proactive and positive, said, 'We can do that.'"

After receiving Tuke's pledge of support, Coppock contacted other conservation organizations for their input. All indicated their support. But when it came to actually writing the legislation, Coppock says she "had no idea how to do it." Don Barger, senior director of the National Parks Conservation Association's Southeast Regional Office, came to her rescue. Along with his assistant, the three of them drafted the legislation.

"We came up with something pretty short and simple," Coppock recalls. "We said there wouldn't be any alteration or disturbance over 2,000 feet for the purpose of mountaintop removal and that the federal stream buffer zone would apply to the state; you have to stay 100 feet out of either side of a stream unless it would improve water quality."

Proposing the legislation, eventually known as the Tennessee Scenic Vistas Protection Act,[5] also required LEAF to incorporate in December 2007, as federal law restricts churches from overt political activity. Coppock registered as a state lobbyist, and along with Tuke, who also registered pro bono, set off to persuade Tennessee legislators to back the bill.

Although Hudson had initially feared that she wouldn't be able to add much to this aspect of the fight, she eventually joined the legislative effort. "The bill from the beginning was bipartisan," she notes. "That was the strength of it. The sponsor in the Senate was a conservative Christian Republican, the sponsor in the House was a Democrat known for a long time as an environmentalist. That brought a coalition."

The framing of the bill by its supporters was crucial. "We promoted it as a pro-business bill," Coppock says. "Tourism is our biggest industry in Tennessee. Development is huge. Nobody wants a condo across from a mountaintop removal site. Pro-business legislators supported our bill."

The group lobbied legislators every week of the legislative session and eventually made presentations before committees in the Senate and House. Although their support in the Senate Environment, Conservation, and Tourism committee was never in doubt—they had more than the five committee votes needed to get it to the Senate floor—the chairman, Senator Tommy Kilby (D), opposed the measure and persisted in delaying the vote.

Kilby's tactics shifted the focus to the House, where support for the bill in the eight-member Environment Subcommittee was much less assured. The vote occurred in April 2008 on the final day the subcommittee met.

"We had a nail-biter," recalls Coppock. "We thought we had four yeses, one no, and one undecided. The undecided wasn't in the room when the vote occurred. He left. One of our yes votes switched and voted no. It was 3–5."

It's clear from the looks on their faces that the narrow loss was a devastating blow. Coppock quickly asserts that they will fight for passage next year, but Hudson turns her clear, aquamarine eyes to the floor, blankly studying the carpet as she gathers her thoughts. "We had both said, 'One year and we're out.' It's hard on the family, the pocketbook. We don't know how we're going to do it, but we know we have to."

"How can you walk away from it?" Coppock interjects. "When God calls you to do something, you can't just say, 'We're done now.' Or in the great Old Testament tradition, 'I can't be a prophet, I have a speech impediment.'"[6]

Hudson continues: "We tried to find an environmental group to take it over, and they all looked horrified. We had to realize that nobody else could bring the coalition we had. We're halfway there now—all we have to do is to move two votes and hold the ground we've gained."

The ground they've covered is considerable. Following the bill's failure, Democratic governor Phil Bredesen indicated that he would actively support the bill when it was reintroduced. Speaking in favor of the stream buffer zone provision in the legislation, Bredesen told the *Knoxville News Sentinel:* "For me, with all the energy I've put into trying to preserve lands for future generations in East Tennessee, to have them strip-mined is not consistent with that goal."[7]

Hudson and Coppock are counting on such pledges to buttress them as they press toward the high mark during the next legislative session. Still, they dread the emotional maze that comes with the territory. They recall that some days their prayer was "Please don't let me cry in public." At other times, they followed the lead of country music singer Kathy Mattea, who came to the Capitol to lobby alongside them and lend support. "She said that sometimes she just prays, 'Dear God, you know I don't mean a word of this, but I need to pray for these guys, and I want to mean this.' *I want to mean it,*" says Hudson.

"It's been a real lesson in faith," Coppock agrees, recalling a particularly trying moment immediately following a contentious hearing. Putting on their best game faces, and reminding themselves of their commitment to building bridges, they approached the members of the coal industry who were present. One of the recurring lines that the coal operators used in opposing the bill was that Hudson and Coppock relied on misleading facts and statistics.

"They were towering over us, but we were telling them that we were open to them telling us what we said that was wrong, what statistics we got wrong," Coppock says. "They never corrected us on anything after that invitation. Coal operators have the reputation of being bullies, and neither of us are physically intimidating, but they were backing up from us."

Hudson and Coppock attribute their strength to LEAF's overall vision, that "light is the best disinfectant," and to their commitment to approaching their opponents as human beings. Coppock continues, "When you're dealing with an industry that is so profoundly dysfunctional, the last thing they want is light."

Both women credit their extended family at Church of the Savior with first setting an example for them. It's a lesson they are making sure to share with their children. Each is a devoted mother; Hudson has two daughters, Coppock one daughter and one son.

"My college-age daughter doesn't talk about how much money she wants to make so she can buy a Beamer," Hudson says. "She talks about being socially responsible, doing for others. If it'd just been me pushing that on her, she might have turned away from it. But she was surrounded by others who believed that, who were examples of that."

"It's the Christian spirit here," Coppock seconds. "Live and let live." She says that kind of acceptance is something that originates from behind the pulpit with Reverend Gill. "He created an environment that allowed us to follow our passions. It's safe to be who you are and to be different from each other. There is no polarizing and no factions. People disagree, but they sit down and talk things out. I don't see how LEAF could've been created in another environment."

Pat Hudson talking . . .

I'm the eighth generation in East Tennessee. My father's side is Scotch-Irish, English, and we even have a Native American branch off of that side of the family. My mother's side, she was a Midwesterner. She was from Illinois, from German immigrants. More recently—not real recently—mid-nineteenth century.

My father's family was from Sequatchie Valley, which we visited pretty much every month, and that was even more rural than where I grew up. It's a little bit west of Chattanooga, and there was really only one main road in. You had to go into Chattanooga, into Red Bank, and then up over what they called the W-Road to get into the valley. I was ill every time we did that as a child. The family had been in that place since about 1815, and so there you were connected not only just with nature but with history, just layer upon layer.

My grandfather had an eighth-grade education—that was pretty much all that was available down in the valley at that time—and so the family had to do just a little bit of everything. My uncle was a carpenter. They did stonework, they were janitors in the school; they just did everything. My grandmother had a greenhouse. Everybody in the family did something to add to the family. It's a pretty common Appalachian story.

There was mining down around Sequatchie Valley, and so certainly my dad's family was aware of it. But my uncle, my dad's older brother, went into the mine for one day and came back out and said, "I'm not ever going to do that." And I think because my dad saw his big brother have that reaction, he never went into the mines. That's the closest our family ever came.

I grew up in what was countryside and is now practically wall-to-wall subdivisions in what's now the Karnes Community. The house that I grew up in, they built it when I was on the way and up to the age of two—my dad built it himself—and we lived there from the time I was two on, and that would've been 1958. It's about halfway between Oak Ridge and Knoxville.

My father didn't like living in town. He came down to Oak Ridge when it was new,[8] moved us out about fifteen miles out of town into the countryside, and so my childhood was spent on around 200 acres surrounding my homeplace there. We didn't own all of it, but it was available; in those days, children just ran.

My father taught me very early on the tree names, how to make hickory whistles, how to make dogwood slingshots, all of that sort of stuff from the Depression-era child. You know, they'd had to make do. I've tried, but haven't done a real good job of passing that along to the next generation. They know it—I've actually had him show them—but it's just not a part of their whole being the way it was for me. We don't let children run the way they used to.

It was a very personal connection to nature. You knew the tree names, you knew the cycle of the trees, you knew what was budding and what was blooming. And it's just been a part of everything that I've been from the beginning. There was no real disconnect; now I think kids have indoors and outdoors.

I can remember, at about the age of ten, standing up on the hill behind my parents' house, which had a panoramic view of this whole valley, and it was fall—which has always been one of my favorite times of year, that crisp feeling in the air—and just knowing beyond a shadow of a doubt that I was connected to absolutely everything. I don't think I labeled it God, really, or I don't think I labeled it in a way that a church person would, but I sensed it, I felt it, and I still remember that day vividly.

My parents both came to Oak Ridge in the very early days and started going to church in the only church there was, which was the Army chapel. And after other churches began to develop, there were a core group of people who really liked that interdenominational way of going to church, so my parents kept us there.

I was a little bit unusual growing up in this area, because I didn't have a label, which was freeing, I think, in some ways but was very difficult for a child to explain because everybody—the majority of the kids I went to school with—were Baptists. That was the primary thing to be, and then if you weren't that, well then, at least you certainly were a Methodist. And if you weren't that, then, well, a Presbyterian, but if you got beyond that, then they didn't know how to take you.

Interestingly enough, it's very much like the United Church of Christ, the church I wound up in as an adult, with a lot of meandering in between. It's Christ-centered, but it's noncreedal, which means there was nothing you had to subscribe to or say that "I am . . . I do believe in these ten tenets" or whatever. So probably the description of it that most people would understand is Congregational: each congregation is free to believe in the way that they feel called to believe. It's different from a lot of denominations, where there are certain specific things that you have to profess to be members.

Going to church as a child gave me a hatred of dressing up. The 1950s, early sixties were unkind to little girls going to church with those little crinolines, where you sat down and it was like sitting on barbwire. I'm being a little flip about that. But I think the church gave me a sense of grounding, a sense of rhythm to the week, which I still find really necessary. If I don't go to church on Sunday I feel like I'm not anchored for the week. It gave me an awareness—and I think I sensed this anyway—a way to frame the fact that there is something much larger than yourself and you have to be aware of that at all times and not be so totally self-centered and egocentric that you don't see that. I think that's real critical for children to realize.

Church also gave me some of the language that I've used to try to discern what's going on in my spiritual journey, but it also gave me language that I've had to run from as well. So there are things that you take away from that childhood experience, and then there are things that you, I would say, grow beyond. And maybe everybody wouldn't feel the need to do that, but everybody has to find their own language and their own way of expressing their spirituality. I've always liked that saying "There is no hand-me-down religion"—each of us has to forge it or form it in our own way.

So church was important, but at about fourteen, I went the other direction, like most teens do, and didn't want to have anything to do with it for a long time.

For a time, I was attending a very fundamentalist Missionary Baptist Church. I did that because the young man I was dating, and whom I actually ended up marrying, was the son of the pastor. He was my first husband. And that was an experience that was very disillusioning. The language was all there, the use of the Christian terms was all there, but it was a pretty toxic experience, just because of the personalities involved. And it actually created problems for me using the language of the church, then, for a period of time afterwards. I'm sure a lot of folks have that experience. I then did not attend church for a period of five years.

I wandered back into a Unitarian Church because of the emphasis on social justice, found myself attending there for quite a long while. The way I've sort of described it to my children, because they've asked me this, the Unitarian Church is a wonderful church for a lot of people, it gives them exactly what they need. But for me, it was like running around on the outside of the circle. And I think of the center of the circle as being God, and there's all these different spokes, all these different paths, to get to the center. And for me, I felt like I needed to choose a path and go a little more toward the center of the circle. I think all of us have to find our own path.

You have to be suspicious about anybody who believes that they have all the truth. And so I want to be really clear: I'm not writing out a prescription for anybody else. But I have gotten to the point where I can talk about what works for me, and that's different from proselytizing and thinking everybody will find the same answers. I don't believe that at all. I think each person finds their own answers in their own way. And it may not look like my way, and that's wonderful, that's great—it's the way it ought to be. A few years ago I would've been hesitant to talk about it 'cause I would think people would think I was trying to preach to them—and I'm really not—but I think at some point you feel like you have struggled with the issues that everybody else struggles with, and this is what I've decided for me, and why not talk about it because you're just explaining yourself or trying to?

After the Unitarian episode—and getting very, very involved in social justice issues, which has been a mainstay, then, of religion, for me; I think they're just intertwined, I can't tweeze those apart anymore, those are all one and the same—the place that I found my sense of spirituality was with the Society of Friends, the Quaker religion. To me, the language, the way that they describe religion, the way that they describe spirituality, just resonates with me in a way that no other terminology has.

We started coming here, to Church of the Savior, largely because silent meeting for children is a very difficult concept, and at the time, [at] the Friends meeting that I was attending when my oldest daughter was about three, there were no other children. And so pretty quickly I realized this was a way for a child to really hate Sunday mornings—to go somewhere where it's silent, which is hard for a child, or where you're shunted off into a room by yourself where there aren't any other children. So that would not work as a family.

And so, to me, I'm a member of a UCC Church, but I told Reverend Gill before I joined, "You do realize I'm Quaker?" And he said, "That's no problem. In the UCC Church, in the Congregational church, that's okay."

This church has been wonderful. There's certain areas that this church is probably more liberal on than a lot of other churches, but there's some that it's probably more conservative on than others, and by that I mean doctrinally; this is a pretty mainstream Christian church. There's a cross up front and we use the language.

It's really given me the sense of spirituality that I needed and my children the sense of community that I think is critical.

There's always been a part of me that hates to see anybody left out, just feels this need to have inclusion for a sense of peace around the people that I'm with. I was the kid who cried on Christmas Eve, driving to Christmas Eve services, to see the Christmas trees that hadn't been chosen.

I remember seeing a child in my second-grade class be picked on and it hurt as if it were me, and I wasn't brave enough—because I'm a pretty quiet person in general—to step in myself. Another child did, and I think that made me, at that pretty young age, examine myself and say, "Okay, what was it about me that I wasn't able to do that? And boy, I want to be like that other kid." I'd say that was the first time I really even recognized you do have to make choices about how you're going to move through the world.

My parents are very quiet people also. It sounds cliché, but I've really never seen them not be stand-up kind of folks, people who, you know, they weren't loud about it—they wouldn't be on a picket line, probably, they're not those kind of folks—but it was just stressed in our house from day one: treat everybody the way you want to be treated. And when you see that pretty much modeled from day one, I think it's a part of you and you don't even really realize it.

I spent a good chunk of a decade working on sanctuary for Central American refugees here in Tennessee and was part of a church—that was actually a Unitarian Church—where we declared ourselves a sanctuary church and kept a couple from Guatemala. At the time, we knew it was illegal and that we could be facing jail time.[9] There were those of us in the group who were pretty sure our phones were tapped. I was younger and I didn't have kids at that point, and so that was an action that maybe now I would be more hesitant to take, but at the time it felt like the right thing to do. And I learned a lot. I learned a lot from that culture about what's enough, about community. So that was an action that we took as a couple, my husband, Sam, and I.

Environmental issues are an ongoing thing in my life. Believe it or not, they were going to site a waste incinerator in downtown Knoxville. Now this is a place that has air quality issues anyway. They were going to site it in a poor neighborhood—surprise, surprise—where we lived on the fringes in one of the older neighborhoods downtown. They were going to put it right near an elementary school that didn't have air conditioning or anything, so their windows were going to be open. And downtown Knoxville sits in a bowl, so we have trouble with air inversions anyway, where everything just settles into the bowl and just sits.

The funding was already in place; the city government was

ready to roll with it. We fought really hard against that and we actually won, believe it or not—it was a group of about twenty, twenty-five of us, I guess, that fought that issue. So that taught me that a small group really, really can have an impact—it was a success story that I think surprised even us. Now, looking back—that's nineteen, almost twenty years ago—what would the city have been like? We aren't in compliance now. The way this incinerator was sized, they were going to truck garbage in from a multicounty area to burn in downtown Knoxville, and the only way that it could operate efficiently was to burn day and night, perpetually, constantly. I think that also taught me that the powers that be don't necessarily have the right answers.

I fail to see how churches have not looked at the environment as a stewardship issue. To me, it's so evident. The reason that we founded LEAF, really, was to try to make what seemed so self-evident to us apparent, or at least accessible, to other Christian congregations in East Tennessee, and to at least spark that dialogue in their congregations, because we realized in many cases that wasn't occurring at all.

For many, many, many Christian churches, it's not even anything that they have even put together or thought about being in combination at all. LEAF brought in Dr. Matthew Sleeth, an evangelical M.D. who wrote a book called *Serve God, Save the Planet,* to speak here to a coalition of a hundred churches. The pastor from one of the largest churches in Knoxville said to a member of his church, "I couldn't sleep for two nights after that presentation because I never thought about faith and environment being connected. Never."

Most of them simply are not aware. In the two and a half years that we've been working on LEAF, I've seen such a change. It's been remarkable, and I don't mean just here in East Tennessee. I think this says it all: HarperCollins is coming out with a green-letter Bible this fall.[10] Can you believe that? I mean, this is a major, national publisher who obviously—they wouldn't be doing it if they didn't think it was going to be profitable—realizes that this issue has reached enough congregations, enough Christians, out there that a green-letter Bible is something that will be profitable for them. I think that's just astonishing.

Look at the faith statements and just take, for one example, the Southern Baptist Convention two years ago versus what's come out just recently—it's like night and day. So it's taken a while, but I believe now that the terms are in place, the way of speaking to each other, the ground of speaking to each other, the foundation for speaking to each other, are there, and I think this is just going to take off from here. It's been really remarkable.

It's really easy to be blind to what you don't want to see or what's uncomfortable to see.

I spent most of the past twenty years, really, traveling the southeast mid-Atlantic as a journalist, and I realize now that I first saw mountaintop removal in West Virginia twenty years ago. And I remember it was south of Charleston, when I was working on a guidebook for the Smithsonian called *The Smithsonian Guide to Historic America,* and so what I was focusing on were these historic sites I had to go from place to place and visit. I remember making a turn on a road, and the mountain was just gone; I'd never seen anything like that. And I remember just driving along the road, and they had this rock that they were trying to hold back the remains of the mountain, I guess, from washing down on one of the main roads, and I kept thinking, "Is this an airport? Are they going to build an airport here?" It was like the end of a runway. "Or is it a landfill? Gosh, it's the biggest landfill I've ever seen." And I kept driving and driving and driving, and to my great guilt I never asked, I never found out what that was. So twenty years ago, I could've been speaking out all this time if I'd only realized.

So it's hard for me to point a finger at somebody else and say, "Why aren't you speaking out?" Well, each of us finds the issue at the point, I think, where we're supposed to find the issue, and each of us is given a task at the point where we're up to the task. You know, I can't beat myself up for maybe not asking those questions then, but what brought me to the issue again was that I have, since 1982, gone to Hindman[11] every so often—not as often as I would like—and watching what has happened in Eastern Kentucky and seeing that place that I thought of as this peaceful retreat, this place that's kind of my Shangri-La or my Brigadoon, you know, the place that's almost mythical to me.

From the air, mountaintop removal is like this little creeping cancer that's come a little way into Tennessee, but you get over into Kentucky and it just explodes. And I'm so sorry. I'm so sorry. If I had only been speaking out sooner.

I have a piece of coal that I picked up on the faith tour[12] off the edge of Mr. Sumner's[13] property there, standing on the remains of his land that had been destroyed, and I keep it on the windowsill in my kitchen, 'cause whenever I do dishes—that's sort of my contemplative time, to stand at the sink and do dishes and look out at the green outside my window and realize that so many people now are living with just destruction outside their windows. To stand on the remains of that ridgeline that just dropped off to nothing, and to be standing there singing "Amazing Grace" and have the mountain across from you just blow up while you're standing there, I mean, I don't see how anybody could've been up there and be the same. That was just heartbreaking and soul-wrenching and life-changing. Although I had been working on the issue for a year at that point, boy, that just galvanized me. For me, that was the point of no return as far as saying, "This is the issue I'm going to work on until something changes." And so we came back and began talking about trying to raise awareness, but is that enough? Do we have to wait until Tennessee is facing this very same sort of devastation? We are facing it now, but it hadn't happened yet to that degree.

It hasn't taken hold here because it hasn't been profitable up till now. We have a little different type of coal here in Tennessee, and it hasn't been something that TVA, for example, can burn and stay anywhere close to compliance.[14] That's going to change, and the reason that this is coming to Tennessee very quickly is because

TVA is getting ready to put scrubbers in some of their coal-fired power plants.[15] And when that happens, and this kind of coal can be burned—the kind of coal that's in Tennessee—the push is going to be on. It already is on, but it's going to be strengthened. So while I'd love to say that, oh, we here in Tennessee are so much more enlightened, that's just not the case. The majority of people in Eastern Kentucky, the majority of people in West Virginia, love this land ever bit as much as Tennesseans do.

Frankly, it comes down to economics.

We heard the president of the largest coal company in Tennessee say in front of a legislative body that he'd come here because they'd heard that Tennessee was a pro-business state. Well, that's true. But what we didn't want to have happen here in Tennessee is that it snuck in through the back door, that it came in kind of riding this pro-business attitude that is the basic attitude out there before the legislature really realized what they were allowing in the back door.

Appalachian Voices now has the place on their site where you can type in your zip code and see what mountaintop removal coal, if any, you are using.[16] Well, guess where the mountaintop removal coal that my electricity comes from? It's from Montgomery Creek.[17] And I'm thinking: *How do you live with yourself?* There's a part of you that says you'd like to just turn off all your lights and go live in a cave—that would probably be the most honest thing to do—but that's not real feasible. So you minimize. My kids are always hollering at me saying it's too cold or it's too hot in the house. You do the best you can to make your footprint as small as you can. But there isn't a day that goes by now that I'm not aware of that. There's a face, now, to all that electricity in my house, and it's Mr. Sumner and his lost property. It's hard.

Besides stewardship of the earth, there's also this idea of taking care of your neighbor, what's good for your neighbor. That's so biblical, that's so basic. If you're polluting somebody else's water, that's not good stewardship and it's not being a good neighbor. If you're decimating somebody else's land because you want to power your television set or whatever, that's not being a good neighbor. At every level, this issue is an object lesson in how not to be a good neighbor, how not to be a good steward, how not to be a good Christian, frankly. I think it's really so clear it's hard for me to see how—if people would pause long enough to look at it, and pause long enough to see their part in it—that they wouldn't be appalled at this particular type of environmental degradation and also appalled at themselves, and I think you have to have equal measures in that.

Again, most people aren't aware of mountaintop removal. Most of the legislators we talked to weren't aware of it. It's very hard to go in and enlighten people quickly on something this complex, and the fact that this legislation that was proposed this year got as far as it did, I think, is a testament to how horrified most people really are when they understand what they're looking at. And so do I have hope that the government, that the state legislature, will make steps this next year to stop it? I really am hopeful. Do I realize that could possibly be a naïve view? Yeah, I'm aware of that, too. Am I aware that business is the tail that wags the dog, so to speak? I mean, sure it is. When you work in the legislature you see some of the legislators, a lot of the legislators, do come from small-business backgrounds, and they're very hesitant to want to regulate, and they're very hesitant to want to put more onerous regulations on fellow businessmen. So there's a mind-set there that's very difficult to get beyond. But many of them are also east Tennesseans, and they love the mountains, too. To see their faces, some of them . . . we carried around a little portable DVD player to pop a little four-minute DVD from *Kilowatt Ours* with the mountains blowing up, and the looks on some of their faces! They had no clue that this was going on and no clue that this was headed their way. So it's been an effort to enlighten folks that's going to take some time.

I speak from a faith perspective when I speak about it. To me, from the faith perspective, we have been given a great gift. God's given us a gift, this marvelous place—and I'm biased, I know, but I think that Appalachia is the most beautiful place in the world.

For every gift you're given, you're also given a responsibility. Our responsibility is to be stewards, and that's clear. That green-letter Bible is going to let everybody know right where those phrases are in the Bible. But I mean, it's just as simple as Psalm 24—"the earth *is* the Lord's." It says it really clearly. And there are a host of other verses.

That's speaking as a Christian, but if you want to speak as a parent, why in the world would you want to hand down something to your children that's not at least as good as what you were given, but is hopefully better than what you were given? That flies in the face of everything that most parents intuitively know.

One of the ways that I did get into this issue kind of sideways is that it grew out of air pollution and talking about passing things down to the next generation. My daughters are ninth-generation Tennesseans, and they both have asthma. Neither their dad nor I have asthma. They've both battled just to breathe sometimes. The doctor looked at me and said, "Your daughters will never be healthy as long as they live in this valley. They'll never be completely healthy unless you leave." And I looked at him and said, "My family's lived in this valley for over 250 years."

What have we done that in one generation we can go from having air to breathe to not? That's horrifying to me. So to me, it's an issue that strikes at the very heart of family and who we are here in Appalachia, and even if you think the mountains are expendable, our children's lungs aren't expendable.

We've got to find a better way. That's also a huge part of this issue: even if you can look at a mountain and not think it's the prettiest thing in this world, there's this whole other level of this issue that people need to be aware of, and I think by pointing out both sides of that we can make a bigger tent and get more people into it. It just kills me to think that my kids may have to move away.

When you look at something as horrific as mountaintop removal, there are really not words—and as a writer there really ought to be words—to describe how I feel when I stand in front of a mountain that's not there and to know that destruction occurred as partly my fault, because I'm a consumer of electricity just like everybody is, so I have a part in that. That hurts. That's painful. But partly because we have this short-term way of looking at everything, I think, in this country, that short-sightedness that we have not been able to step out beyond immediate profit, immediate gratification, what's good for our generation and not what's good for later generations. And to me, that's really, truly what sin is: when you can't look outside yourself and see what's good for other people.

I'm Christian, probably mainstream to fairly liberal Christian. I tend to vote Democratic, I tend to think of myself as a progressive, but I realized when working on this legislation that pigeonholing people like that to me feels very wrong. A couple of the staunchest allies in this fight are some of the most conservative Christians in the Tennessee legislature. And they have stepped out of their comfort zones, I think, to some degree, and have taken on this cause and suddenly you realize, "What are all these labels that we put on people?"

I've changed my own thinking on it. One of the most rabid environmentalists can be the most conservative Christian on other issues. I think if I've learned anything from all this, I just absolutely hate this red state–blue state, Republican-Democrat, religious-nonreligious stuff. These labels are all so detrimental to letting us all work together in the ways that we can. Nobody's ever going to agree on everything, but we're letting all these labels keep us apart in ways they just shouldn't.

It's very, very difficult to be involved in an issue that does create so much anger and frustration and divisiveness in people when, first of all, that's not the way I want to move through life and it's not the way that I've tried to move through life, but here I am in the crux of this now and it's forcing me to have to learn how to respond to people who are very angry. And a year ago, my way of responding to that would probably be to just avoid it, and you can't, really, and be effective working on this issue.

So the way my faith has begun to inform this whole dialogue for me is that I have to try to remember that, from a faith perspective—and this is very Quaker—each of us contains the Spirit of God. I believe that firmly. And you have to try to relate to that Spirit in every individual, whichever side of this issue that they're on. So that's the bottom line for me—that's where the faith part comes in.

The way that this issue has informed how I see my faith is that it's forced me to take a stand on something. And while it would be really easy to just say, "You're wrong and I'm going to continue to be angry with you," my faith tells me I can't do that. "The issue tells me you're wrong and I have to somehow find a way to help you understand without condemning." Does that make any sense? It's very difficult, and it's all wrapped up together for me. And it's daily. It's daily. Because generally I process fairly slowly, so if I have a confrontation with somebody I have to kind of retreat, go inward, and think about it and try to figure out "Okay, how am I going to phrase that next time? How am I going to do better next time? How am I going to approach that person next time?" And sometimes there isn't a next time, and that's very hard for me. I don't like leaving things unsaid or undone. That's a part of my faith as well.

All of the legislators come from very different faiths. All of them have a particular point of view. And in the Tennessee legislature most of them come from a business perspective, which is very different from the way I have lived my entire life. I would be the world's worst businessperson, because money just does not drive me. Obviously, making a choice to be a freelance writer, money is not an issue. And a phrase I've used all my life that's resonated with me is "Enough is as good as a feast."

Think about that: in business, there's never enough. So if I'm operating out of "If you have enough, why would you need any more than enough?" and then they're operating out of "You can never have too much," we talk at cross-purposes just automatically. It's two totally different ways of looking at the world. So you've got that whole scenario.

So the anger, I think, comes when I feel like they're totally dismissing my way of viewing the world and they feel like I'm totally dismissing their way of viewing the world, and what we're really both trying to do, I think—or at least I know I'm trying to do—is try to honor their way of viewing the world, but try to say to them, "That's not the only way to view the world, and your way of viewing the world is running roughshod over my way of viewing the world."

So we've got to figure out how to honor both sides without letting one side totally dominate. And certainly in our culture the business model is what dominates and where a lot of the power is, and certainly where most of the money is, and we on the other side have to do a better job of articulating that and also be a means of holding up a different model. And, frankly, that takes a lot of time and energy and effort, and when you're dealing with a legislator, time is one thing you don't have a whole lot of—you get your ten minutes and that's all they have to hear or really want to hear.

It's so funny. You'd think that your faith would inform the issue, but what's happened for me is this issue has informed my faith in ways that I never would have anticipated.

This year's really taught me all of that.

From the beginning, this whole initiative was launched from a faith perspective, and that has made such a huge difference. The other issues I've worked on in the past were only sort of peripheral; faith was peripheral to the issue. This approach on this issue was steeped in that faith from the beginning, so from day one it was about how do we bring faith into this issue, not how do we bring this issue into our faith.

I always try to be optimistic, because it's not totally in our hands. I try not to be naïve, although people accuse me of that sometimes. It's hard for me to look at any human being and believe that you can't find redeeming parts of them. I just can't see that. I can't walk through the world and not see that everybody's got good in them, so there are no hopeless human beings. So consequently, I can't look at a social justice issue and say that this is a hopeless situation. But I think that because most people in this region really do share a deep-seated love of the land and deep-seated sense of "We're in a special place," that makes me more hopeful than I would be, maybe even on a lot of other social justice issues.

I think we have this shared commonality of living in this incredible place that we all want to see taken care of. Do we disagree on how taking care of it is going to act itself out? Certainly we do. And will I be able or LEAF be able to save every mountain we'd want to save? No, I doubt that's going to be possible. But are the coal companies going to get every mountain they want? No, I don't think so. So I'm hopeful.

Knoxville, Tennessee, May 9, 2008

Jack Spadaro

Appalachian Patriot

If you're gonna lead my country
If you're gonna say it's free
I'm gonna need a little honesty.
—Ben Sollee, "A Few Honest Words"

No matter that patriotism is too often the refuge of scoundrels. Dissent, rebellion, and all-around hell-raising remain the true duty of patriots.
—Barbara Ehrenreich

It's the beginning of the dreaded dog days of summer on the forks of Troublesome Creek in Knott County, Kentucky. Those gathered at the forks for the Appalachian Writers Workshop, held annually on the hillside campus of the Hindman Settlement School, are exhausted from the intense, day-long sessions.

Twenty or so attendees have gone up the mountainside to gather on the porch of Preece, one of the school's cabin-style dorms, where the night air hangs thick with humidity and revelry. Their songs drift down through the pines—tonight the favorite is Gillian Welch's "Orphan Girl"—and mingle with the drone of crickets, heat bugs, and bullfrogs down by the creek. Many of the group sing along, half-full glasses cradled in their hands, their heads thrown back in laughter, while others join in side conversations, catching up with their literary kin.

Jack Spadaro leans against the porch railing, alone, taking it all in. It's the first time some of his fellow attendees have met him, and they are surprised to find him so shy and soft-spoken—especially after everything they've read about him in the press.

Jack Spadaro, Huntington, West Virginia. Photo by Silas House.

Some drift over to welcome him, saying they're glad that he's now part of the Hindman family, and invite him to join right in. Others steal glances at him over their cups, admiring the quiet man who caused such a ruckus in Washington just a few years before. All are proud to be in his presence, thankful for his defense of fellow Appalachians in nearby Martin County against the moneyed interests of the mining industry and their patrons, the George W. Bush administration and Bush's Secretary of Labor, Kentucky's own Elaine Chao.

Everyone in this group, which represents a rainbow of political positions, all know that true patriotism involves more than yellow ribbons, flag lapel pins, and Lee Greenwood singing "God Bless the U.S.A." Many modern-day Americans are disdainful of those who actively question their government, believing that doubters beget radicals, radicals beget extremists, extremists beget terrorists. They do not subscribe to the classical definition of patriotism, best articulated by Thomas Jefferson: that dissent is its highest form.

Jefferson would have liked Jack Spadaro. His brand of dissent is the quiet kind—measured, void of shrill chants, tempered by a résumé of government experience a mile long—the sort that makes you hope, down to the marrow of your being, that he is on your side.

His dissent began with a simple refusal to sign his name.

On October 11, 2000, the bottom of a coal slurry impoundment pond gave way in Martin County. Three hundred million gallons of black sludge chugged its way down Coldwater Creek. Despite the devastation—yards buried, bridges destroyed, water contaminated—no lives were lost. Thirty times the size of the Exxon-Valdez disaster, the Martin County spill generated little coverage in the national media.

Clinton administration officials in the Mine Safety and Health Administration (MSHA) took notice, however. MSHA head Davitt McAteer quickly dispatched a team of investigators, which included Spadaro, to determine the cause of the spill.

"He was real clear," says Spadaro of McAteer. "I won't tell you exactly the language that he used, but he said, 'Go down and find where we messed up so that it doesn't happen again.' So we started interviewing people and doing a drilling program that I was in charge of."

The problem, the investigators soon learned, was that a similar accident had happened before—six years earlier—when 100 million gallons of slurry escaped from the same impoundment pond, owned by Martin County Coal, a subsidiary of Massey Energy. After that spill, Larry Wilson, a MSHA engineer, made nine recommendations that the company needed to implement before the pond could be used again. The recommendations were ignored; indeed, the coal company began filling the pond again on the same day as the spill. "That was the root cause of the accident" in 2000, Spadaro says.

But the incoming Bush administration wasn't interested in causes. Only hours after the new president's inauguration on January 20, 2001, Tony Oppegard, the head of the investigating team, learned that he had been fired. The remaining team members were soon told by David Lauriski, the new Assistant Secretary of Labor for Mine Safety and Health and director of MSHA, to conclude their work.

Spadaro was outraged. "We had more than forty other people we wanted to interview," he recalls. These remaining interviews were expected to confirm what the team had already found: that Martin County Coal and Massey Energy knew that the impoundment was an accident waiting to happen, that they had willfully ignored MSHA's guidelines, that the trail of corporate corruption ran right down Pennsylvania Avenue.

The coal companies knew that they had a friend in George W. Bush. He had, after all, accepted hefty contributions from Massey Energy during his presidential campaign. And it didn't stop there.

"While they were being investigated," says Spadaro, "Massey Energy made a contribution of $100,000 to Mitch McConnell, who was the head of the National Republican Senatorial [Campaign] Committee. And of course, Mitch McConnell is very chummy with Don Blankenship, the head of Massey Energy, and McConnell is married to Elaine Chao, who's Secretary of Labor, who has jurisdiction over the Mine Safety and Health Administration." Spadaro pauses, fixing a steady gaze on the blue West Virginia mountains just beyond the window.

"So they bought their protection," he says.

They also scrubbed the final report of the investigation. Tim Thompson, whom Lauriski had named to take over the investigation, insured that the report would give Massey Energy a mere slap on the wrist. Initially, the investigators had recommended up to ten serious violations, some of them criminal. At Lauriski's direction, Thompson had those reduced to two minor infractions. Then, Thompson and Lauriski began pressuring Spadaro to sign the report.

At that point, Spadaro went public.

"I didn't hesitate at all," he says. "I refused to sign the report. And from then on it was just one attack after another from Dave Lauriski and the people who worked for him."

The retribution was swift. Spadaro was locked out of his office and placed on administrative leave from his position as superintendent at the Mine Safety and Health Academy in Beckley, West Virginia, near his home in Hamlin. After Lauriski's charges that Spadaro had abused his authority didn't hold up—the malfeasance amounted to Spadaro's giving free room and board to a field worker diagnosed with multiple sclerosis—Lauriski transferred Spadaro to Pittsburgh, more than 250 miles away from his family.[1]

Spadaro filed an official complaint with the U.S. Office of Special Counsel in 2003, but he soon learned that the odds were stacked against him: this particular special counsel had found in favor of just one whistleblower. It was unlikely that he would be reinstated to his job at the academy. A deal was finally reached the following year: he would drop the charges in turn for being restored to his original pay grade. And he would retire.

"It was difficult for my family, difficult for my wife having all that public attention, having that conflict," Spadaro recalls. "For me, I at least know that I did the right thing."

The public thought so as well: "I had tremendous support from people in the mining communities, environmental groups, labor unions, all of that," he says. "People demonstrated on my behalf in the streets of Charleston; they wrote letters; they raised hell about it."

The public outcry was so scathing that the Department of Labor was forced to do an internal review of the Martin County investigation. Once again, it was a whitewash.

Spadaro sighs wearily, pausing to run his hand down his face. "One of Mitch McConnell's former staff members[2] was appointed to that investigating team so that Mitch had a direct line straight in to the investigation of that corruption that I had exposed. So he protected Massey Energy, and he protected the Department of Labor with that $100,000 that was contributed by Massey. There's no doubt in my mind."

A ruling by a federal appeals judge further inflamed the situation. The final version of the report fined Massey Energy $55,000 for each of the two violations, but a subsequent court ruling lowered that fine to a mere $5,600.

One would think that after all this drama—the harassments, the threats, the lies—Spadaro might have lost faith in his government. To that, he replies with a quiet but emphatic "No, no." His frustration, he explains, is more specific: "I had never seen such blatant, direct interference ever in government as what I saw with the Bush administration."

It's not your typical partisan rant. Spadaro, after all, has worked under a total of eight administrations of both parties. He gives credit where it's due. In fact, Spadaro cut his investigative teeth during the Nixon administration in 1972 when he was studying another environmental disaster that occurred when a coal slurry impoundment dam burst at Buffalo Creek, West Virginia.

Spadaro was only twenty-three years old when the governor named him as staff engineer to the investigating team. Despite his years of experience working at the Bureau of Mines, he was anxious.

"I was just young and I'd been sent down to investigate this disaster," he recalls. "I wasn't sure I knew enough to do any good."

His support to both the investigation and the grieving community was immeasurable. Immediately, he set to work conducting interviews with the survivors. Their stories haunt him to this day.

"These were people who'd lost their loved ones, they'd lost their homes, they'd lost everything," he says. "I'll never forget their voices."

What Spadaro learned was horrifying: several government agencies were aware of the dam's instability. Each passed the buck to the other, assuming it would be repaired. To make matters worse, residents living downstream also knew the dam was dangerous. Many wrote letters to their government expressing these fears. "They just allowed the dams to exist," Spadaro whispers.

Spadaro's experience in 1972 stayed with him. "The whole time, in all those years when I was working," he says, "the Buffalo Creek disaster was my guiding light. I wanted to do whatever I could to make sure that that kind of thing didn't happen again."

Spadaro lives by the adage that those who refuse to study the mistakes of the past are doomed to repeat them, which is why he found the Martin County spill in 2000 all the more sickening.

"We had a lot of support for Mine Safety and Health during the Clinton years," he says. "We did not have it at all during the Bush years."

Indignant, Spadaro leans forward in his chair and begins ticking off recent mining disasters on his fingers. "First, the Alabama disaster with the Jim Walters mine.[3] Then Quecreek.[4] Then the Sago disaster.[5] Then the Aracoma disaster and mine fire.[6] And then Darby in Harlan County.[7] And then Crandall Canyon in Utah."[8]

He throws his hands in the air. "Senator [Edward] Kennedy's committee[9] found out that there had been a plan submitted to MSHA by the coal company that was unsafe," he says, referring to the tragedy at Crandall Canyon. "It was a roof control plan that was submitted and was unsafe. The district manager from MSHA overruled his own engineer and approved the plan, and within a month six people died in this tragic disaster."

Leaning back, Spadaro shakes his head in disgust, trying to suppress his greatest fear—that another disaster could very well happen again. "I hope not," he says.

Even in his retirement from MSHA, Spadaro is working to prevent other such tragedies. "My career's just a little different now," he notes. "I'm not in government, but I'm still trying to do whatever I can to stop what's happening to people in the coalfields."

Spadaro spends much of his time advising a variety of groups on subjects ranging from mine safety to labor issues to a ban on mountaintop removal mining: "I work with Kentuckians for the Commonwealth, the Ohio Valley Environmental Coalition, Coal River Mountain Watch, the United Mine Workers a little bit, groups like the Anstead Historical Society in southern West Virginia—anybody who needs help that I think I can do some good with."

The fight against mountaintop removal is the issue that has especially taken hold of his energies and expertise. Spadaro decries the devastation every chance he gets. "It's destroying a people, it's destroying the Mother Forest for North America, so it's morally wrong."

Although he notes that there's enough blame to go around for the proliferation of the practice—he makes it a point to mention that mountaintop removal increased dramatically on Bill Clinton's watch—Spadaro harbors extra resentment toward the United Mine Workers of America (UMWA), which his father and grandfather belonged to, and which he still occasionally works with on labor issues.

"Shame on the United Mine Workers for even supporting mountaintop removal," he says. "Mountaintop removal has replaced thousands of jobs in the coalfields. It's the main reason their membership has declined so dramatically over the past thirty years."

Despite its prevalence, Spadaro is confident that the movement to stop the practice will ultimately prevail. "I've always thought we could be successful in Appalachia if we joined together with folks throughout the coalfields who are being affected by mountaintop removal and other travesties of mining."

He says as much on a panel at the Appalachian Studies Association Conference held at Marshall University in Huntington, West Virginia, in late March 2008. Afterward, he finds himself surrounded by audience members who compliment his presentation, ask him questions about mountaintop removal, and express their gratitude for his dissent. Spadaro spends a few moments with each one, speaking with his typical humility and nonchalant attitude.

Later that day, his good friend, filmmaker and musician Jack Wright, presented the Jack Spadaro Documentary Award at the Appalachian Studies Association conference in Huntington, West Virginia.[10] Wright says that naming the award after Spadaro was an obvious choice. "Most of the awards given out these days are named in honor of those who have passed on. We have a hero, and he's a live hero."

The accolades are so strong, however, it does sound like a eulogy of sorts. "Jack has devoted his entire career to trying to make mining safer, looking out for the workers, and has not been afraid to face intimidation from above," Wright says. "He sacrificed his career for an ethical belief and should be recognized for his great sacrifices, humbleness, and his ability to stick to the task through hell or high water."

Spadaro makes light of such heady tributes. "I'm just glad I'm still alive. Somebody who had known me for years but hadn't seen me for a long time came running up to me the day before they gave the first award in Dayton and said, 'Oh Jack, I'm so glad to see you. I'm so glad you're alive!'"

"And I said, 'Well, what do you mean?'"

"And she said, 'Well, I thought when they named an award after you that you were dead.'"

Spadaro laughs when he tells that story, his relaxed posture indicating that he is indeed fully alive. His is a patriotism of the present; his work is ongoing. It hasn't taken death for him to be canonized alongside other prominent Appalachian dissenters such as the Widow Combs, Aunt Molly Jackson, and Don West. He would surely shrug off being included in such hallowed company, preferring instead to focus on the fight at hand. His reward, his assurance, is predictably quite simple: "There's never been any doubt in my mind that I did the right thing."

Jack Spadaro talking . . .

My grandfather was James Spadaro, and he was a coal miner for forty-five years in West Virginia. He worked for the New River Company, one of the big companies in southern West Virginia in a little town called Mount Hope. He worked for them all his life. He came here as a boy; he was eleven years old when he came to this country, and he started working in the mines very young. I don't know exactly how old he was, but he was a teenager. He came from Sicily.

My grandfather was an avid member of the United Mine Workers, and my father also belonged to the United Mine Workers. My father worked for a mining company as well, but he didn't work underground; he worked in a machinery repair shop. But during the fifties, there were strikes that I remember as a child, and so I did see people fighting back then, fighting against the mining companies.

Well, not only my father and my grandfather, but my mother, who worked for the communications workers—she was a union member for the telephone company, the Communications Workers of America—and they went on strike several times. I remember one strike in particular when I was in college—it was real painful and long—but she probably, as much as anyone, instilled a sense that you could be successful in fighting back if you joined with other people of like mind, and the union certainly was an example of that.

I've often wondered how I became what I have. My sister saved a bunch of old things that she thought would be important for me and gave them to me a few years ago. One of them was an essay that I wrote when I was fourteen years old about the importance of clean water.

We lived in the woods, really. So at least as young as fourteen, and even younger, I had been playing in the woods. Preschool age we were in the woods, and I think I began then to get the appreciation for the forests that we have. And these are some of the oldest forests in the world, and the most diverse forests, and I began intuitively knowing that as a child living in southern West Virginia, playing in the woods and wanting to learn the names of trees, flowers.

Later, my wife and I met an old gentleman named Rufus Reed who lived in Eastern Kentucky in the town of Lovely. Mr. Reed was a surveyor, a land surveyor, and he knew all the plants in the woods; he'd studied them all his life. He was in his late eighties or early nineties by that time; I was probably in my late twenties or early thirties when I met him. He would take a bunch of us into the woods to show us the wildflowers that grew in the woods, particularly in April and the spring. One day, just walking with him for a few hours—and he could hardly walk, we had to help him through the woods—we identified something like 250 species of plants. I knew how diverse the plants were, but I didn't know it was that diverse a forest. But it is, indeed.

There are about 250 bird species that breed in these forests. There are about 150 tree species. And there are countless other plant species. I was an engineering student and we didn't study that, but I learned as I grew older.

I knew very definitely [that I was an environmentalist] by the time I was twenty-three years old when I went to Buffalo Creek in Logan County, West Virginia, and started studying the root causes of that dam failure that killed 125 people. I had to interview survivors, people who had lost their families.

We had a commission of nine people who'd been appointed by the governor; we set up down there. We had the very first hearing at the Mann High School gymnasium; Mann was right at the mouth of Buffalo Creek. I had a tape recorder, so I had to really carefully listen to everybody who talked. And these were all survivors of this terrible tragedy. I'll never forget those voices.

One woman had lost six members of her family.

A few years before that had been the Farmington disaster, and I had actually been in that mine a few months before it exploded, so I knew some of those men, and I knew the mine well. But the Buffalo Creek experience was what really transformed me, I think, more than anything.

I was an engineer, and I had been teaching at West Virginia University, doing research work about acid mine drainage. And I was appointed by the dean of the school of mines to go down and do the engineering research to figure out why that dam had failed. Of course I didn't know a lot then, but I went into the records of the construction of the dam and found out how long it had been developing. It had been developing over years. There were a series of dams that were built—three dams had been built in a series up this hollow—and people downstream knew that they were unsafe, and they wrote letters to the governor and other people saying, "These dams are unsafe, something needs to be done about them."

There were several government agencies—the U.S. Geological Survey, the Department of Natural Resources, the Corps of Engineers—that sent people to look at these dams, and they didn't do anything. So I think that's when I realized that in any of the work I would be doing, no matter what happened, I would always make sure that, at least from my end of it, the right thing got done.

First I worked for the Department of Natural Resources, and then I went to work for eighteen years for the Office of Surface Mining, a division of the Department of the Interior, writing and enforcing regulations related to coal mining and the environment.

Naturally, I went and got involved in the strip mining issue back in the early seventies. I helped found a group called Save Our Mountains in West Virginia around 1973 or thereabouts. One of our leaders was a man named Chester Workman, who was an underground coal miner, but he hated strip mining. He worked for Westmoreland Coal Company; he really risked his career getting involved in the anti–strip mining movement. But he had the guts to go ahead and be active. That taught me a lot, watching Chester and his family. That whole family was inspirational. That whole community was called Richmond District of Raleigh County. It's near Beckley in southern West Virginia.

We were actually successful in running the strip miners out of the area. We did some legal action, some demonstrations, some fund-raising, and the community united and drove the strip miners out.

I worked for years for the Office of Surface Mining, and I got frustrated because they weren't really enforcing the law, and I had done switched my job, really, to working abandoned mine lands—trying to patch together remedies to try to fix the lands that had already been damaged—and a chance came for me to go back to the Mine Safety Health Administration.

I had actually started with them way back in the sixties. There was a new appointee to run the Mine Safety and Health Administration during the Clinton years, Davitt McAteer, who's a pretty good guy. And so in 1996, I went back to MSHA and was there just a little while, and they decided that they needed somebody to run the mine academy, train all the mine inspectors, to get them oriented in the right way and build an inspection force that would do the job. So that's what I did. I was the director of the Mine Safety and Health Administration's training facility, called the National Mine Safety and Health Academy, near Beckley.

The people who came to us to be trained were people from the coalfields. So what I did was meet with every group that came in for training—there would be groups of fourteen or fifteen or sixteen people at a time—and I would just get to know them pretty well and meet regularly with them, find out what their needs were, find out how we could improve our training program.

What we were trying to do at the academy was to get and instill in inspectors the idea of their responsibility, and there were some really fine instructors. One guy in particular was Richard McDorman, who had been out in the field as an inspector for many years and really understood the law well. We tried to take some of our very best field people and make them teachers for the new inspectors. We were really successful at doing that. So that's what I wanted to do—I wanted to get the inspectors geared to doing the very best job they could to enforce the Mine Act[11] and protect workers in the mines. And we did well.

In October 2000, I got a call from McAteer, and he asked me to join with a team of people he was appointing to go down to Martin County, Kentucky, and find out what happened down there where the impoundment had leaked 300 million gallons of coal slurry into the Tug Fork River and killed everything downstream on Coldwater Creek and Wolf Creek (from the Tug River and Big Sandy River) for a hundred miles, really. It was coal waste impoundment that was regulated by the Mine Safety and Health Administration, so we had jurisdiction.

He wanted to find out really what had happened. He honestly wanted to find out where we had gone wrong as an agency so we could keep it from happening again. He wanted to know if there were other places like this that could break through, you know, and it was just a miracle people didn't die. If the drainage had not split into two watersheds—if it all had just gone down Coldwater Creek—there would have been people drowned in coal slurry.

We started the investigation in November of 2000; there were about seven or eight of us. We interviewed people through November and December of 2000, and in January of 2001 we continued. We had a drilling program that I was in charge of, to go down, drill, and find out exactly why things had broken through. We were interviewing people, we were moving along pretty well, and then Inauguration Day came along on January 20, 2001, I think it was. And that's when Tony Oppegard, who was the head of the investigation, was fired by the Bush administration.

On day one.

We were told to go ahead and wrap up the investigation. We wanted to find out what Martin County Coal and Massey knew, and whether they knew that it was an unsafe situation to begin with. And we were finding out that yes, indeed, they did know and that MSHA itself knew that there was only about fifteen feet of cover between the bottom of the reservoir and the underground mine workings because it had broken through six years before in May of 1994.[12] We were told not to even look into that aspect of it.

So I went along into the spring of 2001, when we were supposed to be finishing up our investigation and write a report, and then this guy Lauriski[13] showed up. He was the Bush appointee to head Mine Safety and Health. (McAteer had been replaced in January of 2001.) So Lauriski poked his finger in the actual writing of the report, and I finally told Lauriski that I refused to sign the report. And I went public and talked to the press, and told them what the Bush administration was trying to do—trying to cover up the real cause of the accident, trying to protect Massey Energy, trying to protect the Mine Safety and Health Administration.

So time went along, and in October of 2001, the report was due out. And Lauriski himself called me twice and tried to get me to sign the report, because they wanted my name on the report to give it credibility, and I refused to do so and again went public with what my concerns were.

The fight went on from January of 2001 until I was literally kicked out of my office in June of 2003, and then the fight went on for another year and a half after that, so it was about a four-year fight. So that takes its toll on you emotionally.

I thought it was really important that we make it public. I

didn't struggle with it a bit because of what had happened at Buffalo Creek. I knew that I was probably jeopardizing my job, but I felt like it was important enough. We found out that there were 225 more coal refuse impoundments in the country sitting on top of abandoned underground mine workings, so any of those 225 dams could fail in the same way.

The best thing, I think, was the raising of public awareness, people getting involved. So that was good.

The worst thing was that Massey Energy and the rest of the industry has got by with flagrant violations of the law over the past eight years and tragic consequences could've been avoided.

We had proposed as many as ten serious violations, some criminal violations. And when Lauriski got involved and directed the new team leader, a guy named Thompson,[14] they reduced the number of violations—they weren't even serious violations—down to two. And they were fined $55,000 for each of those violations initially, but a federal appeals judge—an administrative law judge—threw out one of the violations and then reduced the fine on the second violation from $55,000 to $5,600.

The EPA called this the worst environmental disaster in the eastern United States in the history of the country, and to be fined only $5,600 for it was just outrageous. And it proved to me that there was, from the very beginning, a conspiracy in the Bush administration to protect Massey Energy and the Mine Safety and Health Administration for its failure to do the right job.

I started my career in 1966 right out of high school. That was the Lyndon Johnson administration. Then came the Nixon administration.

The Nixon administration we know was corrupt, but Richard Nixon at least signed the Coal Mine Health and Safety Act, which was a strong law. He signed it in response to the Farmington disaster. And he created the EPA, signed the Clean Water Act, the Clean Air Act. Some of our best environmental legislation Richard Nixon signed into law.

And then, of course, we had Gerald Ford, who vetoed the

surface mining bill three times, and it was Jimmy Carter who actually signed it into law in 1977.[15] Jimmy Carter was committed to protecting the environment. He said when he signed the law that he knew it wasn't enough, but he thought that it was at least the beginning of regulating the environmental effects of coal mining and that it would lead, he thought, to something better. The Surface Mining Act was actually only enforced for about three years under Jimmy Carter.

And then along came Reagan-Bush.

Then, unfortunately, I have to say Bill Clinton didn't do any better. Clinton did not enforce the Surface Mining Act. In fact, mountaintop removal proliferated during the Clinton years.

But the very worst is this George Bush administration. It is undoubtedly the most corrupt administration in my career, and I've lived through all those administrations. It is utterly corrupt; corrupt through and through. The whole process of investigating a mining accident was corrupted from day one, literally from Inauguration Day on, and then we've seen this string of mining disasters that have occurred since 2001.

The first disaster occurred in September of 2001 in Alabama. Thirteen miners died, and we found from investigation that one of the reasons that disaster occurred was that the philosophy had already changed within the agency. The new head of the agency, Lauriski, had encouraged managers to look away from serious violations, probably just to get along with the mine operators. So they found that months before the accident—before the fire explosion that occurred in the Jim Walters mine had taken place—that the district manager down there had been kind of letting things go, letting the company get by with things.

And then of course we had, beginning in January of 2006, a serious string of disasters, beginning with the Sago disaster in Upshur County, West Virginia. Once again, MSHA had been aware of serious violations at that mine in the months preceding the explosion. It had ignored them and allowed the mine operator to continue operating. They had written violations, but they hadn't actually closed the mine, which is what they should have done.

And then a few weeks after that there was the Aracoma mine[16] fire—where two men died, but nine more could've died—and found again that MSHA had not done its job as an enforcer and allowed conditions to develop that led to that mine fire.

Then there was the Darby disaster in Harlan County, Kentucky, where five people died and, once again, when investigators looked into that they found that MSHA had known of serious problems with mine seals and other violations at that mine, but they had allowed them to continue.

And then this last year, 2007, the Crandall Canyon mine in Utah, where six miners died in a roof fall. MSHA had approved a plan, which they knew was defective, for mining that coal seam, because one of the engineers in the agency that had looked at the plan had said, "This is an unsafe plan," but he had been overruled by people who were supervisors. One of them was a man named Allen Davis, who had been an appointee of the Bush administration, so we were able to show directly the influence of the Bush administration and what it had done to weaken mining safety.

During the Clinton years, we were really successful in keeping down the numbers of fatalities and serious accidents in the mines. There were no mine disasters during that eight-year time period. MSHA had a good reputation for enforcing the laws and doing the right thing, and there had been steady improvement.

When I first started in the industry in the sixties, five or six hundred people a year were dying in the mines. Far, far fewer now are dying. It's still way too many—we shouldn't be having any disasters—but substantial improvement was made with the passage of the Coal Mine Health and Safety Act of 1969, there's no doubt about it. And that was government at work.

Under the right kind of leadership, government can function and people can do their jobs and protect people. You go back to things like the New Deal, Franklin Roosevelt. That administration gives you faith in what government can do and what people in government can do. It's one of the best examples. I mean, the country was in really dire straits and the government really saved the country, the leadership of the country saved the country from some of the excesses of the years before.

We've got great people within the Mine Safety and Health Administration who really want to do their jobs. They've just been hindered in doing their jobs by the management that was brought in by this corrupt Bush administration.

I was depressed for a while about the whole thing, but I've been able to actually speak out more since I don't have to worry about working for the government. I can say pretty much what I think whenever, and I'm helping environmental groups and communities who are doing things like petitions for designating areas unsuitable for mining.

I've been working with a bunch of different lawyers who are suing mining companies on behalf of workers who've been injured or killed on the job, and working with groups in environmental litigation.

I'm working with some lawyers who are representing the people from Rawl in Mingo County,[17] where 653 people had their water polluted for over a thirty-year period by Massey Energy. They went to the records and found they'd pumped over a billion gallons of coal slurry in the underground mine workings, contaminated the whole groundwater system. People have arsenic poisoning and neurological damage, kidney damage, lung disease, all kinds of things from being exposed to this really bad water.

From Martin County, after all the hoopla about the cover-up and everything, I got to work with some attorneys who were suing Massey Energy, and we found a miner who had been the fire boss for the mine that the water drained into at Martin County.[18] He had had to walk through that mine every day for years checking the belt line, to see if it was working right, because it ran coal through that abandoned underground mine—they had a segment of it that was still active—to the prep plant. As he was walking through, he found a lot of water leaking from the impoundment, and he was told by Massey Energy not to report it. He finally told it because he wasn't working for the company anymore, so he wasn't afraid for his job. That's how they covered it up. They knew something was wrong for all those years, from 1994 till 2000. For six years they knew that there was [a] serious problem with that impoundment.

The national media ignored the Martin County coal slurry spill. It was 300 million gallons. That was thirty times greater than the Exxon-Valdez spill. When I got fired, or they tried to fire me, a *New York Times* reporter called me—this is three years after the spill—and he asked me, "How come my paper didn't cover this three years ago?"

I said, "Buddy, you tell me. I'll bet if it was in Connecticut you would have covered it." Or Pennsylvania. Or New York. Or if it had been in New England, it would've been covered. It was because it was in Appalachia that it was not covered by the national media.

It's the *Deliverance* syndrome. People from outside the region still view Appalachia as that dark place over there on the other side of the mountains that you shouldn't even go into. And the people in the Appalachian region are some kind or another backward and deserving of this kind of neglect, and it doesn't matter because they're used to putting up with this. I think that's beginning to change a little bit; I think once people actually see things like mountaintop removal now, from outside the region, they really are appalled by it. They're appalled. So that is slowly changing, but that's been an attitude for years.

We didn't get any real national publicity about mountaintop removal until Penny Loeb did her story for *U.S. News & World Report* in 1997. And how she found out about it was she called me one Sunday night from her home outside Washington and said, "I've heard something about mountaintop removal; I'd like to know a little more about it." So two hours later she got a pretty good earful from me, and she decided to come down and write the story. That was the first national coverage that we'd ever had.

We've destroyed a million and a half acres in the past thirty years with mountaintop removal. It's going on at an accelerated rate now. It's not just destroying the land; it's destroying a whole people. It's destroying a culture. It's destroying towns. It's destroying the most diverse forest outside the tropics in the world. This is the Mother Forest for North America. This is the forest that was still in existence after the last Ice Age, and it was the seeds from this forest that repopulated all the rest of North America. Those mountains won't ever come back, and trees won't ever grow on those places, but it's because it's destroying the people along with the trees and the forests that it's morally objectionable.

I think it's been easier for the industry to do what it's been doing because many of those mountaintop removal sites, especially in Kentucky, are non-union operations. But in West Virginia, I'm sorry to say, the union came out in favor of mountaintop removal a few years ago. I was really disappointed with Cecil Roberts[19] and the leadership of the union because they knew better. They knew that mountaintop removal had actually cost union jobs. So I think it's disgraceful that they have joined with the coal operators to defend mountaintop removal. Shame on them.

I still work with the union and try to help them when I can, but it's really disappointing, and it's weakened the people of the coalfields, the way the union has kind of accepted some of the things that have happened and allowed large operations—like the Massey operation—to keep operating. That really disturbs me.

I really think that the movement in the coalfields is strong enough in and of itself that change can happen. I've been involved since the sixties, really, in resisting strip mining, and helped start Save Our Mountains in the seventies in West Virginia, and this is the strongest I've seen people be. I'm seeing these diverse groups. The broad-form deed was great because it was diverse as well, but I'm seeing people now from the whole region joining together to fight mountaintop removal. I'm very optimistic that we'll ultimately prevail because we have to; it's too precious to let go.

We need some leadership. I've heard that Ben Chandler's[20]

willing to introduce a bill to outlaw mountaintop removal. We get a few more people like that on the national scene, it doesn't matter what Robert Byrd or Nick Rahall[21] say, a lot of other people can join in. It'll take support from outside the region.

It's a real fight; we're up against really powerful forces. You don't get much darker than the coal industry. People who run the coal industry pretty much don't care about the damage they're doing to people or to the land. That's been my experience. They don't see, they can't see.

They're just like Nazis; they don't see what they're doing is wrong. And this Bush administration is a fascist regime. It's the wedding of corporate power and government power. So we're fighting fascism, a modern form of it. We really are.

It's a tough fight, but we can win it.

Huntington, West Virginia, March 29, 2008

Nathan Hall

A Leader, Not a Follower

They say: "Hey, we're gonna put it back,"
We're gonna put it back, just like we found it."
Then they make a wreck and call it reclamation
Take away the beauty and they leave an open sore.

Now you boys know you can't put it back
You can't put it back just like you found it
There's a whole lot of sky where there used to be mountains
And there ain't no mountain where there was before.
—Kate Larken, "Can't Put It Back"

When presidential hopeful John Edwards visited Whitesburg, Kentucky, in June 2007, retracing the steps of Bobby Kennedy's "poverty tour," the first question he answered was one posed by Nathan Hall, a twenty-three-year-old Berea College student from Floyd County, Kentucky.

Hall, looking uncomfortable in a button-up shirt and freshly pressed khaki pants, explained that he wanted to come back to the region after completing his degree in sustainable agriculture and industrial management with a focus on biodiesel. Then he launched into his carefully prepared question: "If you're elected president, how will your initiatives to fight rural poverty and jump-start a green energy economy help young people like me to be able to move back to areas like this and have safe, good, and environmentally friendly jobs?"

Hall never cracked a smile. His face was friendly, but he was there to take care of business, and this was clear during the brief hesitation before Edwards gathered himself enough to answer

Nathan Hall, London, Kentucky. Photo by Silas House.

this serious-looking young man, who didn't look completely convinced that any politician had the answers to the problems plaguing Appalachian youth. Edwards, good-natured, with his ultrawatt smile, did a little joking around with the audience before replying to Hall's question. While the rest of the audience laughed and leaned forward to hear more from Edwards, the young man remained stoic, waiting for his answer.

"Well, biofuel is definitely the answer," Edwards began. He then went on to talk about the way he would reduce carbon dioxide emissions 80 percent by 2050, about how badly the region needed grants to provide proper training and how every person in the country—Appalachians included—is of equal worth. He encouraged Hall to pursue his studies, saying that biofuels could be a godsend for the region.

Hall isn't looking for a godsend as much as he's looking for a solution to the major problem that has been plaguing Appalachia for decades: a mining economy that doesn't give much back to the place from which it takes so very much.

Sitting in a friend's house just before heading off to work mowing yards and doing handyman work—"I need money while I'm in college," he explains—Hall is a study in contrasts. On the one hand, he is so young-looking that his vast knowledge of environmental and economic issues is jarring. There is the suggestion of youth in his mussed blonde hair and the extra cream he takes with his coffee. On the other hand, Hall's face is all straight edges and sharp angles: his is the face of a mountain man, somewhat hard and unsentimental. His gray, weary eyes reveal that he is much more aware of the world's sorrows and major issues than twenty-four-year-olds are reported to be. His is the face of countless Appalachian men staring out at us from old photographs. Even his posture suggests someone much older. His is a confidence born of experience, not arrogance. Nathan Hall knows who he is.

While Hall is in awe of old-time mountain music and old-time ways of life, he is equally fascinated by classic rock music and progressive forms of economy. He chooses his words carefully, his hands restless before him as he prepares to speak. He is, in many ways, the epitome of the modern Appalachian intellectual twenty-something: respectful of the past to the point of near obsession, yet profoundly aware of the future, of progress, of the need for new ideas.

Like many of his contemporaries, Hall doesn't want to leave the mountains, as he told John Edwards. But he also wants more reasons to not leave. And like many others his age, he has briefly left the region only to find that he wanted desperately to return. He has lived briefly in the flatlands of Western Kentucky and Louisville, as well as the even flatter lands of Wisconsin, but he has never been able to rid himself of the mountains that live in his blood. This is something that Hall would have never thought possible during his childhood and teenage years.

"When I was a teenager," he says, "I consciously masked my accent if I was somewhere else. Growing up, I got the impression from the outside world that it was a bad thing to be a hillbilly. A lot of people I grew up with, I only saw the negatives about them, didn't recognize the positives. I was just this stupid, angsty teenager who thought I was so much smarter and cooler than everyone else around me. I get mad at my former self when I look back on that. I grew up thinking that it wasn't good to be from Eastern Kentucky. I thought that I should leave here to better myself, that it was a place you had to get out of."

He wanted nothing more than to get out of Floyd County and go to the bright lights of the big city.

"When I was younger I was a little bit resentful of growing up here because I felt like there'd be more to do if I grew up in Lexington or Louisville, so I moved away when I was eighteen," Hall explains. "But nowhere else felt right until I got back to the place I was from. I went through a lot in that period to . . . come to the place where I really did appreciate the positives of where I was from." It took being away from the region for Hall to completely appreciate and understand it. "For a long time I didn't make the connection between surface mining, where I grew up, and how badly that's affecting the environment. I thought about the environment everywhere else, but not in my own home, where I was from," he says. Once he realized how wasteful Americans were, he started trying to make a difference, mostly because he knew what it was doing to his homeland in the mountains. "I started using less electricity and gas and water, started thinking more about renewable energy and renewable fuels. Once I really thought about what I grew up around, I realized what a unique ecosystem and topography we have, and I thought about the way that's being changed permanently."

He finally couldn't fight his homesickness—or his conscience—any longer. "I'd been doing stuff in Louisville, helping out at the community center and all that, but I didn't really care that much about it, to be honest, because it wasn't home to me," he says. "So, I thought, if I'm going to really do something, then I need to do it where I'm from. I'd definitely say I felt a responsibility to come back."

Once he came back, he decided the perfect thing for him to do was to go into the coal mines. He is proud to have been a coal miner, and he is also firmly against mountaintop removal.

Hall says his parents raised him to be aware of, and to appreciate, nature. They often took him hiking and encouraged his interest in the insect world by helping him with a bug collection that won a statewide prize. Still, as a teenager he became apathetic. "I just wanted to party and play music," he says. But, then, in high school, Hall read *Ishmael,* a philosophical novel by Daniel Quinn that had a lasting effect on the way he saw the world. "It's not really an environmental book, but it made me think a lot more about what we were doing to the planet, the mind-set everyone was caught up in. It caused me to start thinking more. My thought process kept developing as I went on, and I hope it still is."

Hall remains in touch with the natural world. "I do spend a lot of time outdoors, more time than I do indoors. I try to get out in the woods quite a bit, and I work outside," he says. "That connection to the land—well, I think that's part of me whether I want it to be or not."

Hall first encountered mountaintop removal mining as a small child. "You can't hardly leave the house I grew up in without seeing a big job. I grew up with them everywhere around me . . . Lots of people can't tell the difference between all the different kinds of mining, but when you see mountaintop removal, you know it because you'll see a big flat area for miles. In MTR, the whole ridgetop is taken," he says. "When I was growing up, I'd go hunting pretty often, and it was just like another part of the landscape, but I didn't realize that wasn't natural back then. But when I was a teenager I started noticing it quite a bit, and I knew it was wrong."

Hall knew how he felt about surface and mountaintop removal mining, but he wanted to make sure that he knew what he was talking about, so he decided to go into the mines. He admits that a big part of the reason he became a miner was because he needed the money, but he also did it for moral reasons. "The way I looked at it, if I was going to say that we needed to stop strip mining and mountaintop removal mining," he says, "then I had to be able to say that we should do more deep mining, so I decided to be a deep miner."

Hall is clearly a man of integrity, another one of the quiet heroes working toward solutions in Appalachia. He is representative of so many young adults who are trying to make a difference in the world while simultaneously making their own way in it. Defying the popular stereotype, he also represents all those mountain people who are trying to make their region a better place. He may be doing it without fanfare, but he's doing it nonetheless.

In a revealing interview that took place over the course of a drought-plagued August morning, Hall offers insight into what it's like to be a contemporary deep miner. He gives his views for a more economically viable and environmentally friendly Appalachia. He talks with refreshing candor about the trials of starting a true grassroots movement. And he gives a brief but poetic look at his family's history in the region. From his very first words he conveys that age-old connection to the land that Appalachians have, which might just be the major reason that so many are beginning to rise up to speak out against mountaintop removal. Hall, however, has decided to not just talk about stopping mountaintop removal. He's taking direct action, using his college studies to find solutions. Instead of waiting for others to join in, he's ready to lead the way.

Nathan Hall talking . . .

I'm from a small town called Allen.[1] That's where my dad's side of the family has lived since the early 1900s. Before that, they were in Letcher County,[2] after coming in from Virginia sometime in the 1700s. My paternal mamaw's side of the family was from Floyd County. My mother's family is from Johnson County, near Lawrence Creek. Her maiden name is Lyon.

As far as the history of mining, my mother's family was mostly self-sufficient on small agriculture. They farmed, kept hogs and chickens. My papaw, he worked in the oil fields in Johnson County,[3] drilling. But he also had a big garden. On my mom's side, one of my uncles—she had four brothers—he worked for a while in the Pike County deep mines for about eight years. He was a foreman for a while, but then there was a rockfall. Rocks hit him in the head and gave him a concussion that put him in the hospital for a while. On my dad's side, my pappy (who was my mamaw's dad, my great-grandpa) ran a pony mine on Arkansas Creek. The mules had carts that were loaded and they'd walk it out, the mules were trained to turn so that it dumped over the hill and then they came back in for more. Pappy also worked for the railroad. And my papaw, he worked for the gas company. I don't really come from one of those families where everybody is a miner.

Like I said, my mother's people had land over in Johnson County, and I used to spend a lot of time over there. In the eighties, a piece of family land that nobody lived on got strip-mined, and a little bit of it had some gas wells drilled that exposed some people to radioactive material, and there was a big lawsuit over that. I personally haven't set foot on that land, because every time I ask about it they'll say, "Aw, it's grown up in briars," or something like that. I've been trying to get my family to take me over there for a while. That's something I'm real interested in because I'm pretty interested in the family history.

It's strange to know about this land my ancestors lived on for generations, but now it's not fit to visit. In a way it seems like there's a part of my past I'll never get to know.

I went one semester to college right after high school; didn't know what I wanted to do. I just took some basic classes; I did pretty well. Then I spent a year where I just worked, then I thought maybe I knew what I wanted to do, so I went back for one semester, did more basic classes. Then three years of no college, just worked. That's when I worked underground, and at that point I figured out the direction I wanted to go. And so then I decided to apply to Berea because they have a free tuition program and it's close to home, and I got in.

I had been living in Louisville for about three years, from the age of nineteen until I was twenty-two, and I just hated it. I never felt right there. Don't know why I stayed there that long. I finally realized I had to move back to Eastern Kentucky because anywhere else, I just didn't feel right. But, you know, to live you have to be able to make a living, and I wanted to be able to make a *decent* living, didn't want to work at Wal-Mart.

Seemed like the only option to make decent money and be in the area where I wanted to be was to go into the mines. And I hadn't really figured out what I wanted to do with myself in the long term. I had some ideas, but it seemed to me that I could work in the mines, make pretty good money, make anywhere from ten to twenty-five dollars an hour without any kind of specialized training or educational background. I figured I could move back to Eastern Kentucky, work in the mines, make good money, figure out what I wanted to do, be saving up for what I wanted to do, and also get some interesting stories and some good training—mechanical, electrical—along the way.

My family thought it was a pretty bad idea because it was dangerous. My papaw was real upset over it, said it was about as smart as sticking my finger in a light socket. Made my mamaw worry quite a bit. My dad didn't think it was a bad idea, but my mom didn't like it. But at that point I had already made up my mind, and it took a long time to get a job. Before you can work in the mines, you have to get what's called a green card, an inexperienced miner's card. You have to go to forty hours of state training on safety and everything. It's kind of a joke, really. You mostly sat around and watched videos from the seventies, so blurry you couldn't hardly understand them. I think the instructors cared, but there's only so much they can do in the classroom, you just have to start working to get the right experience.

I got my green card in early September 2005, I guess, and in about two months I applied everywhere I could. I went to the unemployment office, the newspaper, but I figured out that I had to ask miners where the jobs were. I wasn't very connected to all that, so eventually I had to move to Western Kentucky to get some experience. A friend's uncle owned a deep mine out there, and I worked until I had my time in. You have to work either forty days or 360 working hours to get your experienced miner's card, and that's what I was wanting.

I don't think I could work on a strip job, I was always so against it. I've been against it for years. I knew that underground mining wasn't perfect, environmentally, since it causes a lot of water problems and so on, but as someone from the area who was environmentally conscious, I felt like deep mining was my best choice if I wanted to stay in the area and hopefully make things better in the area.

To be realistic in the matter, there's no way this country could just stop using coal. It'd take a long time to get to that point, and the way I looked at it, if I was going to say that we needed to stop strip mining and mountaintop removal mining, then I had to be able to say that we should do more deep mining, so I decided to be a deep miner. That's part of why I decided to go into the underground mines.

The work conditions, in my opinion, are worse on a strip job than underground. You're exposed to the weather conditions no matter what, whether it's freezing or burning up. Underground it's the same temp year-round, and in most places they have pretty good ventilation. I'd rather work underground just because of the working conditions, myself.

It was pretty bizarre, going in the mines for the first time. I was kind of thrilled. It's unlike anything else, it's almost like a roller coaster at Dollywood or going through a movie set, except it was a working environment. It was kind of surreal. Interesting, but at the same time you're having to do some real manual labor.

There was one time when I thought there might be a belt fire. Those belts can cause so much friction that it can develop into a mine fire. You can tell when they're about to happen, the air gets really smoky and it smells terrible. I thought we were going to have a mine fire, but the foreman had been through that plenty times and put it out. There's a lot of times I was put in dangerous situations, but I never really felt like my life was threatened. I never thought there'd be a big explosion. I've seen big rock falls within ten or twenty feet of me, but that was always under an unsupported roof, and I knew better than to go where there were unsupported roofs.

I set timbers in the mines, which they don't do much anymore. That's where you take a four-by-four or a four-by-six and you wedge it in between the roof and floor. Shoveled belts a lot, mostly in the places where the belts changed directions; the belts have to change with whichever direction the coal seam goes. A lot of coal will come off the belt and get built up so you have to shovel those out every day. People think you shovel rocks underground, but you're shoveling mud—coal dust mixed with water—so thick you just about have to wipe it off. You get soaked doing it because there's usually water on the floor. I've built brattices—concrete block walls—it regulates the air flow; you have to have intake and return so that you can have good air movement. I've slung rock dust, I've hung cables for people working on the section, brought roof bolters their bolts. I got my shot-firing card—they actually sent me for my training for this. There's different kinds of mining. Most mines have continuous miners nowadays; that's a machine with a rotating drum with offset teeth that breaks the coal up. Other mines you have to tap dynamite in. I was a backup guy for that.

At one point, I felt like I had found my niche. I felt like well, okay, I'm going to do this for several years and that'll be okay. I've had a lot of manual labor jobs before—many of them nearly as physically intensive as underground mining—but there was never the kind of relationships that I had with other miners. At other jobs people just kept to themselves. In the mines you depend on your coworkers for your safety, and that creates a bond. I think a lot of it is that it's just such unique working conditions and nowadays relatively few people are willing to do it. When you're an underground miner, there's nothing else like it. There's a camaraderie to it. Of course there's smart-asses and people who get on your nerves, but for the most part, if you show up on time, if you work hard, if you don't smart off, then everyone gets along.

I met the most interesting characters of my life working underground. The most hilarious, the most good-hearted people I ever met, just really intelligent and interesting people. I mean, you have to be smart to be a miner, have to be on your toes, alert, to take in everything they need to.

Just about any job I've ever had I've felt an environmental conflict. I worked as a Stanley Steemer carpet cleaner for a while and I'd always think about all the gas we'd be running out to clean people's carpet, and how crazy that was. Almost any job there's that conflict if you're environmentally minded, and I really kept it to myself when I was working in the mines, but every now and then a miner would say something to me that would really surprise me. I've had people joke around or be sarcastic about global warming, but some of those miners were against what mountaintop removal was doing to this area.

No miners I know are all gung-ho. None of them are "Woohoo, let's tear stuff up!" Most of them are just trying to make a living, to feed their families. They just think, "This is my job, this is how I buy food, this is how I make my car payment."

The majority of blue-collar jobs are environmentally destructive. I think the majority of people don't want that. I know people on strip jobs who don't like what they're doing to the land, but they needed a job, they had their surface card, and they took the job. I was always kind of thinking of those things while I was working. I was a grunt, I did the low-level stuff that wasn't even production-related, usually. I was getting paid somewhat for it, not as much as people with experience. I just kept thinking I'm going to do this for four or five years and then I'll start a business that's environmentally friendly, so what I'm doing during this time is working toward that.

I think there is a real complacency among a lot of Eastern Kentuckians. A lot of it has to do with the fact that people just want to live their lives, don't necessarily want to start a commotion or be considered radicals or activists. They just want to be friendly to people, have people be friendly back, and not have life be a constant struggle.

Just about everybody knows somebody or is related to somebody who works on a surface mining job, so it can be tough for people to feel like they can speak out when it might upset friends or family. It impacts us all, but we won't know for a long time how badly it's impacting us, and I think that's real hard for people to latch onto.

I always think about the civil rights movement and how it was easier to get people involved because it was so direct and in their face. I mean, people would say, "You cannot sit here," or "You can't eat here," so there was no denying it in that case. Here it's more subtle. The rocks aren't usually flying into your house so you don't think about it. They're not just taking your land, so you don't think about it, so it sneaks in. You have some real outspoken people who are really aware of the long-term effects, but the majority of the people are on the fence. They have a feeling that it's bad, but all those politicians are telling us that it's good for economic development.

So many people have been complacent for so long that I don't really know at this point how to get people to be against that and to really stand up. It's been beaten into our heads for the past hundred years or so that we don't have any choice but to exploit the land and ourselves, because the country needs the resources. There's a lot of complications, a lot of gray areas. People have been told for a long time that there's big business and there's big government and you just have to go along with it whether you like it or not. They're told, "Listen, things are better now than they were fifty years ago," so they're convinced that it has to be this way. So many people just want to exist comfortably.

I think lots of people have similar opinions to me, but they're afraid to speak out. I think a lot of people are afraid of seeming different, like that person who is the crazy environmentalist or something. Most people want to blend in. It's easier. If that's what your friends and neighbors are saying, it's easier to just agree, to be a part of the status quo.

And the coal industry has convinced people that mountaintop removal is good for the economy. But if you look at all the thousands of acres of land that have been stripped, a fraction of a percent of that land actually has something economically productive on it.

A lot of the seams they're getting at by mountaintop removal are so small that I just don't think they're worth all the environmental devastation. We have to start thinking about the costs versus the benefits. It's obvious that in the long term the costs are going to carry a lot more weight. When you consider how much coal those big machines can move at once, well, it's obvious that it's taking jobs away. Even deep mining is more mechanized now, but still, you have to have more miners down there than you do on a mountaintop removal site, to get the coal out, to maintain equipment, et cetera.

I quit the mines last year. I got talked into going back to college by family members who didn't want me working in the mines.

My plan from the get-go was to get a college degree and start some kind of business that could be sustainable, that could provide some kind of alternative for environmental and economic development in the mountains. I got convinced that if I went back to college I'd be in a better position to do that. I do feel a little more at liberty to do those kinds of things, to be in the public eye, to speak out. I do feel more at liberty to do that kind of thing now that I don't work underground; it'd be a little strange to get noticed as somebody who was speaking out in public and be working with people who might not be so happy with me. A lot of people, even if they don't completely disagree with you but they perceive you as being some kind of threat to their economic stability, they're not going to be too happy about that.

I'm really working toward doing something to promote alternative economic development. That ought to be one of the key elements to doing something about the devastation happening in Eastern Kentucky.

I want to create a solution.

So many of the people who are part of this anti-MTR movement want to just talk about the negatives, and we need to be talking about the positives, too. We need to be talking about the solutions. I'm not trying to be a full-time activist or anything, I just want to make a difference somehow.

The movement to stop mountaintop removal involves a lot of people who are not from the affected area, who are against it from an ideological sense just because they're against anything that's bad for the environment or sometimes because this happens to be the hot environmental thing of the moment. In the worst-case scenarios, what happens is that a handful of local token mountain people are put on display and taken around to everything to supply sound bites, but that's not a very good way to build a strong grassroots movement of people from the affected area.

In a lot of ways I think it's really alienating to people from the affected area because they really see this whole movement as being an outsider movement, an "activist" movement, and that's hard for them to identify with. I mean, a lot of mountain people who would sit outside with a shotgun to make sure their land didn't get mined would still never identify themselves as environmental activists. For the most part, a lot of these activists don't know how to interact with country people, and they just perpetuate this sense of confusion . . . it's much like a circus, to me, most of the time.

I wouldn't even say it's their fault, but almost everybody comes to Appalachia with some kind of stereotype in mind. It might be the humble, hardworking, old-fashioned version of what people think America used to be like, or it could be the dumb, lazy hillbilly from TV. The reality is a lot more complicated and nuanced, and I think sometimes outsiders don't realize that.

There are a lot of people who really want to do something good and their hearts are in the right place, they work hard on it, but I don't know how effective they can be if they don't understand this place or have a background here. I just don't really think there is a solution to that. As long as it's a movement that's based on outsiders, then it will always be weak. This has to be a movement that is led by people from within the area. That's what makes it a true grassroots movement, a real effective and important movement.

My mamaw once told me that coal was a curse. That's pretty revolutionary, for this older woman from Floyd County, Kentucky, to say. But most people in my family just don't say anything about it. They don't get mad at me for speaking out against it, but they don't really say anything one way or the other.

I want to have that experience again, to go back into the mines after being in a liberal arts college for the past several months. I need that reality to get back to. But I also need to get my business started here in Eastern Kentucky. At this point I'm thinking of biodiesel or some kind of small-scale agriculture. If that works I won't have much reason to go back into the mines, but if everything I do falls flat and I become hopeless about starting a business, then I'll go back in the mines, if I can't find any other way to make a living.

Appalachia is one of the most beautiful and unique places in the world, and what MTR does to it can never be changed. Even if it can be reclaimed, they're still altering the topography, they're still altering things that we won't fully see the effect on for years, the watershed, aquatic life, all these things that are altered. This is too important of a place from an environmental and cultural perspective to not stop it. We grew up seeing mountains, not plateaus, and that has a real damaging effect on the psyche.

We can fight this, though. One way to fight it is to live conscientiously. If you're someone in the region where this is happening, the main thing you need to do is organize as quick as you can, before a mountaintop removal site pops up close to you. The sooner you can organize, the better. There is a lot you can do to protect yourself. File a Lands Unsuitable for Mining petition. Spread information.

The less demand there is for something, the less supply, that's just the way the market works. We have to be more conscious of how we use energy. I always think, "What if I didn't have this coal? What did people do 150 years ago?" That kind of thinking—it can get a little bit tedious, with every little thing you do—but we should think about the ramifications of our actions. Eventually you just get to where you live conscientiously; you don't even have to think about it.

London, Kentucky, August 15, 2007

Anne Shelby and Jessie Lynne Keltner

Holy Ground

Oh this is holy ground
To me it's holy ground
And nothing but the hand of God
Shall ever tear it down
Take your dozers and your dynamite
And head on back to town
Get off of my land cause where you stand
Is holy ground.
—Jessie Lynne Keltner, "Holy Ground"

It is high summer, and the sisters are picking blackberries on the homeplace.

They amble along this place of their youth, the land that has been in their family for more than a hundred years. In fact, this land is a *part* of their family. They move over it the way someone might run their thumb over the knuckles of their mother in her old age. Although these women walk with determination and purpose, they seem to tread lightly on this holy ground, not so much walking on it as floating just above it, careful not to harm anything that lies in their path.

"Now this here is the proper way to spend a Sunday morning," the elder sister, Anne Shelby, says.

"Picking berries and singing hymns," says Jessie Lynne Keltner, completing Shelby's thought.

They call the old mountain farm "the homeplace." Shelby even wrote a popular children's book entitled *Homeplace,* which

Jessie Lynne Keltner and Anne Shelby, Teges Creek, Kentucky. Photo by Silas House.

details one family's connection to a farm over a century. Keltner has written many songs wherein the farm shows up as well, and it is one of her favorite photographic subjects.

Often when friends speak about Shelby and Keltner, they become one unified force: folks often refer to them as "the Gabbard Sisters." They bill themselves that way when they sing together at libraries, festivals, and the like around central Appalachia. Here, at the homeplace, they are certainly one entity, unconscious of how they match one another's stride.

The homeplace is in Clay County, Kentucky, near the small town of Oneida. The farm is about seventy acres of rolling hills and a couple of steep mountains. There is the house itself, which is really a collection of houses pieced together. First is the original cabin with dogtrot, which was built sometime around the Civil War. Then there is the house that their grandparents built over that in 1940, "when they added onto the back of the house, closed in the dogtrot, and raised the roofline, all with pine from the hillside," according to Shelby. In the mid-1990s Shelby and her husband, Edmund Shelby (general manager and editor of the *Beattyville Enterprise*), built on another log structure that contains a new kitchen, a bathroom, an office, and "some badly needed closet space." This was also done with timber cut from the farm. The house has been lived in by the sisters, their mother, their uncle, their grandparents, and their great-grandparents. It has been continuously occupied since the Civil War, with someone in their immediate family inhabiting it since around 1900.

"Our grandparents and great-grandparents had a working farm here. They had cattle and tobacco, they grew a lot of corn and big gardens, lots of chickens. And hogs," Shelby throws her finger out onto the air, pointing to what is now the backyard of the house, decorated by several of the dozen or so stray dogs that the Shelbys have collected over the last few years. "There was a hog pen right out there. It was a real lively place, not like now, where all you see is yard dogs."

The dogs have been stifled by the heat. It is not even noon but the heat bugs are already screaming this Sunday morning.

On the last rise above the creek the two women reach a knot of blackberry brambles fairly dripping with shiny fruit. The pair drop huge, grape-sized blackberries into their plastic buckets while they harmonize as only two sisters can do:

Pure waters of life there are flowing
And all who will drink may be free
Rare jewels of splendor are glowing
How beautiful heaven must be.

They sway in rhythm just a bit, their movement barely noticeable, their hands dipping into the vines, able fingers plucking the berries away from their roosts like quick birds. These are hands that are used to berry-picking. The Gabbard Sisters use their hands quickly in every matter: using a pencil to jot down a thought, knocking aside a strand of hair that has fallen into their eyes, wiping at their brows with the red kerchief Shelby keeps handy.

"Lord, children, it's gotten plumb hot," Keltner says.

"We ought to go down to the creek, sister," Shelby offers.

All of the land slopes down to Teges Creek,[1] which empties into the South Fork of the Kentucky River a couple of miles away and runs through the property like a slender, winding ribbon. This day, in the middle of the worst drought anyone can remember, Teges Creek is shallow, but it still holds slow-moving water, which is becoming littered with small golden leaves that are falling, apparently from heat exhaustion.

Stepping into the woods feels like stepping into a cave. The temperature is instantly cooler and fresher. Here is the smell of green leaves and mossy rocks and Teges Creek, which flows silently just beyond a gathering of rocks that look as if they have fallen from a giant hand into a neat pile. Shelby pulls herself up on the biggest rock and looks down at the creek, dotting her forehead with the kerchief again. Keltner does not hesitate before wading right out into the creek, however. She rolls her pant legs up to her knees and splashes handfuls of water onto the back of her neck. Sunlight falls in patterns through the still leaves, causing glints of light to speckle Keltner's face.

"I used to love to bring a book to this rock and read," Shelby says. She has produced a hair-tie from somewhere and is pulling her hair up into a ponytail. She takes a deep breath and leans back on the palms of her hands. There is nothing but birdcall here. A redbird: "Birdie birdie birdie." A thin breeze, no stronger than a sigh, moves along the top of the water, breathing coolness that causes a few of the golden leaves to shiver down out of the trees. Several of them light on Shelby's head like a blessing. One falls perfectly onto her hand, which she has been holding palm up. "Oh," she says, startled and delighted to find the weightless leaf there. She holds it up to the light, turns it over. One side of the leaf is as white as a piece of typing paper. "Look at that," Shelby marvels.

Keltner is bent close to the surface of the water, peering at the creek bottom. "I wonder where all the crawdads are?" she says.

"Back in the coldest places," Shelby whispers, perhaps not completely conscious of replying to her sister while she continues to study the leaf.

By way of reply, Keltner cups her hand, dips it into the creek, and takes a drink. She wipes her mouth on the back of her arm. Teges Creek is part of her now. But it always has been.

Shelby and Keltner have devoted their lives to preserving Appalachian culture. Shelby is known as the writing sister who can sing and Keltner is known as the singing sister who can write. Both are renaissance women: they do a little bit of everything.

Shelby has written children's books, poetry, essays, newspaper columns, and songs. She has published six books for children, among them *Potluck, The Someday House, What to Do about Pollution, We Keep a Store, Homeplace,* and, to be published in 2009,

The Man Who Lived in a Hollow Tree. The Adventures of Molly Whuppie, a collection of folktales inspired by stories she collected over several years, was published in 2008. Her work has been honored by being named School Library Journal Best Book and American Bookseller Pick. Her book of poetry, *Appalachian Studies,* and *Can a Democrat Get into Heaven?,* a collection of newspaper columns, were both finalists for Appalachian Book of the Year in 2007, the first time a single author has been nominated for two books in a single year. She has not only written the plays *The Lone Pilgrim: Songs and Stories of Aunt Molly Jackson* and *Passing Through the Garden: The Work of Belinda Mason,* but has also acted in those and other productions throughout the region.

In Appalachian Lit circles, Shelby is considered an underrated writer whose work deserves to be better known. Poet and scholar Marianne Worthington has written that "what Shelby does best is remind us of all the things we need to be mindful of. Yes, quilts and tobacco barns and hardscrabble farming are here, but so is our need to preserve the environment and a culture, a call for fighting domestic abuse and drug trafficking, and the responsibility of remembering and celebrating our foundation myths, place names, Appalachian speech habits, and all of our ghostly ancestors."[2]

Keltner has been less public with her work but just as active in preserving Appalachian culture. She has written dozens of songs, has acted in plays, and writes poetry that she doesn't show to anyone. An avid collector of 78 rpm records (mostly early hillbilly music), she wants to safeguard and preserve the old music. Keltner also has a burgeoning collection of sheet music from the late nineteenth and early twentieth centuries. She works with the elderly and those with memory loss as a social worker at the Laurel Heights nursing home in London, Kentucky. There she often uses music in her work with patients, taking in her fiddle and autoharp to play songs from the past.

Both sisters are members of the singing group the Cosmic Mamaws, a quartet (with Kate Larken and George Ella Lyon) that describes itself as a "bunch of big-mouthed, menopausal women" who sing about everything from the Bush administration to being grandmothers. They are also members of the band Public Outcry (which also includes Larken, Lyon, and the authors of this book), a group that was formed to sing out against mountaintop removal. Public Outcry has performed throughout Appalachia, primarily at colleges and universities, spreading the word about the mining practice to as many listeners as possible.

Shelby and Keltner are fighting mountaintop removal with the two things they know best: words and music. Although they are doing most of their protest together, they first encountered mountaintop removal separately.

For Shelby, it was back in April 2005 when she, along with fifteen other Kentucky writers, accepted the invitation Wendell Berry sent to practically every author in the state to take a mountaintop removal tour. On the first leg of the tour, the authors gathered on the lush mountain behind the home of Daymon Morgan on Bad Creek, in Leslie County. After showing the authors several rare and medicinal plants that grew there, Morgan took them a bit further up the ridge and pointed out an overhang that offered a view of the mountains. The drop-off had been created by bulldozers that were illegally cutting into Morgan's land for the mountaintop removal site that abutted his property.

The authors made their way up the bank with hesitation, careful not only because it was steep and slick with tiny rocks, but also because they were not quite ready for what they were about to encounter. For many it was the first time they saw mountaintop removal up close. Shelby eased her way up; once she reached the edge of the precipice, her face went pale.

Below was a scene of utter destruction. A bulldozer groaned back and forth, piling up green-leafed trees it had knocked over. Another mess of trees was slowly burning, the black smoke curling up lazily on the still spring air. There was nothing else but dirt and exposed rock for acres and acres before the site stopped abruptly at the rich, green woods in the distance. Beyond them were blue mountains that faded away to the horizon like smudges of paint.

"Look, that's like heaven," Shelby said that day to the person standing next to her, pointing to the far mountains. Then she brought her finger down to the mountaintop removal site. "And that's hell."

Shelby remembers the day vividly. "I never will forget that," she says. "Up to that point, I thought I knew what mountaintop removal was, but I didn't. I really didn't know how much damage it does. I didn't know they cut down the forest and burned up the trees. I didn't know what big areas were involved. I didn't know what a desolate landscape it left behind. No, I never will forget that," she repeats, looking away. "Some of us who were there have tried to describe how it feels to stand on a landscape like that, but I really cannot. I have all these reasons that are very practical for opposing mountaintop removal, like sedimentation and flooding and blasting ruining people's homes and leaving nothing for the future, but none of that has anything to do with the way it feels to stand on a piece of land that has been made desolate in that way. There's a sentence in Erik Reece's book that says something like, 'I looked around me and there was not one single living thing.'[3] It was sickening to me, to know I was in a place where nothing was living and that people had done this. To see a little piece of grass struggling, trying to come up through that shale, it just made me sick. That's what really made me want to get involved in it, that overriding feeling of 'This *cannot* be right, not for *any* reason.'"

Keltner was driving up I-75 when she first saw a mountaintop removal site. Her car was snaking its way up Jellico Mountain—a land mass known by anyone who has traveled that stretch of highway as being a defining point between the states of Tennessee and Kentucky. Having reached the crest of Jellico Mountain a driver can see for miles on either side: hundreds of mountains, millions of trees. Up there, it is almost as if all of Appalachia is spread out below, perfect from this distance where blemishes are hidden, where all the little joys and tragedies of the people below are hidden beneath a canopy of leaves. At the summit, Keltner noticed something she had never seen before.

"I'm not real good at telling the difference in mining operations, in how they're doing it. But in this case, it was just so obvious: the mountaintop was *gone,*" Keltner says. "I couldn't believe it. It got me so upset that I had to start writing songs, and the first one I wrote was 'Jellico.' Since then, I've read that Campbell County, Tennessee, is one of the poorest counties in the state, and like in Kentucky, mining has hurt tourism and the environment and the economy long-term. I'm not sure what mine I saw, but after that I read about the Zeb Mountain mine, with a permit to mine 216 acres in Campbell County, so it has to be pretty close by. Then I read that between Jellico and Middlesboro,[4] the Clear Fork Valley, it's 90 percent corporate owned and heavily mined, and 90 percent depopulated.[5] So I just had to write about it and get involved."

At this point, the sisters have long since finished their berry-picking. A gallon of the day's gathering has already been made into a cobbler, which is bubbling in the oven. The gloaming has set in at the homeplace, so the logical place to gather is the back porch, which lies in the shade of old apple trees for the last half of the day. The porch looks out over Teges Creek and the still green mountain, where birdsong has been replaced by the sounds of cicadas, katydids, crickets, and frogs. The heat of the day has crept back into the cool cliffs of the mountain or nestled like a thin mist above the creek, easing down off the farm.

The two sisters laugh often, and this sound carries out over the homeplace. It's safe to say that these trees have heard similar laughter for the last hundred years at least; many a past summer's evening saw the sisters' family members watching night close in like this, too. The two siblings are proud of the stock from which they came, frequently mentioning the strength and resolve of their ancestors.

It's no wonder that Shelby and Keltner got involved in the movement to stop mountaintop removal. They are the daughters of Luther and Jessie Bishop Gabbard. Luther, a soil conservationist, spent most of his life fretting about erosion. Jessie, a teacher, always stood up for what she believed in.

"Dad took the charge of being a soil conservationist very seriously. He was serious about stopping erosion," Shelby says. "He loved to grow these big gardens, and I think he really *loved* soil. He knew the value of it, and he knew what it could do if you took care of it."

Their mother, Jessie, was outspoken about her beliefs and felt that dissent was a responsibility everyone should take seriously. "Our mother was the only person we knew who was against capital punishment, or who would speak up when she thought the school system was doing something wrong," Shelby says.

"She spoke out against World War II some, too," Keltner offers. "Our dad and her brother were both in the war, but she spoke out against it. She felt, as a strong Christian, that she should. To them, that meant that you were to be compassionate and gentle. I think that Mom and Dad exemplified what is good about the mountains. They loved their homeland."

The sisters say they are fighting mountaintop removal not only to honor their ancestors, who worked so hard on this land, but also to help preserve the land for future generations, including their own kin. Shelby is the grandmother to triplet grandsons Luke, Leo, and Ace. Keltner is also close to the boys, serving as a sort of extra grandmother.

The pair look on the current state of affairs in Appalachia with a mixture of hope and frustration.

"I sometimes have a nightmare vision of Eastern Kentucky being left to kudzu, mountaintop removal, and the drug culture," Shelby says. "I always think I would never, ever leave this place because our family has been here such a long time, but if they were to start taking these mountains down around me, this place would be gone, in a way. The thing that I stay for would be gone. It wouldn't be the same anymore. So I might have to leave. But, in another way, they can't blow up culture, they can't run it out."

"But this region could be turned into one big coalfield. That's possible," Keltner interjects. She pauses, listening to an especially loud chorus of cicadas. Darkness has overtaken Appalachia now, and her face is lost to the shadows. "And you know, maybe Appalachia will just exist in one little trailer in Georgia or something. That's drastic, but it could happen."

"Yeah, we'll all take that Appalachian culture with us wherever we go," Shelby offers. "It's always been on the brink of disappearing anyway, as its own particular culture. In a way. But it's proven remarkably resilient and strong. It's defied all extinctions for 150 years. So we'll keep right on."

Anne and Jessie Lynne talking . . .

Anne: There were always hills wherever we went. Seems like if you grow up with hills around you, then you miss them when you leave them—or when they leave you, which is starting to happen more with this mountaintop removal. People from the mountains often try to explain—in songs and poems—why we feel this way about the mountains. But it's hard in a way because it's inexplicable, really, why we feel so much better with hills around us. We lived in Jackson County, and in this town, McKee, it was like a little bowl, with hills all around us. And we felt so secure there.

Lynne: We were at Gray Hawk part of the time, and we always came over here, to Clay County, because Mom's parents were here. Even after we moved from the mountains to central Kentucky for about four years, before we came back to London, Mom nor Dad neither one ever came back to live in Clay or Jackson, but we did. We came back because of the history we had heard from our families, from the stories. We knew that our people had a long history, and you could tell that they were very proud to be from the mountains. They were really conscious of it.

Anne: And we were aware, even as kids, that there was a richness to something here. Our grandparents had this little store—Bishop's Grocery—

Lynne: The sign said: "Bradley Bishop Grocery."

Anne: But everybody just called it "Brad and Carrie's." After they died and our uncle, Millard Bishop, ran it, they called it "Millard's." And after he died and Edmund and I ran it, they still called it "Millard's." People were always coming around here, on account of the store. It was just rich with stories and lots of laughing. There was a common group of stories that everyone knew and told. They enjoyed each other's company, enjoyed making fun of each other sometimes. There was also this shared history that existed. Everyone knew everyone's ancestors and who they had been, and everyone else's families and their histories. When we went other places, pleasant as they might have been in other ways, those places didn't have that. And I think that's partly why we kept coming back over and over again.

Lynne: We knew who we were here.

Anne: That we were Appalachians, even though that wasn't a word that was used then. Nobody used that word until the seventies, I don't think, when there was a sort of movement of consciousness of being Appalachian. Since both of our parents had gone to Berea College, they had, from there, a real strong sense of the region and of wanting to stay in the region and to be of service to the region. That was always part of our growing up.

Lynne: Our parents came back here to teach after they graduated from Berea, Mom at Oneida and Dad over at Jackson County. So they had that regional consciousness and a real love of this place. There was a strong sense of community here, as small a community as it was: one little store, and the church, and at one time there was a mill at the mouth of the creek. People in this area considered themselves as the people of Lower Teges Creek, and they had a real strong sense of that community. We saw them at the store a whole lot. They were always telling big tales about their farms and families. They'd launch into memories or jokes. They'd start talking about the weather or something and end up telling some big, hilarious story.

Anne: A lot of the time there would be big long periods where people wouldn't come to the store, so Lynne and I would play Store. Lot of the time on a summer afternoon people wouldn't come for hours, so this was great to us. We'd act like we had been locked up in the store because that's what we really wanted to happen. 'Cause that way we could eat all the candy and drink all the pop without any limitations passed down on us from the grown-ups. Our mother was always trying in vain to keep us from eating and drinking too much there. She'd say, "Now, no more than six pops a day or four candy bars!" We chafed against those limitations. It was heaven for a kid. You know, Bill Cosby says that a child's life is a constant search for candy. And that was us.

Lynne: Plus, you could walk outside the store and there were apple trees full of apples and men whittling, and there were all kinds of pop lids to play with. There were all kinds of kids who would come to play with us while their parents visited.

Anne: And since it was a public place, the grown-ups couldn't really control who came there and who we would be exposed to, or what we would hear. So we'd hang around, wide-eyed, to see what big tales we might hear.

Lynne: It was real different than when we were living in Burkesville, or Stanford, or London, because as late as the late seventies, there were still people riding mules up to the store after they had been working in tobacco or something. But in the last twenty-five or thirty years it seems like to me the community has really fallen apart. There's very little sense of community left. Everybody just runs to Manchester now.

Anne: Yeah, there's no place where people can really get together as much. There's a little store at Oneida where people get together some, I guess, but mostly people go to Wal-Mart. And when you see somebody you know at Wal-Mart you'll stand and talk to them a while, try to catch up, but everything's just so different. Back then, people worked together, in tobacco and farming. Nobody farms much, so there's not that contact. It's just harder to get up with people. And there's a pretty rigid division in the community between the church people and the drug people. So if you don't fit in with either one of them, like us, you're just stranded!

Lynne: People came to the store to socialize, mostly. There weren't so many other things to do—not that TV or the Internet are good substitutes—so people would come in the evening and just visit. There was always singing, too, seems like. Our mother sang more like Sara Carter than anyone else I ever heard. She actually sounded like her. We listened to a lot of music over and over because we really didn't have very many records. Our grandparents had these old 78s. We had a few religious records, maybe one Disney record. A classical collection that our mother wanted us to be exposed to. Church music was real strong in the little Baptist church where we went. We'd just continue it on after we went to church, we'd go to my grandparents' and sing with our cousins and uncles and aunts. We'd harmonize and they'd play guitars. I still like music of all kinds, but folk music and hillbilly music and old hymns are just something that I have a strong connection to because we did have that culture and that exposure. The first song I ever tried to play on the guitar was "When the World's on Fire."[6]

Anne: A nice children's song! How old were you?

Lynne: Ah, 'bout six or seven.

[They laugh.]

Anne: You know, I never did reject being Appalachian. But I did get away from it. I had a rediscovery. When I was growing up in the fifties, it wasn't a subject of conversation, it wasn't an issue one way or the other. I don't think. But I think that that period in the seventies, when you could get access to the old music again, and the writing, and people were talking about Appalachia and being Appalachian, it became exciting to rediscover and reclaim that. I had mostly identified myself as a hippie more than anything else for a period of time. But I remember one time, I was looking in the back of that book *Yesterday's People,* by Jack Weller.[7] In the back he had these characteristics of what he thought made an Appalachian, as opposed to everybody else in the world. And of course he was thinking of these things on his list as negative aspects—all the Appalachian characteristics he saw as negative—but I was looking at it and I thought, "But this is the list I want to be on." I identified with the list that placed an importance on family and community and being a real person, and not the one that placed importance on schedules and money and ambition. And so, at that moment, I think I began to identify very strongly as an Appalachian, and then to learn as much as I could about what that meant. At that time there were no Appalachian history or literature classes, not a strong sense of what Appalachian music was, in the context of American music. So when it became possible to learn more about those things, people began to learn more about who they were, that they were Appalachian. I began to see all the things that were good about being Appalachian. Before, we had known we were from Eastern Kentucky and that meant a lot of things, some of which were real good and others that weren't good, like when people would make fun of you. I got made fun of terrible when I went off to college because of the way I talked. And so I think I did try to change it. I never tried to cover it up, though. I was proud of it; sometimes I'd even lay it on thicker. But I never rejected it, although at the same time I was young and wanted to be a citizen of the world.

Lynne: You don't necessarily have a consciousness of something so much until there's the threat that you might lose it. I think, back then, we had the security of the land and our family and the history and music. As long as we had it, we didn't have to think so much about it. But this was around the same time that strip mining started coming around, and the old musicians started dying off, and so we became more conscious of who we were as a people.

Anne: The first time I ever saw strip mining I had been hearing a lot about it because in the seventies the *Courier-Journal* was real good at covering what was happening in Eastern Kentucky. We don't have that now, we don't have a strong investigative reporting presence, and I think that's making a big difference in awareness. At that time we lived in Laurel and Knox County, and there wasn't too much strip mining going on, but some. But my husband and I had this little convertible, and we loved driving it around. So one day we decided to drive to Hazard. I had been reading a lot about strip mining and was fairly alarmed by it. I remember going up into Perry and Leslie and Harlan counties, and there were so many mountains, and they were so beautiful. And every once in a while you'd come up on a horrible gash in the mountain, and stuff pouring down, but I remember thinking, "Well, these mountains have been here so long, and there's so many of them that these men and their little 'dozers are not going to do that much damage." And I was really comforted by that. I couldn't foresee, of course, the use of explosives to bring down a mountain, and the big permits and the giant machines they have now. So I'm not comforted anymore.

Lynne: We dealt with coal a lot when I was living out here in the seventies. All the coal trucks and the damage to the roads. More and more trucks. That's when I first became aware and knew that the industry was getting bigger and bigger and that they obviously didn't care about anything but getting at that coal.

Anne: When we were little and Dad was a soil conservationist, we'd be going down the road—

Lynne: —singing and going on—

Anne: Yeah, singing and not paying much attention, but he'd be looking at the gardens and the land. He'd be talking about contour plowing, and he'd knit his brow and frown if there was somebody who had their field on a hillside. This was a major concern of the government, if there was a little farmer plowing on the hillside in such a way that the soil would erode. Because they knew that if you did that, the soil would wash away and there would be no ground cover. So they taught everybody about that. We all knew that very well. They taught it to us in school, and he taught it to us. He was always talking about that, so now it seems absolutely incredible to me that the same government—state and federal—would be allowing this massive erosion to occur with mountaintop removal. It makes no sense.

Lynne: Dad was real proud of "the service," as he called it. At that time, small farms, controlling erosion, and crop rotation were promoted, and the government was concerned with that too. So was the education system. But not anymore. Energy has trumped conservation. So-called conservatives make fun of environmentalists as being weird and weak-minded. The saddest thing in thinking about Dad is that he thought federal oversight was effective and needed, he had faith in that, in federal oversight. He believed that if there was an environmental problem the government would step in and get things right—as opposed to now, when they watch out for business interests. Our father would be real disturbed to know that we can't trust that anymore. He and Mother both had a lot of love and respect for the mountains, and they knew the mountains produced people of good character and humor and strength. Mom used to tell the story of when the commodity program came along. They had everybody go down to the voting house, down at the mouth of the creek, where they were handing out meal. They said that Pa—our grandfather, her father—who was a very strong and silent person, he went over to get a bag.

Anne: This was during the Depression, and the Democrat politicians were the ones giving it out. And right when Pa—who was a Republican—got up there to accept his cornmeal, one of the politicians said, "Maybe you'll vote right next time."

Lynne: So he just took his pocketknife out and sliced the bag of meal open and left it there.

Anne: Our uncle and mother had that type of character. They'd tell you off in nothing flat if they thought you were in the wrong. I think that was a real traditional mountain characteristic. Our grandfather had never been out of the mountains. He was from up on Buffalo and coming this far, to him, was like coming *out* of the mountains.[8] They had a lot of pride. That sort of speaking out, fighting back, was thought to be part of the Appalachian character. But people don't know about their own history anymore. They don't know that mountaineers stood up and fought in the union struggle, and against the broad-form deed, and against strip mining. So maybe that's why more people don't stand up against mountaintop removal. But I think it's also because we're a society of conformity these days. It's the larger culture we live in, a culture that portrays people who stand up for what they believe in as nuts. Around here, there's a lot of pressure to conform. There's this attitude of "Well, nice people don't speak up. Nice people don't stir and make trouble. They just mind their own business; if it's not bothering you, stay out of it."

Lynne: And the worse times get, the less people have, the less they're going to risk losing a job. Even to the point of not listening to an argument about something this big. I think it's strange that more people don't fight back, but people are busy, they're making ends meet. They only see what's in their neighborhood. They don't fly from here to West Virginia; they don't see mountaintop removal enough to get mad about it. There are buffer zones where people don't see the really ugly stuff from the road. And besides, people are not connected to the land. We just drive past the mine sites and go to Gatlinburg if we want to see some mountains. We don't even notice our own. We're not taught about erosion in school as much. I'm not sure they're teaching in schools about how hard it is for topsoil to regenerate, that it takes at least a hundred years for it to come back.

Anne: And the coal companies do a real good job of making people be afraid, and of painting anyone who challenges them as nut-cases or agitators or troublemakers. And they're real good at making people afraid of losing their job. Because when you have a job in Eastern Kentucky and you lose it, you may not be able to get another one. Ever. So the companies use that fear that people have of not being able to put food on the table for their families. They've always done that. They did it with the broad-form deed. They certainly did that with the union, to the point of killing people. They've always made it out like, well, if we're regulated, if we have to follow safer regulations at all it'll ruin the coal industry! We won't never be able to mine coal again! We'll all starve to death! In the seventies they acted like if they had to go by new regulations they'd be destroyed, that no mining would be able to happen. But once those regulations were enacted they managed to struggle on somehow—

Lynne: —from their mansions on the hilltops.

Anne: And they're acting the same way nowadays, with mountaintop removal. They act like if they have to go by any kind of new regulations then little children in Eastern Kentucky will starve to death. Now surely to God there's some kind of middle ground. It can't be either blowing up the mountains or starving children. There's somewhere to meet in the middle, but the coal industry doesn't even want to talk about it, they don't want to meet in the middle. Most of the time, with these politicians, it's Tweedledee and Tweedledum. Most of the time, even if they're not corrupt when you elect them, they'll be corrupt before they leave. We'd love to have some honest, creative, intelligent candidates.

Lynne: I believe most of our representatives don't represent us properly because they get their pockets lined by the coal industry. They say their constituents don't want mountaintop removal stopped, but I don't believe that's true. Lots of people don't know about it and some people don't care about the land, so sometimes people vote stupid or uninformed, but I don't believe most people are *for* it. Politicians'll say anything to justify their support of big money.

Anne: We can get energy in other ways than taking down our mountains. It scares me. Eventually they'll want at the little seams of coal like that are in this country here.[9] It seems to me that mountaintop removal is a violent and unprovoked attack on living things. That's not justifiable. We know what some of the short-term effects are—we know it leads to flooding, that it pollutes the water, there are certain things that we can measure—but we don't know the long-term effects or consequences. I worry about what those will be.

Lynne: I think mountaintop removal takes advantage of diversions and shifts in population and loss of ties to the land and community to drive its own values into the culture; the values of the coal industry are basically nil. It deprives people of a living land, a place with a store, a place with a history. It brings on depression in an economic and emotional sense. If your neighbor's land is torn down, how does that make you feel? That land has no value any more. Its essence, as Kate says,[10] has been taken. The whole changing of culture from a viable and colorful and definitive thing to an economic and marketable thing is a terrible thing that's happening in our country.

Anne: The rest of the country never can quite make up its mind about us. Sometimes they think we're interesting, that we make pretty quilts and have quaint stories and make good music, so they patronize us for a while. But then, when it comes down to it, they think of us as inferior.

Lynne: They think of us as gun-toting and sorry,[11] but I think we're welcoming and docile people, to the point of letting people run over us. We let them come into our country[12] and not show us respect. We do let that happen. We are beaten down, as a people. We keep taking hit after hit.

Anne: But I think that wherever industry—no matter where it is in the country—if industry wants something, they'll run over the people to get it. The same kinds of labor struggles that went on here in the thirties went on in other places, too. And mountaintop removal is happening in other places, too. With that said, however, I think that it's handy that they have such stereotypes of us—that we're poor and not doing good—that they have these excuses to take down our mountains, that we need more flat land for economic reasons. I've lived in Eastern Kentucky for fifty years, and I've never heard anybody else but the industry say we need more flat land.

Lynne: Climbing to the top of the hill up here is a spiritual thing. I remember Mom talking about her father going up there to pray. I walk up there by myself. Anne and I walk up there together. We've trudged up there as a family, to the graveyard. You can see the whole farm from up there. I started thinking a lot about that, and it gave me some way to express my anger and sadness and frustration about mountaintop removal mining to write a song about it. So that's why I wrote my song "Holy Ground." I had just been so frustrated to discover that mountaintop removal existed, when people had exhibited such outcry about strip mining just a few years before. I can't speak out very well, but I can try to write something by myself, to articulate the way I feel.

Anne: I wrote a song, "All That We Have," soon after the author's tour. I wrote it for the *Missing Mountains* book because I thought we needed a song.[13] I was working along on it, and I wrote that part "The land and each other was all that they had." And I thought, well, that's all we really have still, even though we *think* we have all kinds of stuff, like computers and such, but those things are not even real, in a way.

And, you know, I love Aunt Molly Jackson, and she would've written a song about it, no doubt. I had always heard of Aunt Molly Jackson, but I had only a vague idea of who she was—something about Harlan County, the labor struggles, something about Theodore Dreiser. I started doing some research on her and found out she was born and raised right around here in this part of Clay County. And she was a nurse and midwife, that was what she seemed to be most proud of, and she was apparently very good at that. She talks about how many babies she helped bring into the world and about using herbs to cure the sick. But, like so many others, her family left their farm and went to the mines, and after that they were completely dependent on the mines, on the vicissitudes of the coal market and the generosity—or lack thereof—of the coal operators. And then she married a coal miner, so she spent most of the first fifty years of her life in coal camps in Eastern Kentucky: in Laurel County, Knox, Bell, and Harlan. She came from a musical family—Sarah Ogan Gunning was her half-sister and Jim Garland was her half-brother—so when the miners went on strike in the late 1920s and early 1930s she wrote songs to rally the miners, most of them using traditional tunes that she wrote the words for, describing conditions in the coalfields; "Hard Times in Coleman's Mines," "Only a Miner," "Hungry Ragged Blues" are probably her best-known songs. But she wrote a lot, and the songs were poetic and very articulate about the way the miners and their families were being exploited. When the Dreiser Committee came into Bell and Harlan counties to conduct hearings, they were so impressed by Aunt Molly's testimony, which included her singing "Hungry Ragged Blues," that they asked her to come back to New York with them and work as a spokesperson and fund-raiser for the miners and other workers. So she did that, and spent the rest of her life in New York and then in California. For a time she performed with, and was friends with, Woody Guthrie, Leadbelly, and other folk musicians of that time. I think she was a brave woman and a brilliant artist who used her talents well. We need that kind of role model now. People are afraid to stand up. We've forgotten that a lot of the rights we have now, somebody had to fight and sacrifice for them.

Lynne: Reckon what Aunt Molly would have thought about mountaintop removal, Anne?

Anne: She'd a had a thing or two to say about it. It would've just made her so mad. But, like I was saying, people are afraid to stand up. It's the pressures of conformity, I believe. The church is very much an agent for conformity in that way.

Lynne: These days, they don't preach stewardship much in the churches round here. When we were little, they did preach that, they preached respect for the land, and service. I've been to some churches here where the coal operator contributed to the church, too. So that plays a part in it.

Anne: That concept of stewardship of the earth, we heard a lot about that in church in the fifties. The coal industry is an agent of the status quo, and so is the church. The coal association takes that verse from Isaiah and uses it literally.[14] As if the prophet were talking about MTR rather than the coming of the Messiah. It's condescending. It's saying, "Take this, you little people with your little Bibles that you take literally." It's revealing, though, that sometimes they're desperate, to resort to that. They respond to everything.

Lynne: There is ownership, but even in law there is the idea that we're not supposed to waste the land, and our directives from the Bible are to respect the creations of God. It's just so self-centered and short-sighted, to think that if you own the land, if you paid for it, then you can do whatever you want.

Anne: I was talking to some kids at the library the other day about this folktale we had read. And the king in the story thought everything in the world belonged to him. So I asked the children who they thought the world belonged to and one said, "Everybody." One said, "All of us." One said, "Nobody." Another one said, "God." Not a one of them said, "Whoever's got the deed." I mean, in a way, it is just a piece of paper. And as a landowner, as a human being, you have some responsibility to the people who will be here after you.

Lynne: Morally and legally, don't we have a duty to protect children and things that can't protect themselves? I see the land as one of those things. The land deserves protection. The industry wants to put out that we want to stop building of the roads and development and all that. We don't. We just want to stop rampant devastation of the land. The industry has already been allowed so much.

Anne: Even looking at it selfishly, it's really in our own interest to protect it. "Never send to know for whom the bell tolls"—because we cut ourselves off from the earth at our own peril. We're part of that, and we tend to ignore that for some reason.

Lynne: We're taking thirty pieces of silver for our homeland.

Anne: You know, it did surprise me when the press ignored us going up there to Frankfort and how big a crowd we had.[15] I would've thought the press and the state government would have at least *tried* to be neutral.

Lynne: They never even tried to *appear* neutral. I felt rejected by the government when that happened. It seems like they're awfully careful to not hurt the industry's feelings, and the industry—well, they are so sensitive that anyone would challenge them on the necessity for mountaintop removal.

Anne: The governor even came out to talk to them, when the mining industry people went up there about a month later. And the lieutenant governor, too, came out and expressed his opposition to the Stream Saver bill.

Lynne: But you know, that didn't surprise me, that so many miners went up there with them. Because if my boss told me to go somewhere like that and lobby, I probably would, too.

Anne: Especially if they told you that you had the day off and you better go and they said what time the bus would be there to pick you up. Everybody knows that's what happened.

Lynne: Yeah, so you'd think that the governor and the papers would know it, too.

Anne: Well, I think part of it is the overall political atmosphere now, it's so conservative. If you are even moderately challenging something, they portray you as an extremist nut. And the press now, they seem to have this idea that the truth is somewhere in the middle between the extreme somewhere. Every time we say something, they have to give Bill Caylor a chance to respond. And sometimes the truth just *is not* in the middle. Sometimes the truth is on one side only. But they're not doing any investigative reporting enough to know this. They put stuff in that we write and they put stuff in that industry people write, but that's not the same as covering an issue.

Lynne: Can you imagine if they'd been concerned with giving equal coverage to both sides of the Holocaust?

Anne: Or slavery!

Lynne: Not that mountaintop removal is necessarily comparable to those two things, but the point is that it's an important issue that needs newspapers to step up and take a side on it. Let's have Kentucky open for business and commerce—that's all they care about. The newspapers and big business seem to be awful good bed buddies. Sustainable agriculture used to be part of the team, but now that's all out. It's just energy and money that's important to them. So we all just feel like ugly stepchildren.

Anne: And as the price of coal goes up it doesn't bode well.

Lynne: They take advantage of the ignorance people have about the coal-to-liquid issue, or how people don't know how widespread mountaintop removal is.

Anne: You know, I've heard so many stories from people who live around these mountaintop removal sites. Their stories were so awful, so disturbing, so moving. What it's like to live with that all the time. Their rights are being violated so terribly, their quality of life is being ruined by the dust and noise. Their foundations being cracked and the water being ruined. And I've never seen coverage of that—no kind of investigative reporting about that. Now in the seventies that would have been covered by the press in Eastern Kentucky. The press covered all these issues back during the fight against the broad-form deed, and we heard from the people who were opposed to that. And we're just not hearing that about mountaintop removal. There's been some kind of shift in the press; they seem to be more complicit now and to serve the purposes of the coal industry in a way they really didn't before. But it reminds me of in the thirties, when the local law enforcement and the coal companies were so helpful to one another.

Lynne: I think the coal industry is more willing now to stretch their story, too, to go on about how they're doing the greater good and helping people. Back when the political climate was more liberal they weren't able to do that as easily. And I just don't believe they were as underhanded back then, either.

Anne: It's interesting, it's funny even, how they'll sometimes acknowledge the bloody and shameful history of coal in Appalachia. They'll say, "This isn't your grandfather's coal company."[16] That's one of their mottos. It's like they're saying, "Yeah, it's true that we lied and did all kinds of things in the past, but just give us another chance, just trust us."

Lynne: "Yeah, we're on the right track now, we'll do right now."

Anne: They'll say they're only going to take 7 percent of the mountains. But we're never told 7 percent of *what.* And they expect us to believe that they're going to mine that 7 percent and just up and quit. Then we can just trust them to stop, no matter what the price of coal is.

Lynne: "It's over now, we'll see you. Bye." That's not going to happen.

Anne: There's a reason why we don't believe them. Because we know the history—the very complicated and troubled history of coal in Kentucky—we have to question their motives.

Lynne: Somebody started attacking me the other day. They said, "Oh, so you don't benefit from coal-mining, you don't use electricity." I was so hurt and flustered that I just kindly limped away, but I've used electricity all my life and we didn't have to have mountaintop removal for that, and we still don't.

Anne: It's not right here yet, and I'm glad, but when I came back from seeing where it is—which is not far away at all[17]—those images stuck with me. I couldn't get them out of my head, I couldn't help but imagine it. And I could not stand the thought of it being here. I couldn't. I think that would be a loss that would be—

Lynne: —unbearable—

Anne: Yeah, I believe it would be. I know people bear all kinds of things, and I guess one could bear it, but it would be an irrevocable loss. And I'm not immune from that. This place is very much like other places where mountaintop removal has happened. Where I've seen it up close is in Perry County. I used to live there. I know some of those communities that are totally gone now. Like Lost Creek. People lived there. And now I can't imagine that there's any form of life there and never will be again. It's like my love of this place, and thinking of it happening here, that makes me want to fight it. Because I don't want it to happen to anybody else's place, either.

Lynne: I think I'm speaking out because I've feared it happening too close. I think of families going through it. As I grow older, I see the government is failing, it seems to me, very badly. I'm seeing that the coal industry has a strong hold on government and public opinion, and that makes me mad. And I do think people are not aware of the scale of damage. I feel like we're at a desperate time, at a time that we need to plead the case to people who would care if they had the time to understand and had the information. The whole practice evokes a danger and a senselessness to me. It's not practical and necessary like they say. It's being done out of callousness and carelessness and detachment from farming, from the land, from rural people. There's more and more money to be made with bigger and bigger machines. It's all business interests, and none of them want to take responsibility for what's happening to our mountains. It's a big network of people who don't want to claim what they're doing right beside their own granny's place.

Anne: I believe you're right.

Lynne: We have so much a corporate society, and that makes me want to speak out. Corporations operate mines, and the little people who live in the war-torn country or in the ravaged mining country, I feel like we need to stay alive as long as we can and have a voice and at least say, "We don't want this to happen. Why did you do it?" Our country's kind of getting away from us. We're so corporate and so money-hungry. We end up hurting the land and hurting the people.

Anne: And the same corporations that are bringing us the war and mountaintop removal, they also lull us into complacency through all kinds of entertainment that we have. That entertainment, a lot of the time, shows us that people who speak out are kind of flaky. And that the heroes are people who just make money, are part of the corporate culture and are very attractive and pleasant. It's all of a piece.

Lynne: We see something as horrible as war—we thought that when Bush started the war we weren't going to be there long, we were told that they were so happy we were there; and now look, it's been seven years. And now, now what? And we're still at war.

And think about the way they talk about mountaintop removal: "It's only going to be 7 percent and we'll have so much electricity. Just bear with us." And we just end up with an old golf course that nobody wants to go to.

Anne: If I could talk to all my neighbors, I would appeal to what I know is their love of the land and their respect for all the people who lived here before them. I'd try to make that connection for them so they wouldn't perceive mountaintop removal as just something on the news, something they thought of as people being up in arms about without themselves wanting to get involved. I would ask them, "Do you want to see that mountain there blown up and destroyed? Do you want to see that creek full of rocks from the mountain? Or the river down here full of sediment, empty of fish?" It makes it different when you think about it happening to your own land.

Lynne: I'd try to remind them to remember their heritage, their families, how their ancestors worked these hillsides, walked these mountains. I'd encourage them to visualize their parents and their grandparents standing around on these mountains with their hoes and fiddles and mules, saying, "Now you all need to stop this." Because I truly believe they *would* say that.

Teges Creek, Clay County, Kentucky, May 6, 2008

Larry Bush

The Gathering Storm

Now the rich, they get richer, and the poor mine the coal
And the lights must keep burning the cities we're told
But where will we turn to when the boom turns to bust
And the once-living mountains turn to rockpiles and dust
—Anne Shelby, "All That We Have"

The road over Black Mountain winds about like a coiled snake, poised to strike at any moment. At 4,145 feet above sea level, Black Mountain is one of Appalachia's highest mountains. The view from crooked Highway 160 is nothing less than breathtaking on this July evening as a storm front moves in on over the Cumberland Plateau in Harlan County, Kentucky. The seemingly endless acres of trees are dark green beneath the graying sky, a pristine forest that seems untouched by humanity. From up here this looks like a wild, primal land.

After dozens of stomach-churning curves, a small sign announces that the Virginia state line has been crossed. And suddenly, everything changes. Now there is a moonscape below, a barren wasteland of dirt and exposed rocks and yellow bulldozers. From near the summit of Black Mountain can be seen a mountaintop removal site that stretches itself brazenly above the town of Appalachia, Virginia, and it looks like a scar on the face of the earth.

The Kentucky side of Black Mountain was saved, thanks to the public outcry that followed when it became known that a coal company was seeking a permit for mountaintop removal mining on the Commonwealth's highest peak.[1]

Things are different on the Virginia side. There the mountain

Larry Bush, Appalachia, Virginia. Photo by Silas House.

is mostly owned by Penn Virginia, a huge corporation based in Philadelphia that routinely leases out land to coal companies. The mineral rights to these border-straddling mountains were bought up by such corporations as far back as the 1890s.

Where once there was a mountain here in Virginia, now there is a deep, dead hole. Even far past the mine, coal dust and dirt cover the huge kudzu leaves that crowd close to the road. The kudzu has crept onto the houses and trailers, too, as if this place is being devoured by two nonnatives: a plant from Japan and corporations from a place that locals call "Off," a land whose inhabitants don't have to see the damage they're doing, or just don't care.

The road rolls on, through the little community of Inman, the site of one of the most tragic chapters in the history of mountaintop removal. It was here on August 20, 2004, at 2:31 a.m., that a boulder weighing half a ton crashed through the side of a double-wide trailer and two interior walls and rolled over the bed of three-year-old Jeremy Davidson, killing him. The rock went on to rip through two more interior walls and finally came to rest against his older brother Zack's bed. The boulder had been dislodged by a bulldozer that had been operating illegally to widen a road for eighteen-wheel coal trucks on a mine site above the family's house.[2]

Today, the empty lot beside the Looney Creek Memorial Baptist Church, where the Davidsons' double-wide used to sit, is being overtaken by weeds and kudzu. It is haunted by silence on this Sunday, even though most days people in Inman never get a moment's peace because of the constant roar of machinery that is slowly eating away the ridge above.

The eerie silence is punctuated by a burned-out trailer home, an abandoned tricycle in the ditch, and a young woman—her shoulders tired, her face hollow—walking down the road with a baby on her hip. She considers the passing car and then eyes the sky, watching for rain. The gathering storm has moved on to unleash itself elsewhere for the moment, leaving behind the gray clouds that are a disconcerting mix with the humidity seeping out of the woods.

After a turn onto the Virginia Coal Heritage Highway, suddenly there is the town of Appalachia. Past the North Fork of the Powell River, Appalachia's downtown spreads itself out over a couple of gentle slopes, divided by the railroad that was once the lifeblood of the town. Appalachia used to be a boom town, back when there was plenty of underground mining work. In the early 1900s it took on the nickname of "Mineralville" because of its wealth of coal.

But nowadays Appalachia looks like a dying town. Despite the fact that Virginia's seven coal-producing counties pump out more than forty million tons of coal a year, they remain among the state's poorest. In Wise County, for example, about 19 percent of people live below the poverty level, nearly double the Virginia state average of about 9 percent.[3]

Along Main Street one of the buildings has been completely hollowed out, leaving the shell of a once-elegant brick store; now, weeds grow between the cracks in the floor. There is Appalachian Towers, where a group of elderly people sit out front on benches, smoking cigarettes and cracking jokes. Past this is another storefront, which is being used as storage. Through the dirty windows can be seen stacks of boxes. On the corner a large banner from the Appalachia First Baptist Church announces Vacation Bible School and announces not only that "Kids 'R' Kool" but also that "Jesus Rocks." There is the Miners Exchange Bank—its logo a filled coal car with pick and shovel—but close by is another empty building. Built to curve with the street, this was once a beauty, with decorative brickwork and rounded windows. But now most of the windows have been painted over and some are broken; in one an armless mannequin of a little boy peers out, staring maliciously into the eyes of anyone passing on the sidewalk below.

Just across the street is the local chapter of the United Mine Workers and beside it, Mountain Links, the office of the Southern Appalachian Mountain Stewards (SAMS). Inside, the light is dingy and the air smells of damp carpet. The office furniture looks as if it has been donated just to escape the dumpster. On a desk sits a vase full of dead tiger lilies, their brown petals littering the desktop. Despite the dreary conditions, SAMS has established this storefront on Main Street as a symbolic measure as much as a literal one. It's important for people passing by to see that someone is on their side. It's well known here that most people are against mountaintop removal. They just don't want anyone to know it.

Larry Bush, however, doesn't care who knows it. In fact, he wants everyone to know that he's on the warpath to stop what he calls "a crime," and as chairman of SAMS, he doesn't fail to announce that every chance he gets.

Bush got involved with SAMS because he was tired of witnessing what he calls "the daily rape" of the mountains he has loved all of his life. Before his life was overtaken by activism, Bush served a tour of duty in Vietnam and worked as an underground miner for twelve years and as a federal mine inspector with the Mine Safety and Health Administration (MSHA) for over thirteen years. Clearly, he knows what he's talking about. His presence makes this known, too. Bush does everything with an air of defiance. It's in his walk, his firm handshake, the serious scowl that stretches over his face when he talks about the issue.

Yet there is also a humility and vulnerability about him that is reassuring. Although he speaks from experience and wisdom, he sometimes grows so frustrated that he shakes his head and mutters, "Lord have mercy, children," reminding the listener that he's in this fight because he doesn't see any way around *not* being in it. He's committed to the fight and to SAMS.

Based in Wise County, Virginia, SAMS was started by Pete Ramey, a former miner and war hero who lived near a mountaintop removal site at Roda, also in Wise County, and Pat Jervis, a former schoolteacher from Appalachia. After his house was pummeled with rocks from the blasting, Ramey filed complaints with the Division of Mine Land Reclamation (DMLR). When his complaints went unheard, Ramey filed suit against the company. The coal company countersued, accusing him of defamation.[4] Ramey and Jervis responded by forming SAMS.

Since then, the organization has grown to include over 130 members in Southwest Virginia, and has joined forces with other, larger groups, including the Alliance for Appalachia—a coalition of thirteen organizations—and other groups on the East Coast that are fighting against environmental devastation and seeking solutions in energy resources.[5]

SAMS found its central fight—and Bush found his most trying struggle yet—when Dominion Virginia Power announced that they were going to build a "clean coal"-burning power plant in Wise County, at St. Paul, about fifty miles from Bush's home.

"First of all, there's no such thing as clean coal," Bush says, adjusting his baseball cap, something he often does when he's frustrated. "Clean coal is a myth because there's so much in it. They can't take all that out. If they could they wouldn't because it'd be too expensive. For anyone to get out there and tell you—like these commercials you see, talking about 'clean coal'—why, there's no such thing. Once they put it out there, it's subliminal. After a while people say 'Well, maybe it is clean.' We're so gullible, it's a damn shame."

The operation in St. Paul, formally known as the Virginia City Hybrid Energy Center, would be a 585-megawatt, $1.8 billion coal-fired power plant run by Dominion, Virginia's largest energy company, with 2.3 million customers in the state. According to the *Washington Post,* "Dominion refers to the facility as a hybrid because it will be engineered to burn coal, plant matter, and 'gob,' a kind of mine waste made of rock and coal that is piled around the mining districts of southwest Virginia."[6]

Bush and the other members of SAMS have been joined in the fight by people from outside of the region. Dozens of people from northern Virginia, to which 70 percent of the plant's electricity would go (the rest going to North Carolina), have testified in opposition to the plant. In March 2008, a group of Virginia religious leaders banded together to release a statement calling the use of coal-fired electric plants "immoral and destructive."

Protesters from throughout the state immediately converged on the office of Governor Tim Kaine. The following month, three activists chained themselves together to block the entrance to Dominion's headquarters. They remained in the road for about ninety minutes before being dragged away by police, who gave them a ticket for blocking traffic.

In June 2008, only two days before Dominion was to break ground on the plant, twelve protesters—most of whom were students from James Madison University and Virginia Tech—were arrested in Richmond, Virginia, after they blocked Tredegar Street at the headquarters of Dominion. Four of the activists had encased their hands in fifty-five-gallon drums of cement; another dangled from a pedestrian footbridge in a climber's harness for more than two hours. Nicknamed "the Tredegar Twelve," the group eventually accepted a plea bargain to do 200 hours of community service in Richmond to avoid serving jail time.

Conservationists are especially concerned over how the plant will affect the air quality of two national parks that are relatively nearby: the Shenandoah National Park and the Great Smoky Mountains National Park.

"The air quality in the Smokies is already degraded considerably," Don Barger, senior regional director for the National Parks Conservation Association, told the *Bristol Herald Courier* after plans for the plant were announced. "This would exacerbate the problem . . . in a situation that is really overloaded and that we are trying to clean up."[7]

SAMS has been especially active in the fight against the Dominion plant, organizing a petition against the power plant that has been signed by more than 43,000 people. The petition was the brainchild of Kathy Selvage, vice-chair of the organization. Bush and other members of SAMS have also lobbied in Washington, D.C., and have spoken at hearings throughout the country to help stop the power plant and mountaintop removal.

Dominion has replied to the outcry by running a multimillion-dollar publicity campaign that includes print, radio, and television spots emphasizing how the plant will benefit everyone, including the people of southwest Virginia.

Unfortunately, coal companies and their miners have not responded with as much diplomacy. Bush and his family have repeatedly been the victims of threats, obscene phone calls, and harassment.

"A guy blocked me in with a coal truck. I's setting on the side of the truck and he come right up against the door of my truck where I couldn't get out. When I'm coming out of the holler they cross the double lines to crowd me into the creek. They know me and my truck," Bush says, but his defiance seems to bloom instead of be cowed by the harassment.

The only thing that really worries Bush is that someone will hurt one of his three grandchildren or his two daughters.

"I take the oldest grandbaby to school every morning," he says. "It worries me because they crowd me, they come across the road. If one of them ever wreck me and make me hurt one of my grandkids, he's a dead son-of-a-bitch if I can live long enough to get to him. If they ever hit me, they better kill me, 'cause if I've got an ounce of breath in me, if I can get up, I'll kill *them.*"

The phone calls started immediately after Bush testified at a town hall meeting in Wytheville that had been hosted by Governor Kaine. Bush was quoted in the paper as urging the governor to stop supporting the power plant. The first caller left a message on Bush's answering machine: "Yes, I was going to see who your husband thinks he is, like Mr. Larry Bush telling our governor he needs to change his mind about the power plant. He also told the Board of Supervisors to resign. Is this fuckin' man stupid or what?" The second call was answered by Bush's grown daughter Lorrie Stidham. A transcript of the exchange was published in the *Bristol Herald Courier:*

"Hey, you tree-planting bitches."

"What?"

"Hey, you tree-planting bitches."

"Who is this?"

"If it was up your ass, you would know who it is. Where's your old man?"

The caller cursed a couple more times, prompting Stidham to hang up on him. He called back within ten minutes; this time the phone was answered by Bush's other adult daughter, Missy Bush: "I want to talk to your tree-huggin' old man."

"He's not my old man; he happens to be my dad."

"Well, let me talk to your tree-huggin', son-of-a-bitch daddy, sweetheart."

"You are big and bad, aren't you, calling here and won't tell who you are. You're some kind of a man."

"I'll show you big and bad. Where's that tree-huggin' son of a bitch?"

About this time, while Missy was still on the phone, Bush arrived home, but when his daughter handed him the phone, the caller hung up. His number, however, had shown up on Caller ID, so Bush called him right back. A shouting match ensued, but Bush never did find out who was calling.

When the Bushes reported the calls to the Wise County Sheriff's Office, a deputy told them they could file a report if they got the callers' identities from Alltel, their local phone provider. But then Alltel said they were only allowed to report such information to law enforcement. When writing his report on the matter, *Bristol Herald Courier* investigative reporter J. Todd Foster called both numbers that had been recorded on Bush's Caller ID. The second caller never answered, but the first caller did respond to a voice-mail message left by Foster. The caller identified himself as a miner for A&G Coal Corporation and said that he was working on a mine near the Bush home. He claimed that he had every right to voice his opinion, just as Bush did. "We're working our asses off up here to feed our families, and this guy is trying to take our jobs away," the man told Foster.[8] Bush points out that he was a coal miner for twelve years and a mine inspector for longer than that, so it's not like he can't relate to the miners. And while he understands people need to feed their families, he'd rather go hungry than work on something that imposes such devastation on the earth and its inhabitants.

"Nobody in my family or my wife's family has ever worked any kind of strip mines," Bush says. "They'd quit work altogether before they'd work on one of these jobs. There are a couple guys in our organization who actually have quit because they couldn't stand doing that kind of destruction."

Still, he understands that the Appalachian economy has people in a corner. "Coal has been the mainstay of this economy. These coal companies work to keep other industries out of here. Regardless of what people think, they're out to keep ye dependent on them," he says. Bush is not optimistic about the future. "There's not even fifteen years of coal left in Wise County—it's either been raped or is under permit to be raped. They'll fight you tooth or nail to preserve their jobs—and I don't blame them for wanting to provide for their families—but it's so short-term. It's just like this oil thing. How better to get people to holler, 'Drill anywhere!' than to raise the price of oil? 'Let's drill anywhere, save me a dollar.' That's today. But people have to start thinking, 'Damn, what's left for me and my grandkids if we rape it all today?' How we've become a nation of greedy, petty people I don't know."

Bush believes that mountaintop removal is destroying not only the environment and culture of Appalachia, but also the heritage of coal mining. "It's an insult to call these mountaintop removal workers coal miners," Bush says, taking off his baseball hat once again. He rustles around his hair, replaces the cap. "That's not coal mining in any sense of the word. That's just total rape of the earth. Strip mining, even back in the early seventies—which was just bench and auger, when you'd cut a little road and go in and auger it and above and below it nothing was disturbed and they're grown up and you can't even see them any more—was way better. But this, this is just rape. And it's raping it not only for the people living today, but for my grandchildren."

Bush pauses, taking a deep breath. The interview is over, so he ventures on out to his truck, alongside the curb on Main Street, which lies still and silent on this Sunday evening. Down the hill a train, pulling dozens of gondolas filled with piles of glistening black coal, labors by in surges and jolts, its wheels crying out with each jolt. Just over the top of the building with the staring mannequin can be seen a mountaintop, past the railroad tracks and the river, off toward Big Stone Gap. The overcast day makes dusk appear earlier than usual, and now it seems a gray quilt is being pulled up over the town, darkening Bush's face.

The air is charged by the distant storm, and the sky seeps out the clean, sharp smell of ozone. Before getting into his truck, Bush considers the brewing clouds and draws in the scent. "Looks like it may storm yet," he says.

Larry Bush talking . . .

I was in Vietnam in '67 and '68. I was with the Ninth Infantry Division, Eleventh Armored Calvary, Black Horse Regiment. In Vietnam I learned survival, just trying to survive, and it's the same thing here, just trying to survive, just fighting to stay alive. They're poisoning our air, our water, destroying our mountains and our whole way of life.

I'll not quit fighting 'em. I can't stand the thoughts of having died and not having done something to try to protect my grandkids—and their kids—from this devastation. Fighting 'em, dammit, until I die.

When I got out of the military I come right back here. Didn't want to go anywhere else but here. I've lived here all my life except for when I was in the military.

I was born in Big Stone Gap, and from the time I was born, my dad worked in the mines, and everybody in my family has worked in the mines. My father-in-law worked forty-four year underground, my dad worked twenty-two years before a roof fall got him and disabled him for the rest of his life. We lived in coal camps all during my childhood. Roda and Keokee. When I was young the coke ovens was still going over here. I can barely remember them, but they's going full blast over in Keokee. It was all underground mining, though. There was none of this rape happening, this rape of the earth. But, you know, coal has been a part of this part of the country for more than a hundred years. They came through here in the 1890s and bought up all the mineral rights for a quarter an acre. So coal has been the mainstay for this part of the country—still is, to an extent. But it's got to a point where the extraction process is destructive to all life; not just people, but every living organism is affected by MTR-type coal mining. I never saw it, and I worked as an inspector for the federal government. I saw strip mining, but I never saw this, for them to go in and destroy whole mountain ranges. It's the most sickening thing you can look at, and you've seen it if you come down Black Mountain on our side.

My dad bought me a little .22 Remington rifle when I was six years old—and I still have it—and took me in the mountains from the time I was big enough to walk. He used to hunt ginseng all the time, and he'd take me and my brothers in the mountains all the time. I started squirrel hunting and stuff like that with him. I've been in these mountains, hiking and hunting and everything, since I was six years old. These mountains are a part of us, and to see them destroyed is extremely hard to take. When I leave my home in the morning, coming downtown, I look at a high wall above my house, and that's the most sickening thing, to see what they're doing, for what? For a lump of coal, when there's 120-foot coal seams out west. They can move seven foot of dirt out in Montana and the Dakotas and Utah and places, and get 122 foot of coal. I know this from talking to people at meetings. They do that there, but then they come in here and blast away centuries-old mountains to get at a little seam of coal. Why would you do that? These greed-driven—I just don't understand how they justify doing it. I told some of them in a conference the other night, "I don't see how you get up and look at your kids in the morning, knowing what you're doing to this place." I mean, it's *gone.*

I've stood up to them since the eighties, on clear-cutting the forests; that's when I got started on this environmental movement, if you want to call it that. People have been relying on coal for so long it's hard to get anybody to stand up, and the ones who have have been dogged out for doing it. "You're speaking out against coal?" they'll say. "This is all we've got around here."

Nobody likes mountaintop removal. You go to Roda, Stonega, Dunbar, anywhere you want to go, nobody likes what they're doing to these mountains, but if you try to get people to stand up and say, "Stop this," they won't, because people are so beat down, so hopeless, they keep being told that there's nothing you can do. But we're working on it, we're hoping to save something here. I've been three-quarters of the way around this world, but I've never wanted to be anywhere else but here. We live here because we want to. I want to be with mountain people.

My dad preached union to me from the time I was big enough to listen. I was local union president for nine years. When Westmoreland was here I worked union and preached union. I was on the state compact political action committee as a state chairman and county chairman. I've been involved with the union; even when I was working with the government I was vice-president of the union, when I was an inspector.

Strikes. Picket lines. I've lived through it. I've been arrested, my wife's been arrested, thrown in jail because she was out there with us. That was during the '77 strikes, when everybody come out, the whole union, the UMWA, everybody.

Growing up union taught me to respect people's rights. When my dad started, they'd just throw you out in the streets. I've worked three organizing drives with the international UMWA, and it's just about fairness for workers, give 'em a fair share of what you're making. If a company is making $50 billion in profit and you're paying a CEO $120 million, why can't the workers get a part of that? Some of them is still making minimum wage.

Nowadays there's a lack of the union presence here, and it was a well-organized effort. Penn Virginia is the biggest enemy southwest Virginia has ever had, but they sit back like they're the good ol' boys who only do good. They're the landowners here, they're the ones who lease it out to these coal operators, who destroy it. Their headquarters is in Philadelphia. When people way back sold their mineral rights to them for a quarter an acre, they couldn't imagine continuous miners blasting away the earth. If they had, they wouldn't have sold it. Mountain people wouldn't have sold it. People today won't sell it to them.

If I could sit down with [UMWA president] Cecil Roberts I'd tell him that the union needs to be out in full force, fighting this. John L. Lewis would have been in Congress, screaming to high hell about it.[9] He's one of my heroes. There's other mining systems besides blowing these mountains up. There's thin-seam systems; Westmoreland used one here for years before they pulled out of here, they went in on old existing benches that had been augered before, and they went in there. They had twenty-five miles of existing benches they didn't have to do anything with. Deforesting and killing every organism on these mountains—there's other ways to do it.

And this power plant. It's going to make everything worse. The air, and look at all the mining that is going to have to be done to fit that need. I'm against this power plant because it will create more pollution. Go up to the Carbo plant and look at the suffering they've already gone through.[10] We went up there to a meeting in Cleveland, Virginia, and in one week's time, three of their residents were dead of cancer. The air and the water and everything is so dirty from this one power plant. And this one's going to continue to operate and they're going to add on to that with this new plant. One of the specifications on this new plant is that they have to use Virginia coal, two million tons a year, on top of what's being done now. The only result that can come about from that is more of blasting away of our mountains.

Generations. It's affecting generations. There was a feller got up and said, "Mountains can heal from this." Nothing can heal from this, when it's blasted to gravel. I truly believe that our state and federal government have deemed local people expendable. They think they've lived with coal for a hundred years, so just blast 'em away. Let them live with coal or die. That's maybe a harsh statement but, dammit, it's true. They've pretty much written us off; southwest Virginia will eventually be one big waste dump, maybe. I have lost all—*all*—respect that I ever had for any of these politicians.

I've always been for people. You might call that liberal, I don't know, but I've always been for the common man, for working families, as much as possible an advocate for that. I don't consider myself conservative or liberal, I consider myself someone who cares about the earth, the people. We're good people here, and we shouldn't be written off just to satisfy the dollar for a coal operator.

Like Jeremy Davidson and the way they got out of all of that.

Terry Kilgore came down here and represented Jeremy Davidson's parents.[11] He was sent down here for damage control. There ain't a doubt in my mind that A&G and the other coal companies paid him to come down here.[12] And he did, he silenced it. There could have been a whole lot of stink over that. A lot could have been changed. All them renewed laws, that was nothing but a scam, not one thing they rewrote in those laws benefited anybody.[13] If they'd actually wanted to do something, they'd kept them from working half a mile from people's homes. All kinds of things they could've done. The state representatives are bought and paid for by the companies. They're killing us.

We should preach it, about Jeremy Davidson. They're killing us in our homes. They killed the little boy; another two foot and they'd killed his brother. Out of respect to them, none of us want to use that as a theme to do anything. It's a bad situation.

If he'd been a little rich boy, though, people everywhere would know who he is. If it'd been one of A&G's administrators' kids, it'd been all over the news. After all these years, these damn coal operators still have so much influence that the government won't book 'em at all.

But the coal industry is a dying industry. And what do we do then? People can't just pack up and move. We don't have the resources. I'm disabled, on a fixed income, and lots of people are. They can't just pick up and go.

It takes the lowest form of humanity on this earth to do what they're doing to this earth, these coal operators. I'll tell them that right to their face. I *have* told them that.

We have to stop this. If we don't, this area—southwest Virginia, Eastern Kentucky, West Virginia, East Tennessee—we're going to be just one big gob pile. But we're making inroads, we have 140 sponsors on that Clean Water Protection Act. We're trying to get it passed. But our own congressman, Rick Boucher, who professes to be so much for southwest Virginia and does so much for the environment and all this, he won't sign onto this. He's a Democrat. He won't sign onto this because it would probably stop them from shoving the waste—it would change one word in the act, the act was passed, but Bush changed it through executive order, changed it from waste to fill. What we're trying to do right now is to change that one word, to stop valley fills. To stop those valley fills would prevent them from shoving the waste into the valleys, so they couldn't blow the tops off the mountains.

Boucher is coal, he's been a coal advocate since the first. I drove him around to the bathhouses the first two terms he was running, to talk to coal miners to help get him elected. Over the years we've had meetings with him. He's stopped being an advocate for people and started being a full-fledged politician who does what special interest groups—especially coal—wants him to do. He met with us during lobby week, and he wouldn't even talk about it. I hate to say that about him because I had the utmost respect for him the first few terms he run. I've met with him and talked to him personally. He's always been pro-coal; that's not wrong, but don't get it the wrong way, don't destroy the whole universe to get the coal.

We're lobbying up there all the time, getting more and more

people to take notice. The congressmen might not, but there are other people who are noticing.

I'll never quit. It gets frustrating sometime. Especially with the Division of Mines that we have here in Big Stone Gap; they won't help you at all. They're out there supposedly as advocates for the people, to protect the people, but they just enable the coal companies to destroy everything around us. Their primary purpose, I think, today is to act as a buffer. If the federal government was to come down here they'd say, "Our laws supersede . . ." I'm not saying the feds would even come down, though. This Division of Mines and Minerals in this state, and West Virginia and Kentucky, they're just enabling the companies to destroy people's homes and lives and whole communities, and a mountain range that's centuries old and diverse in so many respects, not just the trees, but the wildlife and organisms that's in these mountains. It's criminal what they're doing to these mountains.

Hopefully it won't all be destroyed before we get something done. We're working under the gun. If we don't get something done pretty quick there won't be nothing left to fight for.

Appalachia, Virginia, July 5, 2008

Appendix A

Text of the Petition Letter Circulated by Coal Companies against the Stream Saver Bill

This letter was handed out at gas stations, churches, and even in school parking lots in the days before the coal miners' rally in Frankfort, Kentucky, on March 13, 2008. It was also circulated by e-mail. Most of the statistics in the letter are incorrect, according to reports from the coal industry itself; others are seriously misleading. The text was most likely written by Bill Caylor, president of the Kentucky Coal Association; almost all of it is directly quoted from a column he published in the *Lexington Herald-Leader* and the *Courier-Journal* on January 7, 2008.

TO: Honorable members of the Kentucky House of Representatives and Senate

House Bill 164, the Stream Saver Bill, will seriously impact surface and underground mining in Kentucky by not allowing excess rock to be placed in streams that only flow when it is raining.[1]

Why focus only on coal? Our fills are no different than those needed for highway construction, real estate development, commercial development, other mineral extraction, and farming.

People living in the flatlands take level land for granted. There is no level land outside the floodplain in Appalachia that hasn't been created by man. We need this land for our future economy.

- Only a small percentage, 7%, of the Appalachian coal fields will be impacted by surface mining.
- You cannot surface mine without the surface owner's per-

mission. The surface owner must agree on the post-mining reclamation.

- There are only eight active mountaintop removal permits in Kentucky. Only two mountaintop removal permits have been issued since 2005.
- In the 24 eastern Kentucky coal-producing counties:

    - 6,055 surface miners mine 45.5 million tons of coal
    - $354,629,000 is paid in direct wages
    - 23,000 trickle down or extra jobs
    - $1.9 billion in gross sales of coal (79.5% is exported out of Kentucky)
    - $1.5 billion brought back to eastern Kentucky where 85 cents on each dollar stays and circulates
    - $87 million paid in severance taxes ($43 million back to 24 coal counties)

Coal provides high paying jobs and delivers cheap, dependable electricity. Kentucky has the 4th lowest electrical rate in the U.S., which is critical not only for attracting businesses like aluminum plants and auto manufacturing plants but also for our low income and elderly residents.

The elimination of surface mining will end future farms, airports, housing subdivisions, industrial parks, recreational areas, commercial sites, golf courses, and a host of other actual uses of reclaimed coal mine lands.

Don't let your common sense be swayed by broad-brush, emotional statements. This is about the future of eastern Kentucky, not about remembrances of the past.

[Signature]

Appendix B

House Bill 164, the Stream Saver Bill, as Introduced in February 2008

AN ACT relating to surface mining.

Amend KRS 350.450 to change requirements relating to restoration to original contour of surface mines, and to require that when all requirements of the amended KRS 350.450 are met that the configuration requirements of KRS 350.410 and 350.445 may be altered, but that overburden must be returned to mine area to the maximum extent possible and that other overburden is to be disposed of in permitted areas or previously mined areas, and that no overburden is to be disposed of in the waters of the Commonwealth; amend KRS 350.440 to provide that no spoil be disposed of in the waters of the Commonwealth, and that any spoil not returned to mine area be disposed of only in previously disturbed areas on lands eligible for reclamation under the abandoned mine land program.

Notes

Introduction

1. "Robert Kennedy at Alice Lloyd College, Pippa Passes, Kentucky, February 13, 1968," http://www.rfkineky.org/library/what-happened.htm.

2. Tom Vanden Brook, "Recruits Hungry for Good Jobs Head off to Coal Mines," *USA Today*, Feb. 14, 2006.

3. This exception led to permits for mountaintop removal sites being issued to companies that promised to convert the land for public use, such as airports, subdivisions, golf courses, and industrial parks.

4. "Mountaintop Mining/Valley Fills in Appalachia: Final Programmatic Environmental Impact Statement," U.S. Environmental Protection Agency, http://www.epa.gov/region3/mtntop/index.htm.

5. Vicki Smith, "Activists Slam EPA Decision on Mining Rule Change," Associated Press, December 3, 2008.

6. "Survey Shows Most Americans Oppose More Mountaintop Removal," Civil Society Institute, http://www.700mountains.org/release091307.cfm.

7. "Stream Saver Bill: HB 385," Legislative Research Commission, http://www.lrc.ky.gov/RECORD/07RS/HB385/bill.doc.

8. In addition to serving as a state representative, Gooch is also vice-president of West Kentucky Steel Construction Company. The company's Web site boasts of "erecting the world's largest dragline, 'Big Muskie,'" and notes that Gooch himself is "active in running the business on a day to day basis."

9. This political ambush has not quelled Gooch's opposition to the bill. He has accepted thousands of dollars in campaign contributions from the coal industry, including $2,700 in the 2006 primary election cycle alone. He also opposed a hearing for mine-safety legislation in early 2007 in the wake of mine collapses in Eastern Kentucky and West Virginia. More recently, Gooch was instrumental in passing a $260 million tax incentive package during a special legislative session called by then-Governor Ernie Fletcher to entice energy companies to construct coal-to-liquid gas plants across the state, according to the *Louisville Courier Journal*. In February 2008, newly elected Governor Steve Beshear announced that he had canceled a $400,000 grant to Peabody Energy Corporation, as "the company has made no visible progress toward studying the feasibility of a $3 billion coal-to-liquids plant in western Kentucky," according to the *Lexington Herald-Leader*.

10. As chair of the House Appropriations and Revenue Committee, Moberly cleverly attached the Stream Saver bill to a measure in his committee that would provide tax breaks for camel feed.

11. Don Garvin, "Sen. Hunter Introduces Bill to Ban Mountaintop Removal," *Winds of Change Newsletter,* March 2008, West Virginia Environmental Council.

12. Phil Kabler, "Mountaintop Removal Foes, Supporters Speak," *Charleston (W.Va.) Gazette,* Feb. 28, 2008. Retrieved July 21, 2008, from http://www.wvgazette.com.

13. Art Jester, "Mountaintop Removal Bill Won't Be Considered," *Lexington Herald-Leader,* Feb. 10, 2007. Retrieved Oct. 13, 2007, from http://www.kentucky.com.

14. Ibid.

15. Stephen George, "High on a Mountaintop," *LEO,* Feb. 19, 2008.

16. Critics charged that the miners were coerced to attend the rally, citing some miners who claimed that buses were supplied by the coal companies. Just before the miners' protest, several workers—mostly women who claimed to be the wives of miners—showed up at small grocery stores, schools, and even churches, to hand out petition-style letters that people could sign and send to Frankfort with the miners. The letter, reproduced in Appendix A, charged that the Stream Saver bill would shut down the entire industry instead of simply impose sanctions to protect water. The miners' rally received widespread television news coverage.

17. Although located in a non-Appalachian city, the *Lexington Herald-Leader* is, at 141,019 readers (Audit Bureau of Circulations, 2006), the largest newspaper that is widely read in the central Appalachian region.

18. "Rein In Rapacious Coal Industry," editorial, *Lexington Herald-Leader,* July 29, 2008.

19. Doris A. Graber, *Mass Media and American Politics* (Washington, D.C.: CQ Press, 1997), 99–100.

20. John Gaventa, *Power and Powerlessness: Quiescence and Rebellion in an Appalachian Valley* (Urbana: University of Illinois Press, 1980), 106.

21. Ibid., 107–108.

22. Roger W. Cobb and Charles D. Elder, *Participation in American Politics: The Dynamics of Agenda-Building* (Boston: Allyn and Bacon, 1972), 43–44.

23. www.projectcensored.org/censored_2006/index.htm.

24. Erik Reece, "The Facts Aren't Pretty," in *Missing Mountains: We Went to the Mountaintop but It Wasn't There,* ed. Kristin Johannsen, Bobbie Ann Mason, and Mary Ann Taylor-Hall (Nicholasville, Ky.: Wind Publications, 2005), 61.

25. Information on the Exxon-Valdez oil spill retrieved Oct. 14, 2007, from http://www.valdezalaska.org/history/oilSpill.html.

26. "Coal Silo Protest," *Charleston Gazette,* March 17, 2007. Retrieved Oct. 13, 2007, from http://www.wvgazette.com/section/News/2007031633.

27. Rebecca Bowe, Jon Elliston, David Forbes, and Brian Postelle, "Protestors, Police Amass in Downtown Asheville," *Mountain Xpress,* Aug. 13, 2007. Retrieved on Oct. 13, 2007, from http://www.mountainx.com/news/2007/protestors_police_amass_in_downtown_asheville.

28. Don West, "Romantic Appalachia; or, Poverty Pays If You Ain't Poor," *West Virginia Hillbilly,* March 29, 1969.

29. "Coal Production in the United States—An Historical Overview." Energy Information Association, U.S. Department of Energy, http://www.eia.doe.gov/cneaf/coal/page/coal_production_review.pdf.

30. Energy Information Administration, www.eia.doe.gov.

31. Gaventa, *Power and Powerlessness,* 53.

32. Jeff Biggers, *The United States of Appalachia: How Southern Mountaineers Brought Independence, Culture, and Enlightenment to America* (New York: Shoemaker & Hoard, 2006), 45–46, 56.

33. Robert Shogan, *The Battle of Blair Mountain: The Story of America's Largest Labor Uprising* (Boulder, Colo.: Westview Press, 2004), 4.

34. John W. Hevener, *Which Side Are You On? The Harlan County Coal Miners, 1931–39* (Urbana: University of Illinois Press, 1978), 45–47, 177.

35. Biggers, *The United States of Appalachia,* 162.

36. Hevener, *Which Side Are You On?,* 33–35, 60–61.

37. Ibid., 66.

38. Personal interview, Anne Shelby, Aunt Molly Jackson scholar.

39. The school is now known as the Highlander Research and Education Center.

40. John M. Glen, "Like a Flower Slowly Blooming: Highlander and the Nurturing of an Appalachian Movement," in *Fighting Back in Appalachia: Traditions of Resistance and Change,* ed. Stephen L. Fisher (Philadelphia: Temple University Press, 1993), 31.

41. *Harlan County USA,* dir. Barbara Kopple. DVD. 103 min. New York: First Run Features, 1976.

42. Carol A. B. Giesen, *Coal Miners' Wives* (Lexington: University Press of Kentucky, 1995), 13.

43. "The 'Widow' Combs, Who Made Stand against Strip Mining in '60s, Dies at 88," *Louisville (Ky.) Courier-Journal,* Feb. 26, 1993.

44. Melanie A. Zuercher, ed., *Making History: The First Ten Years of KFTC* (Prestonburg: Kentuckians for the Commonwealth, 1991), 67–68.

45. Ibid., 77.

46. Richard B. Drake, *A History of Appalachia* (Lexington: University Press of Kentucky, 2001), 205.

47. Gerald M. Stern, *The Buffalo Creek Disaster: How the Survivors of One of the Worst Disasters in Coal-Mining History Brought Suit against the Coal Company—and Won* (New York: Vintage Books, 1976), ix–x.

48. Ibid., 302.

49. "Service Today for Coal Country Activist," *Lexington Herald-Leader,* Aug. 11, 2007.

50. "Saving a Mountain" by Silas House, http://www.discoveret.org/tnleaf/materialsforyouth.htm.

51. "Kind Kids Save a Mountain," http://www.kindplanet.org/kindkids/kidsstory.html.

Jean Ritchie

1. The Hindman Settlement School in neighboring Knott County, Kentucky, was the first rural social school in the nation. Such schools offered social services in impoverished areas and grew out of the "settlement movement" that began in England in the late 1800s, which focused on educating the poor instead of simply offering them charity. Founded in 1902 by May Stone and Katherine Pettit, the boarding school provided education, health care, and social services. The teachers there—many graduates of schools like Wellesley—encouraged students to further their education. The Hindman Settlement School is now known for its programs in adult education, an outstanding dyslexia program, and such yearly events as the Appalachian Writers Workshop and Family Folk Week.

2. Now known as University of the Cumberlands.

3. The Henry Street Settlement School has provided social services and arts programming to New York's Lower East Side since 1893.

4. Pickow (pronounced *Peek*-o) is an acclaimed photographer, filmmaker, instrument builder, and artist who has been integral in Ritchie's career. A native of Brooklyn, Pickow was drawn to folk music and became a close friend of such artists as Alan Lomax and Woody Guthrie. As a book illustrator, he worked with Ritchie on her many publications of Appalachian music and later became a partner in recording endeavors. During the folk explosion of the early 1960s he became one of the leading photographers in the nation for album jackets (most famously the cover of Judy Collins's *Golden Apples of the Sun* in 1962). He was also an ardent documenter of the folk music scene. Pickow served as an associate producer and cameraman on the Oscar-nominated film *Festival.* His other films include films include *Oss Oss Wee Oss* and *Ballads, Blues, Bluegrass.* A collection of his photographs taken in Ireland in the early 1950s is permanently housed in the Pickow-Ritchie Archives at the National University of Ireland, Galway. Pickow's photographs of Appalachians are especially notable because of their lack of stereotype, as noted by the *Washington City Paper:* "Above all, Pickow's photographs are respectful, betraying no condescension despite his Northeastern upbringing—a refreshing reminder

of common ground so often missing in today's ultra-polarized age" (vol. 25, July 2005).

5. A ceilidh is a traditional Gaelic social dance held in Ireland and Scotland.

6. David Noebel, *Communism, Hypnotism, and the Beatles* (Tulsa, Okla.: Christian Crusade Publications, 1965). The book was later repackaged as *The Marxist Minstrels* (American Christian College Press, 1974).

7. The song is a whimsical look at the relationship between the Virgin Mary and Joseph, who, when asked by Mary to gather her some cherries, says that the father of her child can gather them for her. Christ commands the tree to bend down to Mary's hand and it obeys, proving Christ's divine parentage.

8. Subsistence farming, as the term implies, raised crops or livestock to maintain the farmer's family, usually not leaving any surplus to sell or trade. Only natural fertilizers were used, and rarely any kind of machinery.

9. Subscription schools were schools that children could attend when their parents paid a monthly fee. After the public school system became more widespread, subscription schools died out.

10. A common Appalachian way of referring to the Hindman Settlement School.

11. According to the Web site of WSGS, a Hazard, Kentucky, radio station, Davis "was one of the most popular personalities ever heard on WKIC and WSGS. He sang songs he composed and worked as a disc jockey on the radio stations in Hazard from 1947 until 1969. But first he was a coal miner, operating a coal-cutting machine from 1920 to 1949. Davis began singing and playing the guitar about 1933, when Eastern Kentucky coal mines were being organized by the United Mine Workers of America. He would practice on his front porch, and miners would gather around his home to listen. The Singing Miner went on to hold shows at schools, theaters, and anywhere he could get an audience. Davis began his career at WKIC with fifteen-minute shows sponsored by various local businesses. At one time he had five shows a day." http://www.wsgs.com/singing.htm.

12. Lines from a traditional song alternately called "In the Pines" and "Where Did You Sleep Last Night" that dates back to the 1870s and has always been especially popular in Appalachia. The song was brought to a national audience most famously by Bill Monroe in the 1940s and by the alternative rock band Nirvana in the 1990s.

13. These lines would later become a catchy refrain in the chorus of one of Ritchie's most popular compositions, "Blue Diamond Mines."

14. As Ritchie explained in an interview with the authors, "Than Hall was a pseudonym I took during that time. My mother was living then and 'protest' was a bad word, not for me in New York, but I didn't want anyone bother-

ing Mom about it. I was with BMI at the time, and they refused my use of my grandfather's name, John Hall, because that was the then-BMI president's name, so I took the end of 'Jonathan' and became 'Than.' Around home that was a common way of shortening that name."

15. Seeger was an integral figure in the folk music revival of the 1950s and one of Ritchie's closest associates in the business. After a string of hits with his band the Weavers, it was revealed that Seeger was a former member of the Communist Party. As a result, his mainstream success faltered. By the early 1960s, however, he had regained popularity as a singer of protest songs, particularly "We Shall Overcome," which he is credited as popularizing. Seeger wrote such modern classics as "Turn Turn Turn," "If I Had a Hammer," and "Where Have All the Flowers Gone." His music was introduced to a new generation in 2006 with the release of Bruce Springsteen's *We Shall Overcome: The Seeger Sessions.*

16. A large mine near Jeff, in Perry County, Kentucky.

17. *Singing Family of the Cumberlands.*

18. The stretch of road named for Ritchie is on Highway 7 between Jeff and Viper, Kentucky.

19. Governor Ernie Fletcher, a Republican, who served as Kentucky's governor 2003–2007.

20. Meaning "against" (dialect).

Denise Giardina

Epigraph: H. L. Mencken, "The Coolidge Buncombe," in *On Politics: A Carnival of Buncombe* (Baltimore: The John Hopkins Press, 1956).

1. Denise Giardina, "Let Us Be Clear: Mountaintop Removal Not about Creating Jobs," *Charleston, W.Va., Gazette,* May 22, 2007.

2. http://www.episcopalchurch.org/1829_ENG_HTM.htm.

3. Cecil Roberts is a sixth-generation former West Virginia miner who became president of the United Mine Workers of America in 1995 and still holds that position, making him the second-longest-running standing president after John L. Lewis. Prior to his election, from 1982 Roberts served as vice-president. He gained wider visibility during the campaign for the 2008 presidential election by working closely with Barack Obama. During the campaign, he famously replied to Republican vice-presidential candidate Sarah Palin's attack on Obama's past as a community organizer by saying, "Jesus was a community organizer."

4. According to the West Virginia Office of Miners' Health, Safety, and Training, McDowell has produced more coal than any other county in the state. However, the 2000 census reveals that the per capita income for the county was $10,174, which is the lowest in the state and the twenty-eighth

lowest in the country. About 33.8 percent of families and 37.7 percent of the population in McDowell County were below the poverty line.

5. A gob pile is "a pile or heap of mine refuse on the surface," as defined by the Internal Revenue Service's glossary of mining terms, created in relation to the Coal Excise Tax, which may be found at www.irs.gov/businesses/small/article/O,,id-139342,00.html.

6. U.S. Steel, now known as USX Corporation, is one of the major steel producers in the world. The corporation owned and operated the town of Gary, West Virginia, until the early 1970s and continued to mine coal there until 1986.

7. The organization's mission statement reads: "Our mission is to articulate the biblical call to social justice, inspiring hope and building a movement to transform individuals, communities, the church, and the world."

8. For information on the land ownership survey, see note 6 in the next chapter (on Bev May), below.

9. One of the founders of Kentuckians for the Commonwealth.

10. Hechler served in the West Virginia Congress 1959–1977 and was known for his support of laws to protect the environment.

11. Surface Mining Control and Reclamation Act. According to the U.S. Department of the Interior, this is the primary federal law that regulates the environmental effects of coal mining in the United States. After President Ford refused to sign the bill, saying it would harm the coal industry, President Carter signed it into law in 1977. The act created the Office of Surface Mining.

12. Larry Gibson is a tireless activist in the fight against mountaintop removal. He frequently gives tours of Kayford Mountain in West Virginia, where he occupies a fifty-acre tract of land surrounded by 12,000 acres that have fallen to mountaintop removal. Gibson has been featured on *CNN Heroes* and the traveling art exhibit Americans Who Tell the Truth, a series of paintings by Robert Shetterly.

13. Giardina is referring to the events of May 4, 1970, when four students were killed and nine others were wounded by the Ohio National Guard at Kent State University in Kent, Ohio. The students had been protesting the American invasion of Cambodia.

14. A German Lutheran pastor who was hanged in 1945—just weeks before the war's end—for his involvement in a plot to assassinate Adolf Hitler. He was very vocal in his opposition to the way Hitler was treating Jews and others. Giardina wrote a critically acclaimed novel about Bonhoeffer entitled *Saints and Villains,* published in 1999.

15. Wallis, editor-in-chief of *Sojourners* magazine, is the author of influential, best-selling books such as *God's Politics: Why the Right Gets It Wrong and the Left Doesn't Get It* (New York: HarperSanFrancisco, 2005).

16. At the time of this interview, John Edwards was still in the running for the 2008 Democratic presidential nomination, but he dropped out in February 2008.

Bev May

1. According to Big Coal, the blasts are from ANFO—ammonium nitrate/fuel oil: "ANCO is a high-tech explosive that is used in big strip mines all over the world, as well as by terrorists such as Oklahoma City bomber Timothy McVeigh . . . Coal mines are responsible for about 70 percent of the 2.5 million tons of industrial explosives that are detonated in America each year."

2. KRS Sec. 350.610, Designation of lands as unsuitable for surface coal mining, U.S. Office of Surface Mining Reclamation and Enforcement.

3. Overburden is a geological term that, according to the American Heritage dictionary, means "material overlying a useful mineral deposit."

4. Lee Sexton is a renowned clawhammer banjo player from Knott County, Kentucky.

5. University of Kentucky.

6. Patricia Beaver, director of the land ownership study, explained the study in an interview on August 28, 2008: "In 1978 a group of citizens and scholars in the Appalachian region began a major research project on land ownership in Appalachia." The research, she said, was "concerned with the collection and analysis of data on land ownership patterns and the impacts of these patterns on rural communities. Funded in 1979 by the Appalachian Regional Commission, over sixty researchers collected ownership and tax data from county courthouses in eighty counties in six Appalachian states: West Virginia, Virginia, Tennessee, North Carolina, Alabama, and Kentucky. The study found ownership of land and minerals in rural Appalachia to be highly concentrated among [a] few absentee and corporate owners whose tax burden was low, resulting in little land actually being available or accessible to local communities for economic diversification and housing, and inadequate funds for education, and civic infrastructure."

7. Somerset is a small town in southern Kentucky that was one of the organizing centers for KFTC.

8. Nellie Woolum was a sixty-five-year-old retired postmaster who was killed in a December 18, 1981, sludge slide in the small community of Ages in Harlan County, Kentucky, when the Eastover Mining Company's impoundment on the west fork of Ages Creek broke, releasing about 125,000 cubic yards of saturated coal refuse, which traveled more than 4,400 feet downstream. Three homes were completely destroyed, with

more than thirty badly damaged. Woolum's body was found in the ruins of her home.

9. In 1968, during Robert F. Kennedy's Poverty Tour, Kennedy was allowed access to a Knott County strip mine owned by Bill Sturgill, a past board member of the Kentucky Coal Association. Photos of the devastated land were widely published.

Carl Shoupe

1. Filmed during 1973 and 1974, *Harlan County USA* documents the Brookside coal miners' strike against the Eastover Mining Company in Harlan County, Kentucky. The strike began with Eastover's refusal to sign a contract with the miners after their decision to join the United Mine Workers of America (UMWA). Directed by Barbara Kopple, the film won an Academy Award for Best Feature Documentary for 1976 and was added to the National Film Registry in 1990.

2. Mountain Association for Community Economic Development, based in Berea, which seeks to create economic alternatives for residents of Eastern and Central Kentucky.

3. Massachusetts Institute of Technology.

4. Joseph Albert "Jock" Yablonski had lost the 1969 United Mine Workers of America (UMWA) race for president and had asked the U.S. Department of Labor to investigate the election for fraud when he was murdered, along with his wife and daughter, in a hit ordered by his opponent, incumbent UMWA president W. A. "Tony" Boyle. The murders occurred on New Year's Eve 1969, and were discovered five days later. The next day more than 20,000 coal miners walked off their jobs in a one-day strike to signify their conviction that Boyle was involved in the killings. Once Boyle's complicity unfolded, the framework was laid for Arnold Miller, a West Virginia miner, to become the new union president. Boyle was convicted of ordering and funding the murders and was sentenced to three life sentences. He died in prison in 1985. Hazel Dickens wrote and performed a song called "Cold Blooded Murder" (sometimes known as "The Yablonski Murders"), which was featured in the film *Harlan County USA.* A popular HBO movie, *Act of Vengeance,* based on the murders, was released in 1986.

5. Arnold Miller, who became UMWA president after Boyle, himself suffered from black lung disease and made fighting for better legislation about the disease his top priority. Initially Miller was widely popular, but his term as president ended in mistrust. He died in 1985 and is remembered for his black lung reforms.

6. Cecil Roberts, President of the United Mine Workers of America.

Kathy Mattea

1. Judd has lent her support to a CD entitled *Songs for the Mountaintop,* which was produced by Kentuckians for the Commonwealth, providing a blurb declaring that the music was "as clear and beautiful as our mountain streams used to be."

2. Shortly after this interview, in April 2008, Emmylou Harris hosted a dinner for the Natural Resources Defense Council at her Nashville home that was attended by such music celebrities as Sheryl Crow, Mattea, Big and Rich, Jeff Hanna (of the Nitty Gritty Dirt Band), and Matraca Berg, as well as representatives from environmentalists' groups throughout the nation. The featured speaker at the event was Robert F. Kennedy, Jr. One of the main topics of discussion was mountaintop removal mining.

3. Country singer Mary Chapin Carpenter was also active at an early stage in making the issue of HIV/AIDS more visible among the country music industry.

4. This bill was put forth by LEAF, whose leaders are featured in the chapter on Pat Hudson.

5. Smithers is located in Fayette County, in southern West Virginia.

6. The 2006 Academy-Award-winning documentary *An Inconvenient Truth* featured Gore's campaign to acknowledge global warming as a serious problem. Mattea was in the first training class conducted by Gore, in September 2006.

7. The Hobet Mine, operated by Arch Minerals, is 10,000-plus acres (about 15 square miles) located about 25 miles southwest of Charleston, West Virginia, near the headwaters of the Mud River.

8. Mari-Lynn Evans, a native of Bulltown, West Virginia, is a documentary filmmaker whose miniseries *The Appalachians* was seen by more than 30 million people when it aired on PBS. During the time she did the flyover with Mattea, Evans was working on a documentary about the history of coal.

9. Mattea describes Friends of Coal as "a big coal coalition for the industry." Friends of Coal describes itself this way in its mission statement: "The Friends of Coal is dedicated to informing and educating West Virginia citizens about the coal industry and its vital role in the state's future. Our goal is to provide a united voice for an industry that has been and remains a critical economic contributor to West Virginia."

10. Mattea is married to Jon Vezner, a successful Nashville songwriter who has created many hits, including songs for Martina McBride, Faith Hill, Steve Wariner, and Reba McEntire.

Judy Bonds

1. According to the West Virginia Coal Association, 32,764,140 tons of coal was mined in Boone County during 2006. This amount is nearly 20 million tons above the second highest producer, Logan County. Of the 32.8 million tons from Boone County, 20 million came from surface mining. Information on Boone County poverty is taken from the 2000 U.S. Census.

2. The Matewan Massacre (also known as the Battle of Matewan) was one of the most famous events in the history of coal mining. It occurred in Matewan, West Virginia, in 1920, when efforts of the miners to unionize resulted in a shootout that led to the death of ten men. The massacre eventually led to the Battle of Blair Mountain, the largest armed insurrection in the United States since the Civil War. Mother Jones was a famous labor organizer, whose involvement in the Paint Creek–Cabin Creek, West Virginia, coal mining strikes led to a federal investigation of conditions in coal mines. John L. Lewis was a revered president of the United Mine Workers; he was president of the UMWA 1920–1960.

3. Roberts is President of the United Mine Workers of America (UMWA); Raney is President of the West Virginia Coal Association; and Caylor is President of the Kentucky Coal Association.

4. According to *Worlds Apart: Why Poverty Persists in Rural America,* by Cynthia M. Duncan (New Haven: Yale University Press, 1999), dog mines are "small, often unsafe operations that pay low wages and have no benefits" (p. 31). Appalachian lore has it that the name comes from the fact that miners in such mines "worked like dogs."

5. Jay Gould was a leading railroad developer, financier, and speculator of the late 1800s who is often named as one of the nineteenth century's "robber barons."

6. Polyacrylamide, according to Merriam-Webster's Medical Dictionary, is "a polyamide polymer . . . derived from acrylic acid." According to the National Cancer Institute (NCI), polyacrylamide has been proven to cause cancer in rats but has not as yet been proven to do so in humans. However, the NCI points out that "the relationship between acrylamide and cancer has not been studied extensively in humans." A 1997 study found that polyacrylamide can degrade under normal environmental conditions, causing it to release acrylamide, which is a known nerve toxin.

7. *Squidbillies* is a wildly popular series of cartoon shorts that currently runs on the Cartoon Network. The network's Web site describes the show this way: "A family of inbred squids tear the ass out of all creation in the North Georgia mountains. It's not all drinking, brawling, and reckless gunplay. Occasionally they use crossbows. There's also hate, love, sex, a multinational drywall

conglomerate, cockfighting, the penal system, and a deep-seated mistrust of authority and all things different." "Appalachian ER" is a popular skit regularly performed on NBC's *Saturday Night Live.* It always includes an Appalachian who has been sodomized by some sort of item. "Hillbilly Moment" is a skit on the popular children's show *The Amanda Show,* which is no longer in production but still regularly airs on Nickelodeon. The skit features two Appalachian dullards hitting each other over the head and talking in thick accents. The skit has proven especially popular with teenagers, who make parodies on YouTube. A recent search of the phrase on YouTube's Web site garnered seventy hits.

8. Neither the text nor the author of this speech could be confirmed despite hours of research.

9. Common Appalachian colloquialism for *scrip,* tokens or paper vouchers with a monetary value given to miners by the coal companies as salary.

10. According to the 2000 U.S. Census, McDowell County had a population of 27,329 people, with 38 percent falling below the poverty level (the national average was 12 percent) even though the county produced 6 million tons of coal in 2007 alone. The 1950 census listed the population as 98,887.

11. Synthetic fuel.

12. Department of Environmental Protection, a government agency.

13. Appalachian Power, a division of American Electric Power, which serves about 1 million people in West Virginia, Tennessee, and Virginia. Despite the coal industry's constant claims that mountaintop removal mining helps to keep electricity rates low in Appalachia, AEP recently filed a request with the Public Service Commission of West Virginia to raise electricity rates by a 17 percent increase in revenues in 2008.

14. "And the Lord God took the man and put him into the garden of Eden to dress it and to keep it."

Pat Hudson

1. II Corinthians 3:17.

2. *Kilowatt Ours* is an award-winning 2006 film by Jeff Barrie that explores the way coal is causing widespread pollution in Appalachia and the rest of the nation. Produced by B. J. Gudmundsson, *Mountain Mourning* highlights personal stories of mountaintop removal through a faith-based perspective. Described as a "summons to moral courage" by the filmmaker, it was sponsored by Christians for the Mountains and released in 2008. *Serve God, Save the Planet* by J. Matthew Sleeth examines how Biblical models of personal responsibility and environmental stewardship can be applied to modern life. It was published in 2006.

3. From the A Rocha Web site: "A Rocha is a Christian nature conserva-

tion organisation, our name coming from the Portuguese for 'the Rock,' as the first initiative was a field study centre in Portugal. A Rocha is now a family of projects working in Europe, the Middle East, Africa, North and South America, Asia and Australasia. A Rocha projects are frequently cross-cultural in character, and share a community emphasis, with a focus on science and research, practical conservation and environmental education."

4. Tuke, a fellow adoption attorney, is also the former chair of the Tennessee Democratic Party. He ran for the U.S. Senate against incumbent Lamar Alexander (R) in 2008 and was defeated.

5. SB 3822 and HB 2248.

6. Coppock is referring to Moses' fear that he was not worthy to be a prophet because, he says, he is "not eloquent . . . I am slow of speech, and of a slow tongue." He tells God to choose his brother Aaron instead (Exodus 4:10–16).

7. Tom Humphrey, "Bill on Surface Mining Halted," *Knoxville News Sentinel,* April 3, 2008.

8. Oak Ridge, Tennessee, was a town established in 1942 as part of the Manhattan Project, which developed the atomic bombs that were eventually dropped on Japan. The population of the town grew to nearly 73,000 over the course of World War II, during which the town did not appear on maps and was completely surrounded by a fence and guard towers. After the war, the population greatly decreased. At the time of the 2000 census, there were 27,387 people living there.

9. According to the book *From Welcomed Exiles to Illegal Immigrants* by Felix Roberto Masud-Piloto (New York: Rowman and Littlefield, 1995), "the year 1980 also brought an increase in Central American asylum-seekers, namely Salvadorans, Guatemalans, and Nicaraguans escaping the political turmoil." This led to some churches stepping forward to house the refugees.

10. HarperOne, a division of HarperCollins, released *The Green Bible* in the fall of 2008; the publisher's catalog copy describes it as "the first Bible to highlight how the scriptures teach the importance of caring for God's creation . . . and will specifically focus on creation care, with input from leading Christian conservationists, theologians, and practitioners, showing that creation care is not just a calling, but a lifestyle."

11. Meaning the Appalachian Writers Workship at the Hindman Settlement School. Appalachians refer to both the school and the workshop as "Hindman."

12. The Mountaintop Removal Tour for Interfaith Leaders.

13. McKinley Sumner, resident of Montgomery Creek in Perry County, whose family land is being lost to mountaintop removal.

14. The TVA is the Tennessee Valley Authority, a government-run corpora-

tion that serves as a flood control device, an electricity provider, and a regional economic development agency in Alabama, Kentucky, Georgia, Mississippi, North Carolina, Tennessee, and Virginia. The TVA has been a controversial entity, especially because of its legal employment of eminent domain.

15. According to the Kentucky Coal Association's "Coal Facts" Web site, which includes an extensive glossary of coal-mining terms, scrubbers are "any of several forms of chemical/physical devices that remove sulfur compounds formed during coal combustion. These devices, technically know[n] as flue gas desulfurization systems, combine the sulfur in gaseous emissions with another chemical medium to form inert 'sludge,' which must then be removed for disposal." http://www.coaleducation.org/glossary.htm#S.

16. See www.ilovemountains.org, a Web site dedicated to providing information about mountaintop removal, made up of a coalition of seven grassroots organizations from five Appalachian states. Those organizations are Appalachian Voices, Coal River Mountain Watch, Kentuckians for the Commonwealth, the Southern Appalachian Mountain Stewards, Save Our Cumberland Mountains, the Keeper of the Mountains Foundation, and the Ohio River Environmental Coalition.

17. The Montgomery Creek mine was the culminating site for the Mountaintop Removal Tour for Interfaith Leaders and the place where Hudson saw a mountain blown up.

Jack Spadaro

Epigraph: Barbara Ehrenreich, "Family Values," in *The Worst Years of Our Lives: Irreverent Notes from a Decade of Greed* (New York: Harper Collins, 1991).

1. Erik Reece, *Lost Mountain: A Year in the Vanishing Wilderness* (New York: Riverhead Books, 2006), 133.

2. Erik Reece names Andrew Rajec as McConnell's former aide who was appointed to the investigative team. Ibid., 131.

3. On September 23, 2001, thirteen miners were killed by a methane gas blast in the Jim Walters mine no. 5 in Brookwood, Alabama. Chao personally promised the victims' families that MSHA would investigate the explosion in order to help prevent future mining accidents. The miners' widows have since been active in protesting for safer deep mining and for faster payment of benefits.

4. Nine miners were trapped underground for over seventy-eight hours, July 24–28, 2002, in the Quecreek mines in Somerset County, Pennsylvania. The disaster galvanized the nation as everyone watched the rescue with hope that all nine miners would be saved. They were, in the process becoming national heroes. The event led to the creation of many books, a high-rated TV mov-

ie (*The Pennsylvania Miners' Story*), and several songs (perhaps the best known is "Quecreek," written by Julie Miller, performed by Buddy Miller). The Quecreek disaster cast new light on the issue of safety in the mining industry.

5. The Sago disaster occurred on January 2, 2006, when thirteen miners were trapped for nearly two days. Only one survived. The accident led to widespread outcry for better safety regulations and a Senate investigation. Perhaps expecting another hopeful story like that of Quecreek, top journalists converged on the scene.

6. The Aracoma Alma mine accident occurred on January 19, 2006, when a conveyer belt in the Aracoma Alma mine no. 1 in Logan County, West Virginia, caught fire and killed two miners.

7. Five miners were killed in the Darby mine disaster, which happened on May 20, 2006, in Harlan County, Kentucky. According to *The Nation* (Erik Reece, "Harlan County Blues," June 28, 2006), "the majority of miners at both Sago and the Darby Number One Mine in Harlan survived the initial blast. They died because their self rescuers held only an hour's worth of oxygen. In the late 1990s . . . MSHA proposed installing more caches of oxygen inside the mines. But the Bush administration, under former mining executive David Lauriski, withdrew that idea in September 2001, calling it cost prohibitive." A lawsuit filed by the sole survivor and relatives of four of the five miners killed charges the coal company with putting production over safety. News of the disaster was carried on page 28 of the *New York Times* and did not become a national story.

8. Six miners and three rescuers were killed at the Crandall Canyon mine in August 2007. The mine owner, Bill Murray, became the subject of ridicule after he blamed the accident on the land itself. "Had I known this evil mountain, this alive mountain, would do what it did, I would never have sent the miners in here," Murray said, according to an Associated Press report filed on August 23, 2007.

9. Senate Health, Education, Labor, and Pensions Committee.

10. According to the Web site of the Appalachian Studies Association, the Jack Spadaro Documentary Award "honors the activist and whistleblower . . . who has spent his entire professional career working within the coalmining industry for the betterment of the Appalachian community . . . the award is given to recognize the best film, video, radio, television, or other media presentation on Appalachia and its people." www.appalachianstudies.org.

11. The Coal Mine Health and Safety Act of 1969.

12. In 1994, the same impoundment released 100 million gallons of coal slurry. Larry Wilson, an MSHA engineer, made nine recommendations to Martin County Coal before the pond could be used again. They were never implemented.

13. David Lauriski was the Assistant Secretary of Labor for Mine Safety and Health from January 2001 to November 2004.

14. Tim Thompson.

15. The Surface Mining Control and Reclamation Act (SMCRA).

16. Another Massey Energy mine, located in Logan County, West Virginia.

17. West Virginia.

18. A fire boss is someone employed by the mine or a state official responsible for examining a mine for potential dangers.

19. President of the United Mine Workers of America (UMWA).

20. U.S. Representative from the Sixth Congressional District of Kentucky.

21. U.S. Representative from the Third Congressional District of West Virginia.

Nathan Hall

1. Allen is the county seat of Floyd County, Kentucky.
2. Kentucky.
3. Kentucky.

Anne Shelby and Jessie Lynne Keltner

1. "Teges" is thought to be a colloquial distortion of the word "tedious," according to Shelby.

2. Marianne Worthington, "Anne Shelby's *Appalachian Studies: Poems* and *Can a Democrat Get into Heaven?*" *Appalachian Heritage,* Fall 2006.

3. Shelby is referring to Reece's book *Lost Mountain: A Year in the Vanishing Wilderness* (New York: Riverhead Books, 2006).

4. Middlesboro, Kentucky, is located where Kentucky, Virginia, and Tennessee meet.

5. The Clear Fork Valley in Clairborne County, Tennessee, is an area often cited in arguments for new legislation in that state, due largely to the vast size of the MTR sites there and the depopulation being caused by the practice.

6. An old traditional song about the Rapture, the biblical end of time. The first verse goes: "Oh my loving mother, when the world's on fire/Don't you want God's bosom to be your pillow/Hide thee over in the rock of ages/Rock of ages, cleft for me."

7. Although Weller's 1965 book has proven popular (it became a best seller upon its initial publication), it is largely seen in contemporary Appalachian literature circles as presenting the region in a stereotypical fashion from

the point of view of an outsider. Such an approach has lessened in popularity as Appalachian studies became more widespread and scholars native to the region published their own studies.

8. Buffalo was once a small community in northern Clay County, Kentucky.

9. "In this country": a colloquial expression meaning the area close to her home.

10. Kate Larken, a singer/songwriter/activist who wrote the song "Can't Put It Back," in which is the line Keltner is referring to: "You see them strip away her essence."

11. "Sorry": colloquialism meaning "lazy."

12. "Country," meaning Appalachia.

13. *Missing Mountains* is a collection of writing that includes essays, news articles, poems, and other forms of writing that was put together immediately following the 2005 Kentucky author's tour hosted by KFTC. The book was edited by Kristin Johannsen, Mary Ann Taylor-Hall, and Bobbie Ann Mason, and published in Nicholasville, Kentucky, by Wind Publications in 2005.

14. Shelby is referring to the fact that the Kentucky Coal Association's Web site has used Bible verses to justify mountaintop removal mining for the last few years. One such verse is Isaiah 40:4: "Every valley shall be exalted, and every mountain and hill shall be made low and the crooked shall be made straight and the rough places plain." This sentiment is repeated in Luke 3:5: "Every valley shall be filled, and every mountain and hill shall be brought low; and the crooked shall be made straight and the rough ways shall be made smooth."

15. Shelby is referring to I Love Mountains Day 2008, when about 1,200 people marched on the capitol to support the Stream Saver bill and to oppose mountaintop removal.

16. This is a much-used mantra by coal industry officials, mine operators, and politicians who support the coal industry.

17. Shelby lives about thirty-five miles from the site she is speaking of, and there are more mountaintop removal sites much closer to her home.

Larry Bush

1. The Kentucky side of Black Mountain was saved largely thanks to the efforts of a fifth-grade class in Harlan County, led by their revered yet modest teacher, Judith Hensley. In 1998, Jericol Mining, Inc., petitioned for a mountaintop removal site on Black Mountain. Hensley's concerned class wrote letters and even converged on the Office of Mining in protest. Others across the Commonwealth rallied to their cause. The following year, the state caved to political pressure and purchased mineral and timber rights to the summit, thereby ending the threat to the Kentucky side of the mountain.

2. According to the Virginia Department of Mines, Minerals, and Energy's final report on the Davidson case, "after the rock penetrated the rear wall of the residence and struck the child's bed, it struck the floor, went airborne again, traveled through two interior closet walls, and came to rest against a bed in which the Davidsons' eight-year-old son, Zachary, was asleep." For details on the cause of the dislodgment, see Tim Thornton, "Southwest Virginia Family and A&G Coal Settle in Three-Year-Old's Death," *Roanoke Times,* Sept. 8, 2006.

3. Data on poverty taken from 2004 U.S. Census.

4. The Virginia Department of Mines, Minerals, and Energy claims that "a petition for expenses and fees" was filed against Ramey. Virginia Department of Mines, Minerals, and Energy, Accident Investigative Final Report, Surface Coal Mine Offsite Fatality of August 20, 2004, report filed December 17, 2004, http://www.npr.org/documents/2005/feb/vamine_report.pdf.

5. The Alliance for Appalachia describes itself as "a collaboration of thirteen organizations in Central Appalachia working to bring an end to the devastating coal mining technique known as mountaintop removal . . . and seeks to promote a just and sustainable economy and a clean, renewable energy future in the region" (www.ohvec.org/alliance_for_appalachia/index.html). AFA members include the Coal River Mountain Watch, Kentuckians for the Commonwealth, the Ohio Valley Environmental Coalition, Save Our Cumberland Mountains, the Southern Appalachian Mountain Stewards, the West Virginia Highlands Conservancy, the Appalachian Citizens Law Center, Appalachian Voices, Appalshop, Heartwood, the Mountain Association for Community Economic Development, the Sierra Club Environmental Justice Program, and Southwings.

6. David Fahrenthold, "Dominion's Coal-Fired Electric Plant to Advance," *Washington Post,* June 26, 2008.

7. Debra McCown, "Conservationist Says Coal Plant Emissions Could Damage Smokies," *Bristol Herald Courier,* June 18, 2008.

8. Todd J. Foster, "Power Plant Opponent's Family Threatened by Phone," *Bristol Herald Courier,* April 6, 2008.

9. President of the UMWA from 1920 to 1960, Lewis was known for his rallying speeches and his commitment to the welfare of coal miners.

10. "Carbo" is a local reference to American Electric Power's Clinch River Power Plant, which is also located in Wise County, less than fifteen miles from the proposed site for Dominion's new power plant.

11. Terry Kilgore served as an attorney for the Davidson family and currently is serving his eighth term as delegate of Virginia's first legislative district, which includes Scott, Lee, and a portion of Wise and Washington counties. He was recently appointed chairman of the Virginia Coal and Energy Commission

and is currently being investigated by the Virginia state bar for possible ethical misconduct. Kilgore is the twin brother of Jerry Kilgore, former attorney general of Virginia and present chairman of presidential candidate John McCain's Virginia campaign. Jerry also ran as governor of the state in 2004, losing to Tim Kaine.

12. A&G Coal Corporation.

13. Bush is referring to the Virginia General Assembly's toughening of state mine safety laws, which require plans to protect people living in areas that could be hit by mining debris.

Appendix A

1. The bill's language says nothing about streams that "only flow when it is raining." Instead, the bill specifies "that no overburden is to be disposed of in the waters of the Commonwealth."

Selected Bibliography

"Activism in Appalachia." Special issue, *Now and Then* 7 (Fall 1990). Johnson City: East Tennessee State University.

Appalachian Task Force. *Who Owns Appalachia? Landownership and Its Impact.* Lexington: University Press of Kentucky, 1983.

Applebome, Peter. *Dixie Rising: How the South Is Shaping American Values, Politics, and Culture.* New York: Times Books, 1996.

Baber, Bob Henry, et al. *Old Wounds, New Words.* Ashland, Ky.: Jesse Stuart Foundation, 1994.

Bachrach, Peter, and Morton S. Baratz. *Power and Poverty: Theory and Practice.* New York: Oxford University Press, 1970.

Barret, Elizabeth. *Stranger with a Camera.* Directed by Elizabeth Barret. DVD. 58 mins. Whitesburg, Ky.: Appalshop, 2000.

Barrie, Jeff. *Kilowatt Ours.* Directed by Jeff Barrie. DVD. 64 mins. Nashville, Tenn.: Southern Energy Conservation Initiative, 2005.

Biggers, Jeff. *The United States of Appalachia: How Southern Mountaineers Brought Independence, Culture, and Enlightenment to America.* New York: Shoemaker & Hoard, 2006.

Billings, Dwight, Gurney Norman, and Katherine Ledford, eds. *Back Talk from Appalachia.* Lexington: University Press of Kentucky, 1999.

Burns, Shirley Stewart. *Bringing Down the Mountains.* Morgantown: West Virginia University Press, 2007.

Carawan, Guy, and Candie Carawan. *Voices from the Mountains.* New York: Knopf, 1975.

Cheaves, John. "State Revokes Peabody Grant." *Lexington (Ky.) Herald-Leader,* Feb. 28, 2008. Retrieved May 2008 from www.kentucky.com.

Classic Labor Songs from Smithsonian Folkways. Various artists. Smithsonian Folkways compact disc, 2006.

Clavel, Pierre. *Opposition Planning in Wales and Appalachia.* Philadelphia: Temple University Press, 1983.

Coal Mining Women. Various artists. Rounder Select compact disc, 1997.

Cobb, Roger W., and Charles D. Elder. *Participation in American Politics: The Dynamics of Agenda-Building.* Boston: Allyn and Bacon, 1972.

Crow, Peter. *Do, Die, or Get Along: A Tale of Two Appalachian Towns.* Athens: University of Georgia Press, 2007.

Dearing, James W., and Everett M. Rogers. *Agenda-Setting.* Thousand Oaks, Calif.: Sage Publications, 1996.

Derickson, Alan. *Black Lung: Anatomy of a Public Health Disease.* Ithaca: Cornell University Press, 1998.

Dickens, Hazel. *Hard Hitting Songs for Hard Hit People.* Rounder Select compact disc, 1980.

Dickens, Hazel, and Bill Malone. *Working Girl Blues.* Urbana: University of Illinois Press, 2008.

Douglas, William O. *Points of Rebellion.* New York: Random House, 1969.

Drake, Richard B. *A History of Appalachia.* Lexington: University Press of Kentucky, 2001.

Dunbar, Anthony P. *Against the Grain: Southern Radicals and Prophets, 1929–1959.* Charlottesville: University Press of Virginia, 1982.

Duncan, Cynthia M. *Worlds Apart: Why Poverty Persists in Rural America.* New Haven: Yale University Press, 1999.

Edelman, Murray. *Political Language: Words That Succeed and Policies That Fail.* New York: Academic Press, 1977.

———. *The Symbolic Uses of Politics.* Urbana: University of Illinois Press, 1985.

Eller, Ronald D. *Miners, Millhands, and Mountaineers: Industrialization of the Appalachian South, 1880–1930.* Knoxville: University of Tennessee Press, 1982.

Fisher, Stephen L., ed. *Fighting Back in Appalachia: Traditions of Resistance and Change.* Philadelphia: Temple University Press, 1993.

Forester, William D. *Harlan County—The Turbulent Thirties.* Self-published, 1986.

———. *Harlan County Goes to War.* Self-published, 1990.

Gaventa, John. *Power and Powerlessness: Quiescence and Rebellion in an Appalachian Valley.* Urbana: University of Illinois Press, 1980.

Giardina, Denise. *Storming Heaven.* New York: Ballantine, 1988.

———. *The Unquiet Earth.* New York: W. W. Norton & Co., 1992.

Giesen, Carol A. B. *Coal Miners' Wives.* Lexington: University Press of Kentucky, 1995.

Graber, Doris A. *Mass Media and American Politics.* Washington, D.C.: CQ Press, 1997.

Guthman, Edwin O., and C. Richard Allen, eds. *RFK: Collected Speeches.* New York: Viking, 1993.

Hall, Bob, ed. *Environmental Politics: Lessons from the Grassroots.* Durham, N.C.: Institute for Southern Studies, 1988.

Hansell, Tom. *Coal Bucket Outlaw.* Directed by Tom Hansell. 27 mins. Appalshop, 2002.

Harlan County USA: Songs of the Coal Miner's Struggle. Various artists. Rounder compact disc, 2006.

Hevener, John W. *Which Side Are You On? The Harlan County Coal Miners, 1931–39.* Urbana: University of Illinois Press, 1978.

Higgs, Robert J., Ambrose Manning, and Jim Wayne Miller, eds. *Appalachia Inside Out.* 2 vols. Knoxville: University of Tennessee Press, 1995.

Hoffman, Edwin D. *Fighting Mountaineers: The Struggle for Justice in the Appalachians.* Boston: Houghton Mifflin, 1979.

Horton, Aimee I. *The Highlander Folk School: A History of Its Major Programs, 1932–1961.* Brooklyn: Carlson, 1989.

Iyengar, Shanto. *Is Anyone Responsible? How Television Frames Political Issues.* Chicago: University of Chicago Press, 1991.

Jester, Art. "Authors Call for End to Mountaintop Removal Method." *Lexington (Ky.) Herald-Leader,* April 21, 2005.

Johannsen, Kristin, Bobbie Ann Mason, and Mary Ann Taylor-Hall, eds. *Missing Mountains: We Went to the Mountaintop but It Wasn't There.* Nicholasville, Ky.: Wind Publications, 2005.

Jones, Loyal. *Appalachian Values.* Ashland, Ky.: Jesse Stuart Foundation, 1994.

Kennedy, Rory. *American Hollow.* Boston: Bulfinch Press, 1999.

Kingdon, John W. *Agendas, Alternatives, and Public Policies.* Boston: Pearson Education, 1984.

Kopple, Barbara. *Harlan County USA.* Directed by Barbara Kopple. DVD. 103 min. New York: First Run Features, 1976.

Loeb, Penny. *Moving Mountains.* Lexington: University Press of Kentucky, 2007.

Long, Priscilla. *Where the Sun Never Shines: A History of America's Bloody Coal Industry.* New York: Paragon House, 1989.

Masud-Piloto, Felix Roberto. *From Welcomed Exiles to Illegal Immigrants.* New York: Rowman & Littlefield, 1995.

Montrie, Chad. *To Save the Land and Its People: A History of Opposition to Surface Coal Mining in Appalachia.* Chapel Hill: University of North Carolina Press, 2003.

Norris, Randall, and Jean-Philippe Cypres. *Women of Coal.* Lexington: University Press of Kentucky, 1996.

Nyden, Paul. "Mining Appeal Moving Along." *Charleston (W.Va.) Gazette,* May 16, 2008.

Pancake, Ann. *Strange as This Weather Has Been.* Berkeley: Shoemaker and Hoard, 2007.

Reece, Erik. *Lost Mountain: A Year in the Vanishing Wilderness.* New York: Riverhead Books, 2006.

Reel World String Band. *Mountain Song: Reflections.* Reel World compact disc, 2002.

"Robert Kennedy at Alice Lloyd College, Pippa Passes, Kentucky, February 13, 1968." http://www.rfkineky.org/library/what-happened.htm.

Salyer, Robert. *Sludge.* Directed by Robert Salyer. DVD. 40 mins. Whitesburg, Ky.: Appalshop, 2007.

Savage, Lon. *Thunder in the Mountains: The West Virginia Mine War, 1920–21.* Pittsburgh: University of Pittsburgh Press, 1990.

Schattschneider, E. E. *The Semisovereign People: A Realist's View of Democracy in America.* New York: Holt Rinehart & Winston, 1960.

Shainbaum, Barry. *Hope and Heroes: Portraits of Integrity.* Toronto: London Street Press, 2001.

Shelby, Anne. *Can A Democrat Get into Heaven?* Louisville, Ky.: MotesBooks, 2006.

Shifflett, Crandall A. *Coal Towns: Life, Work, and Culture in Company Towns of Southern Appalachia, 1880–1960.* Knoxville: The University of Tennessee Press, 1991.

Shnayerson, Michael. *Coal River.* New York: Farrar, Straus and Giroux, 2008.

Shogan, Robert. *The Battle of Blair Mountain: The Story of America's Largest Labor Uprising.* Boulder, Colo.: Westview Press, 2004.

Songs for the Mountaintop. Various artists. Kentuckians for the Commonwealth compact disc, 2006.

Steitzer, Stephanie. "Energy Bill Wins Final Legislative Approval." *Louisville (Ky.) Courier-Journal,* Aug. 25, 2007. Retrieved October 14, 2007 from http://www.courier-journal.com.

Stern, Gerald M. *The Buffalo Creek Disaster: How the Survivors of One of the Worst Disasters in Coal-Mining History Brought Suit against the Coal Company—and Won.* New York: Vintage Books, 1976.

Still, James. *From the Mountain, from the Valley: New and Collected Poems.* Lexington: University Press of Kentucky, 2001.

———. *River of Earth.* Lexington: University Press of Kentucky, 1978.

Straw, Richard. *High Mountains Rising.* Urbana: University of Illinois Press, 2004.

Titler, George J. *Hell in Harlan.* Beckley, W.Va.: BJW Printers, 1972.

Webb, James. *Born Fighting: How the Scots-Irish Shaped America.* New York: Broadway Books, 2004.

Weller, Jack E. *Yesterday's People: Life in Contemporary Appalachia.* Lexington: University of Kentucky Press, 1965.

Whisnant, David. *All That Is Native and Fine: The Politics of Culture in an American Region.* Chapel Hill: University of North Carolina Press, 1995.

Woolley, Bryan. *We Be Here When the Morning Comes.* Lexington: University of Kentucky Press, 1975.

Zuercher, Melanie A., ed. *Making History: The First Ten Years of KFTC.* Prestonsburg: Kentuckians for the Commonwealth, 1991.

About the Authors

Silas House is the author of the novels *Clay's Quilt* (2001), *A Parchment of Leaves* (2003), *The Coal Tattoo* (2004), and the plays *The Hurting Part* (2005) and *Long Time Travelling* (2009). He is the winner of the Appalachian Book of the Year, two Kentucky Novel of the Year prizes, the James Still Award for Special Achievement from the Fellowship of Southern Writers, the Chaffin Prize for Appalachian Literature, and the Appalachian Writer of the Year award, among other honors. A contributing editor for *No Depression* magazine, House has written press kits for artists Kris Kristofferson, Lucinda Williams, LeAnn Womack, Buddy Miller, and others. He wrote the draft of the authors' statement at the first authors' tour of mountaintop removal and wrote the introduction to *Missing Mountain,* a collection of writing on the topic. In 2008 he was awarded the Helen Lewis Award for Community Service from the Appalachian Studies Association for his work in the fight against mountaintop removal. A graduate of Eastern Kentucky University and Spalding University's MFA in Creative Writing program, House serves as writer-in-residence at Lincoln Memorial University in Harrogate, Tennessee, where he directs the Mountain Heritage Literary Festival. His fourth novel, *Eli the Good,* will be published in late 2009. House lives in Eastern Kentucky, where he was born and raised.

Jason Howard is a writer and musician from Eastern Kentucky. His works have appeared in such publications as *Paste, Kentucky Living,* and *Louisville Review.* While serving as senior editor and staff writer for *Equal Justice Magazine* in Washington, D.C., he wrote investigative articles on such subjects as miners' fights for black lung benefits in Eastern Kentucky, an eminent-domain case before the U.S. Supreme Court, and assisted adoption in New York City. Howard can often be found on the road as half of the roots music duo The Doolittles and with the band Public Outcry, along with House, Jessie Lynne Keltner, Kate Larken, George Ella Lyon, and Anne Shelby. He graduated from George Washington University with a degree in political communication, an interdisciplinary major of political science, journalism, communications, and electronic media.

Index